PRAISE FOR *FAR*

"Jolyn Canty movingly unveils ___ __ _____,, ____g_ MacDonald. Thoroughly researched and compellingly written, we follow Louisa Powell who became MacDonald's wife and bore him eleven children. As committed Christ-followers, the MacDonalds had an amazing spiritual journey. Jolyn reveals the strength upholding George's capacity to fulfill his God-given purpose while frequently and seriously ill – certainly the Holy Spirit – but greatly manifested through Louisa! Truly, a remarkable achievement to bring to light the determination, duty, humility, and yes, force of a woman dedicated to her Lord, husband, and family. You will be captured by *Far Above Rubies*. I couldn't put it down."
– *Dave Gresham, The Navigators Ministry*

"Jolyn Canty's biography of Louisa MacDonald is a delightful and spiritually thought-provoking book. The words in letters and conversations between George and his beloved captivated me, as it was from an era when language was eloquent, beautiful, and deeply meaningful. Jolyn has captured the sensibility and love between two joyful and sincere Christians. Sorrow followed them, not because of their own sins but because of the treatment of many Christians who criticized George's theology in preaching. May the reader delve into their story with humility and thirst for the Truth."
– *Valerie Elliot Shepard, author of Devotedly, and daughter of Jim and Elisabeth Elliot*

"Jolyn Canty has captured a most beautiful love story in this captivating novel about Louisa MacDonald, wife of George MacDonald, preacher, poet, and author of so many well-known books of the 1800's. I was inspired by her love for the Lord, her husband, her children and anyone God would bring into their lives. She was talented in so many ways and used her God-given gifts to love and nurture George throughout his

life. I want to read this book again to continue being inspired by this amazing woman of God."
– *Gloria Wellman Walters, Peninsula Bible Church*

"This book is meant to be read slowly and savored—the life of this indomitable woman is painted with a magnificent description of nature, wildlife, historical settings and people (common and famous) that will come alive for the reader. The way Louisa lived her life has made a deep impression on my heart and mind. By giving herself completely to her Savior and opening her arms to a lifelong and profound marital love with her husband, she allowed God to use her to deeply encourage her husband's heart and provide him the gift of time and space to share his Godly insights through his spoken and written words. Her children, too, were discipled in the knowledge and practices of what it means to live as a follower of Christ, whatever the cost. Her legacy is still felt today through Jolyn's use of her own gifts of writing and creativity, which has given her profound insight into the life of this incredible saint."
– *Wendy Egelkamp, Olney Christian School*

"When I read *Far Above Rubies*, the story of George MacDonald's wife, I realized I had missed the richness behind his writings--two hearts woven by the love of the Lord Jesus. Louisa, talented in her own right, provided encouragement and read all of his manuscripts. Through poverty, tragedy and loss, their faith shines forth, depending on each other but especially on the Lord Jesus. Jolyn Canty does a magnificent job of bringing Louisa to life. This is a great read for anyone who knows the Lord can do mighty things through lives dedicated to Him."
– *Marjorie B. Hill, author of children's, juvenile, and adult fiction*

"The gentleness of George MacDonald's life and his tender commitment to his wife, Louisa were exquisite models too often absent in many marriage stories. This is a family book on how to live the Christian Life. Let us learn what God's

grace can do to build a family and a marriage! Well done Jolyn Canty!"
— *Barbara Tompkins, teacher, seminar leader, and inspirational speaker*

More Reader Reviews of *Far Above Rubies*:

"Canty's writing beautifully captures George and Louisa's enduring love and sets a new bar for anyone seeking a supernal marital relationship that can only exist in partnership with Deity. The portrayal of Louisa, without whom George would not have been George McDonald as we know him, reads like 'lovely cream poured over pudding.'"
— *Cheri Peck*

"A remarkable story of goodness, love and faith in a 19th century woman."
— *Carol Nowling*

"Jolyn Canty's biography of Louisa MacDonald is unique. Although I have read many of George MacDonald's writings, I knew little about his wife and family life. This book changed that. In Louisa, readers will find a godly wife and mother. Her message about purposeful parenting is a timely one for readers today. I highly recommend this book."
— *Tara Reilly*

Far Above Rubies: The Life of Louisa MacDonald

Jolyn Canty

A Production of The Works
of George MacDonald
worksofmacdonald.com

Prov. 3:15-18
Jolyn Canty

Copyright © 2021 Jolyn Canty
Foreword by Christopher MacDonald
Preface by Rolland Hein
Photographs and illustrations courtesy of Christopher MacDonald
All rights reserved.
ISBN: 9798723766716

With love to my husband, Earle, whose life is a testament of a faith that ardently trusts and obeys, and who loyally answered the call to "Come follow Me" no matter the cost.

Many who knew her, thought it a pity that so substantive and rare a creature should have been absorbed into the life of another, and be only known in a certain circle as a wife ....But the effect of her being on those around her was incalculably diffusive: for the growing good of the world is partly dependent on unhistoric acts; and that things are not so ill with you and me as they might have been, is half owing to the number who lived faithfully a hidden life, and rest in unvisited tombs.
George Eliot, *Middlemarch*

TABLE OF CONTENTS

Foreword x
Preface xi
Introduction xiii
The Near Loss of Everything 1
The Becoming of Louisa 3
Struck From the Eternal Light 12
The Whole Universe Is Tented with Love 25
Called to Preach: Te Deum 40
By and By Becoming Thoroughly One 54
For Richer, for Poorer, in Sickness and in Health 61
Salted with Fire 72
The Chalice and the Paten: Parenting, Poverty,
and Pilgrimage 87
Limping toward Jerusalem 101
Adeste Fideles 113
Faithful Forever Friends 124
Do the Next Thing 147
The Sound of a Far-Off Song 157
America 170
Tethered to the Cross 189
Through the Valley of Shadows 200
A Slow and Certain Light 212
A Rough Shaking: Shifting Ground
and Gathered Fragments 225
The Perfection of Selfless Love 234
The One Who Is the Life and Light 240
Acknowledgements 249
Notes 250

FOREWORD

by Christopher MacDonald

I have woken up every day with an Edward Hughes portrait of Louisa MacDonald watching over me. I have to admit to occasionally asking her advice as her family legacy is one of common sense, compassion and ability.

Jolyn Canty's insightful and sympathetic work, looks at my great-great grandmother's life and devoted support of her husband. For us in the 21st century, so much of Louisa's tale is strange, as different to how we live now as can be imagined. Even the role of wife has changed beyond comparison, and these differences, being retold in the context of a historical life, makes for a fascinating read.

I am very happy that Jolyn's excellent book, the first to concentrate on Louisa, shines new light on her, and her position of "power behind the throne".

It is high time to show that George MacDonald's success might well not have happened without the determination of his petite, strong, and deeply loving wife by his side.

PREFACE

by Rolland Hein

Perhaps chief among the many features that shaped the life and ministry of George MacDonald was his marriage to Louisa Powell. She was a person of remarkable character and abilities. After thorough and perceptive research, Jolyn Canty has given us a vivid and inspiring portrait of this remarkable woman.

It is indeed fortunate that the many letters that were exchanged between George and Louisa remain intact in various collections today, chief among them is the collection of the Beineke Library on the Yale University campus. Jolyn Canty has made a careful search for the letters at her disposal and has composed a biography that enables us more fully to appreciate the depth of Louisa's character.

George and Louisa's life together contained an awesome quantity of hardships and difficulties. The exigencies of the early years of their marriage forced them to live apart for periods of time in dire circumstances. Louisa was forced to accept the hospitality of her more opulently secure sisters. She then had to nurse her husband during extended periods of ill health.

As the children kept coming–they had eleven in all--she undertook to teach them how to act out various fairy tales. When the family's delight and enjoyment grew, Louisa turned several fairy tales into dramas, and in 1870 Strahan published her collection Chamber Dramas for Children. When they had remarkable success giving dramatic entertainments for their friends, Louisa conceived the idea of securing public facilities and charging entrance fees for their dramatic presentations.

Success followed success, and for several years the family was an acting troupe giving public performances throughout London and elsewhere. Their most successful play was their version of John Bunyan's *Pilgrim's Progress*, Part Two, with MacDonald himself playing the part of Great Heart. Even the Princess Louise attended a performance.

The added revenue was much needed to supplement the family income, since the royalties from MacDonald's many novels had been greatly diminishing due to pirating. His works were very popular in America, but there were no international copyright laws, and pirated copies forced MacDonald's British publishers to greatly reduce his royalties. Louisa's inspiration, ingenuity, and energy, therefore, provided the family much needed revenues.

In the final chapter of the Book of Proverbs, a passage celebrating the godly woman certainly applies: "An excellent wife who can find? She is far more precious than jewels. . . . She looks well to the ways of her household . . . . Her children rise up and call her blessed; her husband also, and he praises her." MacDonald and their eleven children had great reason for doing so, as he could not have had the great ministry which he did-- and keeps on having--had it not been for Louisa.

Rolland Hein, a professor emeritus from Wheaton College, received a BD from Grace Theological Seminary and a PhD from Purdue University. He is the author of several books, including George MacDonald: Victorian Mythmaker.

INTRODUCTION

When I think of Louisa MacDonald, I am reminded of an old Chinese proverb about oaks and strawberries. A ripe strawberry is a lovely red fruit, adorned with seeds perfectly placed outside, and beautifully topped with a hat of green. But if you drop or squeeze it, it becomes mushy uselessness. In contrast, the Chinese oak tree grows stronger because of the most contrary winds and the harshest winters. Louisa was certainly not a strawberry.

I met Louisa through her husband, George MacDonald. I was first introduced to his books when I was in my twenties. I devoured every novel of his that I could get my hands on. His words showed me the shape of godliness. In fact, his book "Diary of An Old Soul" was my wedding gift to my husband. Wanting to learn more about MacDonald and his family, I looked for whatever information I could find. Fortunately, I came across an old copy of the biography written about him by his son, Greville. What I found most interesting was how Greville attributed so much of his father's success to his mother, Louisa. She was the oak that upheld the family through many storms. Who was this mysterious Louisa? How is it that she had such a profound influence on her family?

Today, being an "influencer" is a fashionable vocation. Our society is enthralled with the social media "Influencers" who inundate our feeds. Courses are even taught about how to become a successful influencer. Seemingly perfect and always pictured in the loveliest of settings, Influencers can make an awful lot of money based upon how many followers they have and how well they influence these followers to purchase sponsor's products. An "influencer's" goal is to be seen and known as a "name" and a "face."

Louisa MacDonald would never be hired as an Influencer because Louisa, like John the Baptist, was a Voice, not a Name. When asked if he is the Messiah, John the Baptist could have answered "I'm not the Messiah, but he's my cousin," which would have called attention to himself. But he did not. He wanted to be known as the "voice of one crying in the wilderness." He had come to point them to Jesus. That is how I think of Louisa. She was a voice, not a name—but she was a profound influencer.

She was not a beauty who turned every head when she entered a room. Rather, she was a simple, plain, petite, and demure woman. But within her tiny, simple frame was a mighty strength that had been shaped through pressure and pain, like a diamond is made. A brilliant musician and vocalist, she was also a writer, a teacher, a wife, a mother to many, and a faithful friend. Much of her strength came from being content and happy to do, to the best of her abilities, what God had gifted and given her to do. Throughout her life she endured hardships which few of us will ever face, but she emerged a diamond, polished and shaped to reflect His image.

Now, Louisa is my hero. Her life has taught me that even I, an ordinary woman, can do hard things, and that God will always be faithful in whatever circumstance I face. In many of her letters to her children, Louisa included the ancient Latin phrase of praise to God "Te Deum," and her life certainly modeled Te Deum: O God, we praise and acknowledge Thee.

On the following pages you will come to know Louisa, the mighty oak and voice. She was ordinary, plain, sometimes insecure, and often overwhelmed. But she had a remarkable husband who believed in and shouldered the plow with her, and a Savior Who always upheld her. As you read, I hope you will get a glimpse of His grace and will be encouraged that this same grace that sustained Louisa will also help you to do hard things for the Master.

CHAPTER 1

THE NEAR LOSS OF EVERYTHING

Everything difficult indicates something more than our theory of life yet embraces, checks some tendency to abandon the strait path, leaving open only the way ahead. But there is a reality of being in which all things are easy and plain—oneness, that is, with the Lord of Life; to pray for this is the first thing; and to the point of this prayer every difficulty hedges and directs us.
George MacDonald, "The Word of Jesus on Prayer" from *Unspoken Sermons*

Although spring was in the air at the end of May 1853, despair gripped Louisa as she grasped little Lilia Scott and gazed out the window onto the narrow street below. The scent of honeysuckle drifted through the windows of their little red brick home on Tarrant Street, but the lovely fragrance failed to bring Louisa the expected hope of renewal. Even the sweetness of her blessed baby girl could not lessen the hopelessness she felt.[1]

Gone were the exhilaration and joy Louisa had known when, having just married George MacDonald, she had fastidiously arranged and furnished their new home. Rentals in Arundel were hard to come by, but they had found a lovely little cottage, perfect for the two of them. Narrow and terraced, the Georgian home was just a few doors down from the church where her beloved George was the new minister.

She looked about their honeymoon abode and recalled the elation she had felt when she chose the furnishings, the kitchen range, the window blinds—all purchased by her father, James Powell, as a wedding gift to help her and George begin their married life. She contemplated the garden, in which she had lovingly sown her favorite flower seeds, and their only tree, which George often said would whisper sweetly to him about God. Would God whisper to him now, to guide them and help them?

George and Louisa had shared two years of married bliss

by then. They'd faced the expected challenges through which all newlyweds must work, but neither Louisa nor George ever anticipated the catastrophe that had just befallen them. What would become of them? Where would they go? Must she leave her lovely home behind?

Jesus lived a grand simple life in poverty and love. Why should not I?
George to his father, June 3, 1853

CHAPTER 2

THE BECOMING OF LOUISA

That no keeping but a perfect one will satisfy God, I hold with all my heart and strength; but that there is none else he cares for, is one of the lies of the enemy. What father is not pleased with the first tottering attempt of his little one to walk? What father would be satisfied with anything but the manly step of the full-grown son?
George MacDonald, "The Way" from *Unspoken Sermons*

The Bow Bells chimed, and young Louisa awoke to a new and busy day in the Powell household. Those lovely bells of St Mary-le-Bow Church in London's East End comforted Louisa and gave her a sense of time and belonging. Her childhood days were lively—with so many sisters and brothers, it was impossible to be bored.

Little Louisa looked in the mirror and frowned at her wide nose and large mouth. She hated how plain she looked in comparison to her sisters, and her habit of parting her hair in the middle and keeping it tightly pinned behind her head did not alleviate her austere appearance. However, she did have one attribute that her sisters lacked—she was petite, and they envied her tiny waist. Her blue eyes twinkled with mischief as she found endless ways to bring wit and glee to her family's energetic yet carefully managed home.

Lou, as her siblings liked to call her, was raised in a magical, stately Georgian house known as The Limes. She loved to sit underneath the branches of her home's namesake, the single lime tree that grew out front, and smell the blossoms above her. Just a few blocks away, she could see the River Lea that marked East End's boundary. To the north, the River Thames carried boats into the bustling city of London. To the east, fragments of medieval Roman walls beckoned her to grow in strength and fortitude. Although the East End was notorious for its poverty, The Limes was an oasis of luxury. Elegant and vast, it had a three-acre garden and large stables that housed the children's horses. Louisa's father, an avid gardener, was particularly fond of his tea roses.

Louisa noticed everything, especially nature. Throughout her life and in all her letters, she wrote of God's creation, lovingly applying the truths of nature's beauty to her correspondence. From her bedroom window, she could hear the trilling of the wood pigeons, house sparrows, starlings, magpies, and robins that flitted around the East End and brought her endless delight. On her walks in nearby Springfield Park, she looked for the flowers that made her giggle when she repeated their amusing names: magenta corncockle, white wood anemone, purple columbine, and "day's eye" daisies. She delighted in the delicate, powder-blue harebells that flickered in the summer breeze, the late-spring milkmaids with their pastel hue, the lilies of the valley peeking up from limestone pavement, the tall foxgloves that were always irresistible to bees, and of course England's May glory, the bluebells.

It was not easy to find a niche in a family with thirteen children. Louisa's dear Mama, after giving birth to so many children and losing four when they were just infants, was always frail. But the children managed to mother and herd each other quite well. Mama was their touchpoint, their refuge. Her tenderhearted ways were the glue that bonded them together. She made it easy to be comfortable with and enthusiastically admire one other.

As the third of six girls, Louisa wasn't considered the most gifted, nor was she the family favorite—that honor was given to her older sister, Charlotte. Dear Charlotte—how could anyone envy or resent her? Everyone in the family looked up to her, and why wouldn't they? She stepped in and bore the brunt of the work that Mama couldn't do. She had the purest soprano voice, and whenever she sang, everyone would declare that the only singer better than Charlotte was Clara Novello, the acclaimed opera star. Louisa loved to hear Charlotte sing "Rejoice Greatly" and "He Was Despised" from Handel's *Messiah*.

Charlotte's ability to describe and mimic people also entertained her family. "How I wish I were more like

The Becoming of Louisa

Charlotte," Louisa would often think. Charlotte didn't know it, but Louisa marveled that she never complained when the burden of responsibility was placed on her shoulders as Mama's health continued to fail. Charlotte even found time for charity work in several missions around London.

Charlotte never flaunted being the family favorite. In fact, she made sure to highlight Louisa's petite waist. All her life, Louisa carefully kept a poem that dear Charlotte had lovingly penned for her:

> *List ye who would a marvel hear,*
> *Whilst I a story tell;*
> *Come look upon this waist so dear,*
> *And mark this wonder well.*
>
> *A little waist it always was,*
> *A man might well it span;*
> *But now 'tis smaller than it was:*
> *A child I'm sure now can?*
>
> *Yet more this flesh and skin surround*
> *Than ere they did before:*
> *Of old one heart, alone was found*
> *Now two are there—Oh, Lor!*

Not to be outdone, their sister Phoebe also penned an amusing poem in praise of Lou's dainty waist and perfect proportions, and Lou treasured this one as well:

> *You know that our Lou has grown graceful and slender;*
> *Like the breeze on the aspen, a zephyr may bend her:*
> *Is it squeezing and pulling, and tugging and pressing*
> *With steel and with whalebone, with jaen and with lacing?*
> *Oh, no! But give ear and the reason I'll tell*
> *Why a finger and thumb her waist may span well:*
> *She has lost her large heart, and there's nothing within*
> *But back-bone and ribs, nerves, muscle and skin.*[1]

"Louisa! Come quickly, Tiny One! We need you to slip through the porthole and grab the cat again!" Charlotte shouted one day.

Louisa soon appeared at the window, where she squeezed through the frame, caught the kitty by its scruff, and easily slipped back inside. After giving the cat a lecture on obedience, she skipped downstairs to breakfast. She hoped she wasn't late—Father was a stickler for punctuality, and his stern look of reproof would cause petite Louisa to shrink even more.

The table was set, and all were waiting. Fortunately, Father did not notice her late arrival. Glancing over at her mother, who was propped up in her wheelchair, Louisa noticed that she looked weaker and paler than normal.

"She's not feeling well this morning," said Charlotte as she noticed Louisa's concern. "Why don't you read to Mama from *Pilgrim's Progress* after breakfast?" Louisa nodded and smiled. *The Pilgrim's Progress* was her favorite book, and oh, how she wished Father would let them perform it for evening entertainment.

Louisa looked lovingly around the table—she adored all her siblings. Alexander, the oldest, was a practical joker who delighted in teasing his little sisters. He roughhoused sometimes, but Louisa liked his sense of humor and they orchestrated a few fiendish pranks together. Charlotte was next oldest, then Phoebe.

Phoebe was the messy one—she could care less about her dress or being tidy, especially if it interfered with chapel or prayers or her passion: philanthropy. Louisa was always happy when Phoebe took her to Bethnal Green, the very haunt of poverty and sin, to bring food and money, and most of all, love for her Savior. "Oh, to be more like Phoebe!" Louisa thought.

Next in line was George, Mama's pet. Mama often held George up as the model whom Louisa should copy. This did not help her insecurities one bit. George was certainly a very pretty child, but if only Mama knew how naughty he could be! Louisa giggled to herself as she remembered the time he persuaded her to pull the hair of an old gentleman sitting in the pew in front of them the last time they attended chapel.

"See if his hair is real or just a wig," George prodded.

Carefully, she reached up and pulled.

It was real. And its owner was not happy. He turned around to see who had tampered with his tresses, only to find two innocent-looking children, their heads down, reading their Scriptures. Louisa knew that if she returned his gaze she would burst into laughter.

The next oldest sibling was Angela, affectionately called Annie. Sometimes Louisa felt bad for Annie, who struggled with spelling and reading and whom Mama called "Little Needlewoman," as though needlework were the only thing she could do. Mama and Father wondered about Annie's intelligence, but Louisa knew in her heart that Annie was gifted and able.

Across the table sat Florentia, or Flora, as her family liked to call her; she was the quietest of them all, and, thought Louisa, perhaps the most submissive to Father's rules. Flora could play the piano like no other, and her loving ways and warmth endeared her to everyone.

Finally, Louisa's eyes rested on Caroline, whom she affectionately called Carrie. Carrie was the baby and the most delicate member of the family. Although her health was always weak, she was certainly the dearest and would become Louisa's closest, most beloved friend.

At the head of the table sat Father, who led his home with an orderly, profoundly religious demeanor. James made sure that the household was carefully run by four servants, including the children's governess. Louisa loved her father, and although he kept a distance and his business required much of his time, he was a bulwark and refuge for Louisa and her siblings.

By the time Louisa reached her teens, Mama used a wheelchair permanently. As Louisa grew older, she tried to emulate Charlotte and help Father around the home as much as she could. Her greatest desire was to please him. She loved to see him smile, though sadly his smiles were rare.

"Papa carries so much on his shoulders," Louisa would think. "With Mama's poor health, his work stress, and so many children to oversee, his burdens are massive mountains he must climb daily."

James Powell was a prosperous leather merchant who had inherited the family business, Messrs. T. J. and T. Powell Leather Trade, which imported tanning materials and hides from all over the world.

His children always delighted in listening to him tell their family history. Hearing the pride in his voice made Louisa proud, too.

"Remember, our ancestors were Knights of the Shire in Wales, which means that the Powells are related to the first members of Parliament," he would remind his brood, "and you must behave accordingly."

All their ancestors were conventional, chapel disciplined, and proud to come from a long line of Congregationalists.

Father expected his children to behave in a friendly, genteel manner both at home and in public. However, he was not all work and stern demeanor—he had exceptional taste in music and was himself an accomplished violinist. Louisa loved to hear him play, and she always looked forward to the frequent quartets and dinner parties held at The Limes, at which many notable musicians were guests. Louisa and her sisters were well trained musically and were even blessed to have Mendelssohn's favorite pupil, Clara Macirone, for their very own piano teacher.

As a proficient carpenter and bookbinder, James Powell always kept himself busy. All the Powells were busy bees, because Father stressed through his words and actions that industry and frugality must rule the home.

The men of the family were expected to gain a good education and continue the family prosperity, while the young Powell girls were educated at home and focused their studies on music, literature, needlework, and home management. College was not in the cards for the Powell sisters. Louisa's parents expected her to be feminine, graceful, adept at music, and perfect in manners, all of which she mastered well, but the most trying expectation of all was the Victorian requirement that she assume she was intellectually deficient compared to her male counterparts.

Despite the Powell family's rigid tenets, daily life was still sweet and tender. Mama's gentle countenance and Father's wonderful music permeated the family's home and hearts. Growing up in such a strict environment didn't stunt Louisa's creativity or passions—instead, her wit, the twinkle in her eye, and her enormous sense of fun kept the family in stitches.

Every Powell was fond of charades (though playacting was forbidden), and singing and piano-playing were often heard through the windows of their home. Louisa developed a beautiful mezzo-soprano voice and mastered the piano and organ. Music was her source of solace, and sneaking away to play the piano was her favorite pastime. Her love of charades, literature, and music would be put to good use later, and their comforts would sustain her through many difficult times.

Christmas was Louisa's favorite season. Father would gather the family around the table, then cue them with a note, and they would sing Milton's hymn of thanksgiving in exquisite harmony:

> *Let us with a gladsome mind*
> *Praise the Lord, for he is kind:*
> *For his mercies aye endure*
> *Ever faithful, ever sure.*

> *All things living he doth feed,*
> *His full hand supplies our need:*
> *For his mercies aye endure*
> *Ever faithful, ever sure.*

Although she was lighthearted, Louisa had a keen sense of the ridiculous that hid behind others' guise and falsehood. This sense dictated her conscience and would not allow her to excuse pretensions in dress, manner, or especially religion. She just didn't understand why people put on airs. Because of her honesty and innate ability to sense others' guile, she avoided joining her parents' church until she was older than was customary. Angela often told of an amusing incident during which Louisa and Flora met with the elders to finally become members of the church.

"Louisa, Flora, the elders are here!" called their mother from the landing.

The two sisters were ushered into their father's study, where two grave deacons waited patiently.

"We've come to ask you a few questions and to pray with you," one said. He was an undertaker, very old and fat.

"Flora," he asked, "do you wrestle in prayer?"

Louisa quickly covered her mouth, barely stifling a giggle. She almost couldn't conceal her naughty delight as she pictured her sister, with whom she shared a bedroom, as Flora so often was—fast asleep while kneeling at her bedside. However, both Louisa and Flora realized the solemnity of the meeting. Flora kept her composure and attempted to answer the question as honestly as possible. Despite her amusement, Louisa was able to make a decisive commitment that she meant from her heart.[2] After the elders left, Flora playfully pinched Louisa, and they both howled with laughter.

If only Louisa knew how dearly she was loved by all. Her insecurities often tainted her ability to see herself the way others did. Her siblings lamented how dull the home was when Louisa was away. Just like the radiant twinkle in her blue eyes, her life brightened everything and everyone around her. Her family especially enjoyed the way she could immediately see the ridiculous in any situation.

And so little Louisa grew and flourished in her home at The Limes, but deep inside she always felt profoundly inferior and often worried that she was merely floundering in her relationship with God. She desired truth in all things, but she despised her inability to control her temper, sometimes felt spiritually cold, and was frequently discouraged by spiritual turmoil. She knew she needed to practice self-forgetfulness, and caring for her younger siblings helped her to do so. But as she gazed at her plain self in the mirror, she longed for something more—to step into a freer and holier air. She was restless for spiritual freshness.

"There must be something more than this," she thought.

And that Something More arrived when her new sister-in-law, Helen, introduced the family to Mr. George MacDonald.

Trust to God to weave your little thread into the great web, though the pattern shows it not yet.
George MacDonald, as quoted in *The Way to Win: Showing How to Succeed in Life*[3]

CHAPTER 3

STRUCK FROM THE ETERNAL LIGHT

A stronger desire to do the will of the Father . . . is surely the best thing God himself can kindle in the heart of any man. For what good is there in creation by the possibility of being yet further created? And what else is growth but more of the will of God?
George MacDonald, *Far Above Rubies*

Something More's light first dawned for Louisa in 1844 when her brother Alexander married Helen MacKay. Helen was a vibrant woman, full of life and ideas, and she took the Powell home by storm. A great beauty, she was charming, with captivating eyes, a radiant smile, and a sweet, tender voice that floated through the home whenever she spoke or sang. The young Powell girls were bewitched by her loveliness and enthusiasm, and it was clear that Alexander was crazy about her.

Louisa adored Helen. She could not quite put her finger on it, but there was something different about her new sister-in-law. Helen was not demure or submissive, but she was also not permissive or inappropriate. She was a fiercely devout Christian and made sure that Alexander could clearly formulate his views on the atonement before she would even agree to marry him! "How bold! She's so confident in herself and her beliefs," thought Louisa.

"Come back soon!" Louisa called as Helen left The Limes. Then she thought, "We need more of her here. She's fun, and she makes me laugh—and think!"

Helen brought to The Limes a new way of looking at the world and at faith. She demonstrated a surety and a confidence that were unusual for Victorian women, and her vivacious personality lit up every room she entered. The Powell girls had not been allowed to act this way nor even been exposed to a woman who exhibited such certainty. Helen's simple, joyous outlook was the fissure—the crack that opened up the Powell sisters. Her self-assurance and depth prompted them to emerge from their shells and venture out into the glorious dawn of true womanhood. Their mother had always been demure and deferred to her husband, so it had never occurred to the Powell girls that confidence and thoughtful opinions were admirable and even appropriate traits for a Victorian woman.

Louisa's Something More finally arrived in 1845 when Helen visited The Limes once again, this time with her cousin George. Helen and Alexander had been married for about a year when she introduced George MacDonald to the Powells.

"I want to be known as the first person who recognized that my cousin George will do great things for the world's uplifting," she said by way of introduction.

But Louisa was out of town when George arrived. Although she missed his first introduction, her family's excitement about him lingered long after he left.

Angela in particular approved of this bringer of light.

"Louisa, you've just got to meet him! He will explain everything that puzzles you and will make your life so happy!" Annie raved in a letter to her sister.

Father and Mama had always been concerned about Annie's intellect because she struggled with reading and all forms of academics. Most troubling to her parents was that she could never spell above the level of a ten-year-old. However, she and Louisa were the most brilliant of all the sisters when it came to creativity and originality.

When George met Annie, he formed a more positive perspective; he found Annie to be surprisingly receptive to learning and understanding.

"Annie is quite bright and teachable," he boldly announced to her family.

George's confidence in her abilities changed Annie's world. Many years later, she would look back and write, "He came not a conventional youth, with polite smooth talk, but like a prophet of old. Long before we thought of him as having any religious message to us, gradually we found he knew about everything and could put any difficulty right, be it to answer 'Is there a God?' or 'What is poetry?' or 'What about ghosts or fairies?"[1]

Annie marveled that George cared about her and her mind, and that he actually believed she was teachable. "He showed me new life in everything, understood me as an equal. This was very wonderful to me, as all my life I had been the fool of the family for my inability to spell and commit to memory. Great was my astonishment when he wished me to learn mathematics and began himself to teach me."[2]

Annie could not contain her excitement regarding George. She just had to let Lou know what she'd missed while away.

"Louisa, the greatest thing is he actually read to us on Sunday—not from the old hymn book that Father will only allow on Sundays, but from Wordsworth and Tennyson and a wonderful poet named Browning! I was so sick of the small pretty little bits of books that Father allowed us to read during the week, and now George has opened my eyes to all these wonderful writers who live all around us in London!"

"Who is this man, this marvel who invaded our home? When will he return?" Louisa wondered after Annie told her all about the tall Scotsman.

George's return was inevitable because the Powells were lavish with their hospitality and because he sorely needed a home away from home. The vast city of London was so different from his home in the Highlands of Scotland. His funds were limited and he needed a safe haven—the Powells' warm meals and welcoming atmosphere made The Limes his sanctuary. Besides, Helen was his favorite cousin, and he loved spending time with her and her new family.

George was a breath of fresh air at The Limes. He delighted in even the smallest parts of nature and thoroughly enjoyed spending time with the Powell children. He carefully observed their family habits and looked for ways in which he could be helpful. This is why the children loved him so and awaited his visits: he noticed them, even though they were young.

Visitors to The Limes could tell just how much the children liked them by the way they were greeted when they returned for a second visit. If the children disliked a returning visitor, they would hide until forced to come downstairs and extend limp hands in greeting.

"Not the pompous old elder again," they would moan to one another.

"He always smells like cabbage and tobacco," one would lament.

"Nevertheless, you must shake his hand and act like ladies and gentlemen," Charlotte would remind them.

The older ones would coach their younger siblings to ask polite questions, and the younger children would comply with monosyllabic responses. But if the children liked the lucky visitor and had agreed to allow the returnee into their inner circle, they would greet them at the entrance to The Limes with yells and cheers, like little scamps who had been let loose for the day.

Not surprisingly, George MacDonald was immediately made a member of this coveted inner circle. He entered the Powells' lives like a meteor and lit up their whole world with rich glory during his brief visits.

Annie recalled, "Once when I was ill he came to see me in the old schoolroom because I was naughty and would not take my castor oil. He had not talked to me for many minutes before I gulped it down without a murmur, and was rewarded next day with a box of sugar-candy—a rare luxury at that time."[3]

Fortunately, after hearing all about Helen's mysterious cousin, Louisa did not have to wait long to meet him. When George visited again, Louisa was introduced to a tall Scotsman with kind eyes and a patient demeanor.

"How odd," she thought, "that he is so unconcerned with the opinions of others. He even goes to the theater! He was calm and composed when speaking with Father, and so equanimous is this Meteor who has entered our atmosphere with his lovely Scottish ways and wisdom."

George's confidence intrigued Louisa because she was so self-deprecating. He was so open, frank, sensitive, and imaginative. She marveled that he could speak so kindly to and about others and that he was free from anxiety and had such confidence in his faith in God. He hated deceit and mean-spiritedness and desired above all purity and moral courage. In addition, he was a true scholar, having nearly finished his degree at King's College. Surely such a man would never notice plain old Louisa.

But to her great surprise, George was actually attracted to her.

"But I'm two years older than he, and so very common and simple, and so terribly flawed!" she thought. If only she could have seen herself through his eyes, she would have seen a humble and demure girl with wonderful blue eyes, a keen intellect, and a joyous heart—a woman without guile, a conscientious follower of Christ.

Because George was often away at King's College, his visits were random and unpredictable. Louisa waited impatiently for him to return, and her impatience bothered her.

"I hate the way my thoughts continually focus on him," she lamented.

But then it happened—George sent her a letter! It was March 27, 1846.

"Louisa, you have mail," the housemaid called.

Louisa grabbed the letter, rushed up to her bedroom, and shut the door so she could read in private.

"Thank goodness Flora is out and about!" she thought, grateful that no one could observe or comment or ask to read the letter too. Carefully, she opened the envelope, noticing George's exquisite penmanship.

> *My dear Louisa,*
>
> *Will you let the inclosed apologize for carrying off your thimble—I did not mean to do so—but I have not time to explain. I am sorry the bits of poetry are not more worth offering you, but perhaps I may succeed better some other time. Of course you will not put them in your book if you do not like them.*
>
> *Your affectionate cousin(?)*

Evidently, George was not sure whether he was considered a cousin of the Powells, because his familial connection was through Helen alone. Louisa chuckled as she remembered the thimble he had borrowed to mend and sew his own clothes.

Smiling to herself, she decorated the letter with sprays of stars and wrote, "My Dear, my Dearest. I am an overgrown baby with manners like a bear vexed." A bear, yes, she liked that metaphor. "It's certainly an apt description, but more so of him," she mused, and decided to use that nickname for him from then on.

The ice now broken, George and Louisa began to correspond in earnest, carefully keeping each precious letter tied with ribbon.

George's letters grew more hopeful and his affection for Louisa more evident. The personal, introspective poetry he included gave Louisa the confidence to share more personal thoughts of her own. How it surprised her that she could pen her deepest thoughts so easily, and soon she began to share all her fears and self-doubts.

George received each letter with anticipation. In the beginning of their relationship, George took the role of willing teacher, and Louisa of his eager student. She was in awe of his wisdom, spiritual intensity, and nearness to God. But as their relationship grew, George began telling Louisa about his struggles as well. She was not alone. All was well and all would be well.

> *I am not yet going to write you a long letter, for indeed I am not very happy myself, having been struggling for some time with wrong and painful thoughts, which seem to take from me all right to look to Jesus. But I hope to be delivered from them, and triumph over them. Pray for humility for me, dear Louisa, and the feeling that my salvation is entirely owing to Christ Jesus.*[4]

This was the something more for which Louisa had longed. She decided to share even more of her insecurities, especially in regard to George's growing faith and his desire and respect for the Scriptures. He was saying such strange things, things she had never heard before: that God is the Creator and Father of *all* mankind, that God's disposition from eternity is forgiveness and steadfast love, that God will judge everyone with justice and without partiality, and that God's purpose is to bring man to Himself by grace because of His all-consuming love. This was so different from what she had been taught. But was she worthy of George's attention and guidance? She wrote to him of her growing fear:

> *If I cannot appreciate and love your enthusiasm for all that is high, holy and beautiful, for all that is above the common ideas of the multitude most truly you must feel unhappy at the prospect before you and thought of my being a hindrance—a fear oh! The thought is what I cannot bear. What a terrible word that is, what a monster I must be—You say 'deliver you from this bondage'—how can I—oh! What very terrible words for you [to] use to me—I could write no more just now, but have been trying to ask God to help me to be meek and humble—You have helped me much already but oh do not let anything of all that has passed between us—beautiful as it has been to me make you feel obliged to live with one whose temper he would lead a life of bondage. I cannot bear the idea.*[5]

Having wrestled through the same spiritual turmoil, George was devoted to helping Louisa by sharing his spiritual thoughts and findings:

> *You promise in your last note to try to strive. A fear is upon me that you have tried and tried earnestly and tried again, since writing that, and have failed, or seemed to fail, and have become discouraged and are again ready to tell me it is no use. It might well seem to us often to be no use, if we had not hope of help from above. But God wants to have us back to himself, and he will help us. I wish I could think to you the thoughts of encouragement which I could give you. How often has it seemed to me as if it was no use trying, and how often have I been helped to go on. . . . my difficulties are of the same nature as*

> *yours—those which a heart far from God must feel, even when the hand of the Heavenly Father is leading it back to himself, as I trust He is with me—it seems a wonder that he can bear with one. In all temptations and trials the readiest help is to try to pray to God for help and to think of the Man Christ Jesus.*[6]

Louisa grew. She thrived. She blossomed. Soon she was able and happy to be a comfort to and sounding board for George as he struggled with poor health and a lack of funds. To help finance his studies, he had agreed to be a tutor for the Radermacher family, an unpleasant position that entailed teaching unruly children.

"The worst bother is ill brought up noisy children—especially the younger ones who scream frightfully," he once wrote.[7] It wasn't that he wasn't thankful for the work, for it did keep him fed, and he was well aware that he had been chosen to teach the children, but their entitlement and lack of desire to learn irked him, and Louisa listened and gave advice.

Each day she looked forward to another letter from him. She tried not to seem too excited, lest her brother George tease her with his silly kissing noises or try to snatch the letters away. With a casual air, she would walk up to her room and lock the door. Only then would she allow herself to show emotion. She enjoyed every letter, every note, every silly Scottish word George MacDonald penned.

Their letters were not always about serious matters. Louisa shared her wit and sense of humor. When George wrote about his enthusiasm for chemistry and his scientific experiments at college, she had great fun teasing him: "I am so glad dearest George that you are really going to begin the wonders of our cabalistic art—I hope at least you discover the Rosicrucian secret of prolonging life. . . . I shall not be afraid of the magic of your bottles and crucibles and liquids and essences and shall only be too delighted to be admitted into your mystic chamber or laboratory sometimes."[8]

Their growing intimacy, expressed through letters and George's frequent visits to The Limes, was curious to Louisa. Why her? Why did George value her opinions and treat her so differently than every other man she had ever known? Clearly, he did not think of women the same way her father and brothers did. George believed in her; he believed in her sisters, too. He even taught them mathematics and science. Was it possible George believed in emancipating women from the confines of the drawing room so they could stand next to men as equals and co-partners before God?

As they grew closer and communicated more freely, Louisa began to see that George viewed marriage and women as sacred. When George heard that an acquaintance of theirs, George Searle, had become engaged, he was clearly unhappy. Louisa was glad that her George did not support the engagement, because Mr. Searle was a domineering man, and she knew he would not treat his bride the way George treated her—kindly and as an equal. George wrote to Louisa:

> *I am much more disappointed in the news of George Searle's engagement. How could he do it? I hope he may not repent it. Just fancy—if she be as orthodox as her father! However perhaps he only wants her for a piece of house furniture, like a sofa or a carpet—not as a fellow-heir of eternal life.*[9]

Heirs together in the grace of life—was it truly possible? Louisa's George was never pompous or domineering. He was careful to share lessons learned and remedies gleaned from his personal experiences and walk with his Savior. He eagerly confided in her about everything—his health, his studies, his observations on nature walks, and even simple daily events. He treated her as his best friend and appreciated her wit and creative ideas. Was it possible that she could enjoy life so much now that George had appeared at The Limes? Dared she even think he would consider marriage?

What Louisa enjoyed most about their correspondence were George's musings and descriptions of nature. Here was someone who loved God's creation as much as she did. Here was someone who found rapture and truth in the simplicity of God's handiwork. George had always delighted in walking along the sandy shoreline of Aberdeen. During raging storms, he loved to be smack-dab in the middle of the howling winds, watching the powerful waves break against the beach.

When George could get away from his studies and visit the Powells, he and Louisa would often take long walks together, sometimes with Annie, sometimes alone. At the entrance to The Limes, they would turn toward the river, the trees and flowers guiding their way. Birds would twitter while they kept their eggs warm or looked for worms, and the fullness of nature would call out to the couple and draw them together.

George excelled at pointing out biblical truths while they walked. "It's the show of things that God cares for most, for their show is the face of far deeper things than they. What they say to the childlike soul is the truest thing to be gathered of them. To know a primrose is a higher thing than to know all the botany of it—just as to know Christ is an infinitely higher thing than to know all theology, all that is said about His person, or babbled about His work. Nature, as well, exists primarily for her face, her look, her appeals to the heart and the imagination. But that's a lovely primrose over there along the bank, isn't it, Louisa?"

George found kinship in Louisa's shared appreciation of God's creation. He especially enjoyed her detailed descriptions of nature:

> *Here I am my dearest friend, encamped on a stone with a bit of a rock for my desk, the sea blue and green sparkling in the bright sun, before now that same bright sun over my head and the softest most refreshing breeze blowing round me. I have just been paying a most delightful visit to the sands and beach below the waters though I certainly did not stay there long enough to find out whether I should like to live always with Undine and Neptune.*[10]

Only George could fathom what she meant about living with Undine and Neptune. He wrote back: "The sun is low—and the drops on the needle of a fir tree before my window, are sparkling so beautifully."

Once, she found in the mailbox a sweet poem about nature

and the night, addressed to her from her dear Bear:

> *The mysterious night*
> *When but a light of the low horned moon*
> *Looks o'er the rest of a peaked cloudy night*
> *Edging it with a glory—fading soon*
> *And few pale stars are mid the cloud rifts strewn*
> *And the low wind is running to and fro,*
> *Like a forsaken child, that knows not where to go—*
> *Oh! To have the silence of such a night*
> *Around us once more!*

Louisa's heart soared! She loved this man, her best friend, who shared her interests and responded to the deeper promptings those shared interests brought to light.

"Louisa," George would often say, "We must choose faith-filled eyes that see nature through His lens, because nature is the truest true—the only way to see God and to rejoice!"

He once asked her: "Tell me again about everything round about you; every expression the beautiful face of nature puts on. Tell me, too, about the world within your own soul—that living world—without which the world without would be but a lifelessness. The beautiful things round about you are the expressions of God's face, or, as in Faust, the garment whereby we see the deity."[11]

George's letters gave Louisa so much clarity. They were a means of grace, grace that had been unknown to her and that blossomed through their relationship—abundant grace to grow together and to be filled with divine purpose.

Autumn arrived, the air was brisk, and the fallen leaves crunched beneath Louisa's feet. As she walked along the river, she took George's advice and pondered what truths nature was trying to speak to her. Were the falling leaves telling her to let go of something? Was the river challenging her to flow toward something new?

In the mailbox she found the sweetest letter from her Bear; it answered the questions and unspoken longings she had carefully hidden in her heart. She sat down on the nearby bench and began to read.

> *G.M.D. to Louisa Powell,*
> *Highbury College,*
> *My Study, Oct. 23, 1848.*
>
> *... I meant to write a much longer letter to my Louisa and many, beautiful and wise things (to me) I wanted to say, but now the impulse has left me. May our Father in Heaven be with you and bless you, and make you better of your present sufferings.*
>
> *Is love a beautiful thing, dearest? You and I love, but who created love? Let us ask him to purify our love to make it stronger and more real and more self-denying. I want to love you for ever—so that although there is no marrying or giving in marriage in heaven we may keep each other here as the best beloved. It is to heaven I look as the place where I shall have most enjoyment in you—both from my perfection and yours. Oh Louisa is it not true that our life here is a growing into life, and our death a being born—our true birth? ... And in our life together ... when the cloud is over my head, I may see the light shining from your face, and when darkness is around you, you may see the light on mine, and thus, we shall take courage. But we can only expect to have this light within us and on our faces—we can only expect to be a blessing to each other by doing that which is right. ...* [12]

Marriage?

Had he just written about marriage? And in such a lovely and holy way!

Thrilled by each word, Louisa agreed with George that their sexuality was intimately related to their spirituality, and that through marriage they would meet God together, every day, with every event.

It had been two years and four months since they had first met. She had kept count. And now her Bear had decided that it was time to become formally engaged.

The river and the trees had spoken: it was time to let go, time to leave and to cleave and to flow together. George knew Louisa was the answer to his lifelong prayers, and he was ready. But was she?

There is more love in the world than anything else, for instance; but the best love and the individual in whom love is supreme are the rarest of all things.
George MacDonald, *Sir Gibbie*

CHAPTER 4

THE WHOLE UNIVERSE IS TENTED WITH LOVE

Our selves are ours that we may lay them on the altar of love.
George MacDonald, *Paul Faber, Surgeon*

The year 1848 brought with it much change for England and the rest of the world. The threat of Napoleon had been subdued, but the hunger and poverty that permeated England, and the devastating famine in Ireland, had forced a quarter million people per year to emigrate away from England in search of a better life for their families. The Industrial Revolution was ramping up, railways were speeding up life in England, and Chartism had emerged,[1] demanding a vote for every man. These changes did not go unnoticed by George and Louisa.

"Louisa, we must do something that will calm this turmoil," George said. Louisa's tender, receptive heart agreed.

She loved hearing George talk about his studies and fascinations, from Greek and Latin to Jewish antiquities. These subjects, his devotion to studying the Scriptures, and all the suffering he observed around him led him to his final decision about his future vocation. At first, he had thought he could help alleviate suffering by becoming a doctor. But besides his love of chemistry, he neither enjoyed nor excelled in the required fields, and now he knew why. Now he knew his purpose: Christian ministry. But first he wanted to make sure he had his father's approval—and he received it.

George quickly enrolled at Highbury College, a theological school in Highbury Park, London. Because he had already earned his master of arts, he only needed to spend two years at Highbury instead of the usual four.

Louisa was proud. She knew George's decision was the right one. "Imagine! He will be near us here in London," she thought.

His vocation decided, George was finally ready to make a sweeter, more important decision: finally getting his "wee wifie." His family had often told the story of little Georgie's early desire for a wife. His father loved to remind him of the time he was "strutting about in his first pair of trousers before his Uncle William, when the latter vowed he now needed only a watch and a wife to make a man of him." Young George replied, "I can do well enough wanting the watch, but—but, I would like that I had a wee wifie!"[2]

Late in the evening while Louisa lay in her bed, surrounded by her childhood treasures and memories, George sat at his desk. They shared the same view of the moon and shining constellations that peeked through the clouds above them. With trepidation conquered by sheer determination, George picked up his pen and composed the most important letter he would ever write:

Dear Mr. Powell,

I feel considerable embarrassment in writing to you, and the only way I can get over it is to come to the point at once. The continued improvement of Mrs. Powell's health, of which I need not say I am glad to hear, encourages me to write to you on a subject about which I have communicated with you before. Will you permit me to visit your daughter Louisa, with the hope of one day making her my wife? My expectations as far as the things of this world are concerned are none of the greatest and I need say nothing of them, as you can judge of them more accurately than I can. However you may regard my request, I beg you will forgive me, if my present note is at all deficient in propriety, and be assured if so that it is the result of ignorance—which I hope you will excuse.

I am, my dear sir
Yours most truly,
George MacDonald[3]

A short while later, George's letter lay open on the desk in James Powell's study, which had always been the one room that was all but out of bounds to the Powell children; it was his special domain, and he spent a good amount of time closeted there. Bookshelves lined the walls, and his chair and writing table sat in the middle of the room in front of a window that looked over the gardens.

Louisa knocked on the door, only to find the study empty. She crossed the room and looked down at George's beautifully scripted letter.

"It's happened," she realized. "We are now more than mere friends, we are the best of friends, and as such we will become the best as man and wife." But would Papa approve of this tall Scotsman for his tiny Welsh daughter? She really did not know what his answer would be. How she hated the wait and the worry. Fortunately, she did not have to wait long. Within hours, Papa called her to his study.

"Louisa," he said, "You know that I have never been excited about George or his somewhat unorthodox ways. However, his decision to become a minister will give him a respectable, if not prestigious, position. More importantly, with the way he adores you, I am certain you will be loved and cared for properly. Write to that young man and tell him I approve and will allow him to court you."

Louisa darted out of the study as quickly as she could manage and rushed to her bedroom, where she wrote to George: "Papa wishes me to write to you!!!" The extra exclamation points were necessary—she intended them to bring him immediate relief when he opened the letter.

The splendid dawn of hope engulfed Louisa. The longing of her heart had been granted, but she still had to patiently endure a time of waiting and separation. Even so, her father's blessing was a relief to the two lovers.

Years later, their son Greville wrote of his parents' betrothal and explained as best he could how his grandfather decided to agree to the union:

To the heads of the house no less than to the daughters, it was

> something different from any that had hitherto come into their home. The austere merchant who could put his soul into his violin-playing, recognized with sure instinct that a daughter given to this lover of God, this poet who opened the eyes of all who were not slaves to pharisaic convention, was in good keeping indeed. There was always a mystical quality in my father's influence: to come within it was to be convinced.[4]

"I knew he would say yes," Louisa told George. "Mama loves her young Scot dearly, and Papa would not dare question what she believes to be right. And besides, you are quite persuasive, whether you acknowledge it or not!"

As Louisa walked the moss-scented paths around The Limes, she pondered and planned. There would be a waiting period, she quite understood this, while George finished his master's degree at Highbury, and then he would certainly need to be hired by a congregation before Father would allow the marriage to go ahead.

"This could take a while," she thought with a sigh, "but how wonderful that no matter where we are, or how far apart, we are always aware of each other's supporting presence. I'll just keep doing what I've been given to do each day and be at peace."

It was as if she could actually hear George's beautiful Scottish brogue whispering to her heart, saying, "My Dear One, take courage and remember that an active patience is a heavenly power."

When spring arrived, with all the excitement and planning, Louisa began to feel ill and was ordered by her doctor to get away and rest. Accompanied by her close friend Josephine Rutter, and Josephine's younger sister, Hannah, Louisa traveled to Hastings. Oh, how she loved and needed the sea air. Slowly, it strengthened her.

Of course, she kept in touch with George through many letters. When he could, George would visit The Limes and write to Louisa with an update of what was happening at her beloved home. His letters amused and moved her. "Louisa, Phoebe wrapped me up in her boa; and your mother is helping Annie more with her reading, and if Annie allows, I will teach her more mathematics. I think that Flora could help her too. Also, I've been working on getting your concertina mended while you are gone," he informed her. But as always, the letters she enjoyed most were about nature:

> *You tell me about the sea and the sky and the shore so beautifully, so lovingly, so truthfully, that I love you more for it. Tell me again about everything round about you; every expression the beautiful face of Nature puts on. Tell me, too, about the world within your own soul—that living world—without which the world without would be but a lifelessness. The beautiful things round about you are the expression of God's face, or, as in Faust, the garment whereby we see the deity. Is God's sun more beautiful than God himself? Has he not left it to us as a symbol of his own life-giving light? But I cannot now explain all that I mean.*[5]

"I see George's heart in every word he shares; he shares his very being with me, both in voice and in letters," Louisa thought. "I want to understand all that he thinks and feels, on topics from nature to theology to art."

She treasured this letter most of all:

G.M.D. to Louisa Powell
Highbury,
May 15, 1849

> *I have just read your letter dearest. My hands were cold, and when I opened the bit with the flowers they felt warm. . . . I have had a letter from you every day as yet. Only a week to-day since you went! Well, I would not have you back one hour sooner, if your heart were like to break with its longing. You have beautiful things around you, and beautiful things are creeping into your soul, and making a home for themselves there—and my wife is growing more beautiful for me. Does not He deserve thanksgiving who made man male and female? . . . Write to me about the sea and sky, which are common to all*

men—like those great truths the sense of which makes a man feel great too—those truths ever the same yet ever presenting new aspects of beauty, different to different minds, different to the same mind at different times—yet ever in essence one and the same. I am indeed glad to hear you are so wild!

I have been trying to translate a little poem of Goethe's, entitled

Nähe der Geliebten

I think of thee when of the sun the shimmer
From the sea streams;
I think of thee when of the Moon the glimmer
From deep wells beams.

I see thee, when upon the far Way's Ridge
The Dust-cloud wakes;
In the deep Night, when on the narrow Bridge
The Wanderer quakes.

I hear thee there, when with a rushing low
Falleth the Wave,
In the still Thicket loitering oft I go
Quiet as the grave.

I am with thee, and tho' thou art so far,
Yet thou art near!
The Sun doth sink, soon lighteth me each Star—
Oh! wert thou here!

What a strange picture of Turner's I saw yesterday at the Exhibition. A Rainbow over a stormy sea, ships far and near, boats and a buoy. I could make nothing of it at first. Only by degrees I awoke to the Truth and wonder of it. I lost much enjoyment, however, by going without any optical assistance.[6]

Louisa's life with George would be so different from her life at The Limes. Always looming at home was her constant desire for her father's approval—she was never at rest, always afraid of not living up to his expectations. George, by contrast, had an open, frank relationship with his father; instead of living in fear, George delighted in pleasing him and often used his relationship with his father to describe the characteristics of God the Father to Louisa.

"Louisa," George reminded her, "God is our loving, nurturing, encouraging Father, not the tyrant that Calvinists portray. He is like my father, who as much as was possible never refused me anything I asked, poor though he was. I hope our own children will be able to say the same of me. God will never refuse us anything we ask unless it will harm us. All He asks is that we trust Him, even if we don't understand what He is requiring of us, for trust and obedience are essential to growth and understanding."

"Oh, George, sometimes I do feel like such a child," Louisa lamented. "I have so much to learn from you about God and about what love really is."

"Well, my dearest Darling, falling in love often awakens deep religious questions. This really isn't surprising, and the psychic importance is in no way lessened if in later years all sense of passion's relation to the Divine is forgotten."

"I don't understand."

"Surely few are able to call their wives their own, as I shall call you if it pleases our God who made us and made love," he assured her. "When we love truly, all oppression of past sin is swept away, and two become one. Love is the final atonement. You no longer need to be afraid, Louisa."

"Oh, my dear Bear, I do so hope you will find that the love of your wife and the love of God become simply aspects of the same Love, and that we will have a mutual love and affection that is deep and enduring."

At Highbury, George immersed himself in his studies, read the required books, and wrote tedious essays, but late at night when everyone else was asleep he always took the time to sit at his desk and write long letters to Louisa. The two wrote to each other every day and shared deep thoughts about their daily doings and their future together. On the weekends, George often had to preach. He welcomed these opportunities as a way to hone his rhetorical skills, and the pay was an appreciated supplement to his nonexistent income.

He was learning so much, and Louisa loved when he shared his gleanings with her. His two years of school flew by.

"Oh I have two such pieces to read to you—One of Tennyson's *Poems*—and the other a translation from Jean Paul Richter—oh! oh! oh! The last is—I hardly know what to call it—They were both to me worth hundreds of sermons—of some kinds at least," George wrote to Louisa.[7]

George also made lifelong friends during his time at Highbury. Spence, Moir, and Chancellor, as well as James Matheson, were his closest companions at college. Through his friendship with James, he met James's older brother Greville, who would become his most intimate friend. The Mathesons' mother was a widow who lived close to Highbury College, and George often accompanied James and Greville when they visited home.

"Louisa, I can't wait for you to meet this family," George exclaimed. "They have barely enough to live on, but Mrs. Matheson has achieved wonders in educating her family—seven boys and one girl! Can you imagine? She keeps her door open to any of her sons' friends who want to pop in from the college. Would you be willing to invite them to The Limes for me?"

Louisa's closest friends were Josephine and Hannah, and she was glad George was making close friends too. Though meeting new people was quite out of her comfort zone, Louisa took the initiative, called upon Mrs. Matheson, and delivered formal invitations to a charade party. George, as a studious theologian in training, was unable to attend.

To Louisa's surprise, she actually had fun choosing the menu and finding the perfect plots for charades. Her sisters were excited, too, and the house buzzed with preparations. The evening was a success, and Louisa couldn't wait to write to George and tell him about it:

Louisa Powell to G.M.D.

> ... I do not think I sat down for more than ten minutes altogether last night, and I was galloping about into all the corners of the house for dresses, etc., to dress up the actors. We had two excellent charades—Countryman and Bradshaw. David Matheson acted to immense admiration as a most absurd little French valet—he perfectly convulsed the whole room. ... I never saw Papa laugh more.[8]

So began many happy Powell-Matheson expeditions. They frequented the forest, Greenwich, Richmond, and Rosherville. Unbeknownst to Mr. Powell, they even spent an evening at the Sadler's Wells and Grecian theaters.

"You'd better not let Papa know," Louisa advised George. "We don't want his disapproval. But yesterday, I overheard him telling friends how proud he is of you and of your breeding."

Papa's opinion was soon altered, however, when George returned to The Limes after a three-month absence with, horror of horrors, a beard.

"Papa walked into the drawing room, hesitated for one moment, gave George a second look, then, without saying hello to him, Papa turned around and left the room. Without hesitation, George immediately went to his own room and, with soap and razor, obliterated his offence," Louisa recalled to her sisters.

"You do realize that when we are finally married, Louisa, I'm growing a beard," George told her.

"Of course you will," she replied. "You are my Bear, you know."

George's love and confidence in her gave Louisa confidence in herself. His guidance and patient assurances helped her form the traits she needed most as the time of waiting dragged on: pluck, gumption, and endurance. Her first opportunity to practice pluck came when George asked her to attend some lectures for him because he would be away preaching in Whitehaven. He did not want to miss the lectures of A. J. Scott, and Louisa promised to attend and take notes.

"I felt 2 or 3 times as if I should have cried because I could not follow him—really I do think it is rather too strong meat for such as I," she wrote to George.[9]

"But I am determined to do my best," she told herself. And she did.

Another occasion to use her newfound pluck arose when George's brother Charles came to London and Louisa was invited to meet him at the house of her sister-in-law, Helen. George had accepted an apprentice pastorate at Whitehaven and then worked in the ancient and beautiful city of Cork, Ireland, so he was unable to join them.

While visiting Charles and Helen, timid Louisa surprised herself when she came to her sweet George's defense. Apparently, Charles thought that George had made a mistake in taking the position in Cork and that his prospects would have been much better in Manchester.

"I do hope I wasn't lacking in modesty for the way I disagreed with them. I guess I am already strong in my devotion to you," she told George, fearful that his family would not approve of her after she had defended him.

"My Dearest Louisa, you only break out in thunder and lightning! I have a cold smile deep in my heart like a moth-eaten hole when I feel really wronged.[10] You are introspective, yet so comical, so satirical, sometimes cruelly so, and yet you are often moved to tears by others' sufferings," he reassured her.

"Like all great souls, you can give much because you can suffer much, and you so ardently love Truth that hypocrisy often needs to be met with its penalty in satire or scorn. If only you knew how much I already depend on you, and how much your deep love grants me the opportunity to express my own emotions, sympathies, longings, and understandings. How I wish you could see yourself through my eyes! You call yourself plain, but you are lovely in my eyes, for the loveliness is yourself. You are victorious over any plainness, and your face, so far from complete and yet serving you loveliness, has in it room for completion on a grander scale than most handsome faces. Consider how you have reassured me, when I say that I cannot carry a tune, that in my soul I am truly musical. You see my heart, and I see your beauty."

As Louisa grew in grace and strength, she realized that the lessons she was learning during this time of waiting would help her become the woman God meant her to be. Her insecurities, especially regarding Helen, needed to be slayed. This came to a head when George asked Louisa to retrieve some books he'd left with his cousin. The books were full of his boyhood musings, including verses written to Helen, and he didn't think they should remain in her possession.

There was nothing inappropriate about George writing those verses as a child, but it was natural for Louisa to be jealous. It didn't help that Helen couldn't keep from bragging about George's favor toward her. For Louisa, the errand was a mixed blessing. She needed to deal with her fear that Helen was more beautiful and thus more loved by everyone, even George. And his request showed both women that he wanted his precious books to be kept for him by Louisa.

Because Helen was leaving for Banff the next day, Louisa had to retrieve the books immediately. She gathered up gumption and went, then wrote to George afterward:

> . . . *I went to Helen's last night. . . . I felt very much inclined to beg you to write to her, instead of my asking about the books; but when I thought how seldom I can show my love to you by doing anything I do not quite like, I determined not to miss this opportunity, and I found it indeed much easier than I expected. She pretended not to know what I meant at first. She thought I meant some of her note-books that you had of hers and which, as I understood her, you had returned to her. However, she soon understood me, and when I asked for them, saying Papa would perhaps take them, she said, "Very well, Louisa, I will make up a little packet for him." We are* all *going to tea there tonight—for the last time. She was very pleasant and more natural than sometimes, I think, and so we were more cordial friends. I suppose she was afraid of my seeing your letters. . . . I should not like her to go away with all the uncomfortable feeling*

> that I am sure has existed on both sides.... I hope your pocket-books have not shared the fate of the poetry she told me was for no eyes but her own and was therefore put on the fire....

George's reply gave Louisa the confidence she needed.

> ... You were not obliged to say a word about those pocket-books, and, had you loved me less, I am sure you would not.... The better part of me would choose rather to be loved, as I believe you love me, than with the more intoxicated admiration-love that at first sight seems so enviable. What could I ask for more than the enduring affection I believe you have for me which you know is appreciated and treasured by me?... It is dear of you to say we will love each other for ever—it makes my heart happy every time you say so; for it is a strange one for fancying miseries and dreading the time when you will have got tired of me, and I shall have no genius, no talent, no poetry, no beauty to win back the dear, cherished love. My real hope is in growing better and in trusting that goodness may do what the others could not.
>
> But enough of this. Your dear, dear letter requires no other answer than that I too love you more than ever—and that is saying a great deal. I feel so frightened sometimes putting such thoughts on paper, but no one knows but you—and you will not be shocked. The thought of our Heavenly Father knowing every word and seeing my thoughts does not distress me, but the opposite....[11]

George and Louisa's letters reveal the lovers' mutual confidence; they hid nothing and had nothing to hide. From the pocketbook event onward, affection and understanding also grew between Helen and Louisa, and this was noticed by everyone who knew them. Louisa's pluck had worked.

Each day brought fresh challenges that nurtured the spiritual growth Louisa so desired. She was learning to climb out of her comfort zone and discard her timidity, and she was standing up for George. But her next lesson, the most difficult lesson every person must learn—the lesson of endurance—was yet to come. It would begin that fall with sorrow and loss.

Louisa's first test of endurance came in July when her Aunt Sarah and cousin Charlotte both died within twenty-four hours. The loss of both women so close together deeply grieved Louisa. Soon afterward, a greater test began with the slow death of her mother.

"Oh, George, it's such heartache to watch her decline," wrote Louisa. "This September, Papa is having us take Mama to Lynmouth in Devonshire. I do wish you could come. He's been told that the climate there will be good for her."

A few weeks later, Louisa wrote of how overjoyed her father was when he joined them by boat: "It was a truly beautiful picture to see them meeting and their tears of chastened love, thankfulness, and something too like fear."

The respite did help, but it was short-lived. While George was preaching in Whitehaven, Louisa wrote to him and told him she feared he would not see her dear Mama alive again. Mama was hemorrhaging from her lungs daily, and the doctors were unable to stop the bleeding. "They've even put her on a board in bed to keep her chest from bending even a bit; and we keep ice packs on her chest and cold cloths on her head," Louisa informed him. "I take turns sitting by Mama's bedside. Oh, please come my Dearest, please ask the congregation to release you from your commitment to them. You are the only one of her children that has not seen her.... I fear you will not see her alive."[12]

But George could not leave his church, and their beloved Mama passed away without ever seeing him again. The family was devastated. Grieving with Louisa and the rest of the Powells, George sat at his desk in Whitehaven and penned a lovely letter of sympathy and encouragement:

> *I cannot think of length of days as a blessing—but you must all be tired of hearing this same thing over and over again from me. Death is not the end—but a fresh beginning, the grandest birthday of all, the getting out of the lobby, and into the theatre.*[13]

Aware of Louisa's tender heart and her profound loss, George knew he must take great pains to write frequently and try to comfort her. "Death is a beautiful birth into something better, so do not grieve, my Dear. It is a hopeful sign, a good sign, a sign of God's unalterable promise and unfailing love. But I do understand, truly I do, for I was so very forlorn when my own dear mother died."

Worried that her sorrow and grief were burdens to George, Louisa allowed her lingering insecurities free rein when she wrote to him:

> . . . *if God will keep my heart pure by his Spirit I shall ever be able to love you and when I am ugly and commonplace and stupid, my love for you will still be of some value to you. After writing this I want to hide my face with your hands or arms.*[14]

During those days of sorrow, her sister Annie was a comfort and sounding board.

"I never felt the use of religion, of love and trust in God, so much before," Louisa confided. "I am learning that it is through the gentle austerity of my troubles that Jesus comes knocking. He is using this painful loss and my utter helplessness to enter deeper into my heart. Even in the midst of my most futile and useless moments, He wants to fill the cracks and corners of my heart with Himself, with His joy, and with the fullness of His life. My fervent prayer is to grow in His grace and to mature spiritually so that I may be an asset and helpmate to George. I know that all we are asked to bear is what we can bear. That is the law of the spiritual life, and the only thing that hinders me from bearing burdens and growing spiritually, Annie, is my fears."

"We have each other, and we will bear this together," replied Annie quietly.

Behind the doors of The Limes, the family patiently endured their anguish. Eventually, Louisa realized God was using her grief for good—to help her grow and to extinguish her insecurities. Her sorrows would point her to the One who was answering her prayers and granting her heart's desire to develop wisdom, maturity, and grace.

Sorrow herself will reveal one day that she was only the beneficent shadow of Joy. Will Evil ever show herself the beneficent shadow of Good?
George MacDonald, *Alec Forbes of Howglen*

CHAPTER 5

CALLED TO PREACH: TE DEUM

Be thou the well by which I lie and rest;
Be thou my tree of life, my garden ground;
Be thou my home, my fire, my chamber blest,
My book of wisdom, loved of all the best;
Oh, be my friend, each day still newer found,
As the eternal days and nights go round!
Nay, nay—thou art my God, in whom all loves are bound!
George MacDonald, *Diary of an Old Soul*, February 12

For everyone who loses a loved one, life continues and healing slowly begins. To facilitate his family's healing, James Powell rented a furnished home in Brighton, a lovely seaside town overlooking the English Channel. "We need to get away from the memories and the pain," he told his children.

"Yes, Papa, we need to grieve, and to rest and heal." Always ready and seeking divine service, Louisa helped her younger siblings pack and prepared the household for travel.

Although her heart was still mending from the loss of Mama, Louisa was relieved to get away and was also glad that George had returned to Highbury to finish his studies. When the Powells arrived at Brighton, they found a quaint town with a stylish resort and Brighton Palace Pier, a promenade where the locals, holiday-seekers, and day-trippers could swim, sunbathe, and picnic. Originally a fishing village, Brighton had recently emerged as a health resort and was becoming one of the largest coastal towns in East Sussex. It was quite popular with the rich, the famous, and the royals, and a number of imposing seafront hotels had popped up along the sandy shore. Especially fun to visit was the Royal Pavilion, a seaside palace built by the prince regent.

Louisa's early-afternoon beach strolls refreshed her soul. The summer sea breeze, the endless immensity of the salty air, and Brighton's natural scenery and wildlife seemed new and magical every day. She was enthralled by the birds: the rustic buntings, the lesser whitethroats, and the busy sandpipers darting along the beach. "George would love this place," she thought. "It really has cast its net over us and washed away our tears."

While Louisa was at Brighton, George received an invitation to take temporary duties at Trinity Congregational Church in Arundel. This was great news because Arundel is only twenty-five miles away from Brighton, and the assignment meant that George and Louisa were able to visit each other without much difficulty. Once George was settled into his lodgings at Arundel, Louisa determined that she would visit him and actually sit in a pew and hear him preach. George, being lonely and anxious to see his Darling Dearest, did not take long to send an invitation: "Please come, Louisa. I long for you to see where God has put me."

"I'm overjoyed!" Louisa told Charlotte. "I can't wait to get to Arundel and see my Bear!"

On August 27, Helen, Charlotte, and Louisa set out to hear George preach. Although she couldn't wait to see her fiancé, Louisa's insecurities always came out when she was with Helen. She had worshipped her sister-in-law for so long that she was naturally timid and introspective around her.

"I wish I were as bewitching!" she wrote to George. "But I must learn to be content."

The visit was good for Louisa because it brought out more of her spunk and confidence. More importantly, it gave her the opportunity to see the lovely town where George was ministering, which would perhaps become her future home. Their letters during this time were filled with excitement and expectation.

> *What a wonderful time with you, dearest George. I did not go to bed before we had unpacked our treasures, looked at the figs and butter, put the sweet flowers into water, and gave the bits of wild roots and flowers a little too; I felt so happy. I cannot imagine ever living in so lovely a place; so near to such beauties. I felt so happy being there. . . .*

George responded:

> *Dear Louisa, I do wish you could have seen more of Arundel. Behind the town there are very low hills, with the sweet short grass, on which numbers of fallow deer are feeding. Here and there are plantations of very fine trees, and down in one of the hollows rises and runs a stream of water, clearer than the Bogie, and so nice to drink in the hot days. . . . We have a river that runs through the town, up which vessels come of a good size, bringing things and taking away things; but it is a very quiet little town—not so much bustle. . . . The fields grow much richer crops than with you, and there are many more trees growing about the fields; but it is not such a beautiful country to my mind, nearly, as the one I left in Scotland.*[1]

"Louisa, I must visit Arundel with you. I've been wanting to hear your future husband preach," Mr. Powell informed his beaming daughter after she returned from her first trip. This could certainly be a great opportunity for George to entrench himself more firmly in Mr. Powell's good graces, but Louisa was uneasy.

The following weekend, as the sun lit up the dew, Papa and Louisa left for Arundel. When they arrived at the church, a simple square building with a steeple, the bell was chiming sweetly, beckoning the townspeople to the wooden pews.

George met Louisa and her father as their carriage pulled up, and he helped Louisa down the slim steps to the ground. She looked about her curiously and watched the parishioners as they entered the chapel. Serious and somber, they kept silent as they passed through the solid wooden doors to find their seats. George guided James and Louisa to a pew at the front of the church, then assumed his place in a chair next to the pulpit.

Looking around, Louisa noticed that the building's simplistic design matched its congregants. They were clean and properly dressed and did not appear to entertain any airs. She could smell the linseed oil that had been carefully applied to each pew, and though she knew she shouldn't fidget, she ran her fingertips over the grain of the wood. Bold notes from the organ rang out and called the congregation to stand and sing. Focusing on the words and notes as she shared the hymnal with her father was a welcome distraction for nervous Louisa. Then they sat, and George began to speak.

Mr. Powell was silent and solemn.

"I wonder what Papa is thinking," Louisa thought, before realizing that her concern over her father's opinion of George was keeping her from listening to the sermon. But the melody of George's Scottish brogue and the sincerity in his kind eyes overtook her, and she was drawn back to his preaching.

Sitting in the pew and hearing George teach was a balm for Louisa's sorrowful spirit. George spoke of Jesus, of His doings, His words, His thoughts, His life. "Jesus Christ is no object of so-called theological speculation, but a living Man who somehow or other hears us when we call to Him and sends us the help we need," George preached. Louisa's meek, timid heart overflowed as George's words penetrated it, and at length her whole soul was full of Jesus.

Louisa's receptiveness and affectionate nature brought her and George closer together. George appreciated her desire to learn from him and grow in understanding, but he realized that Louisa's ultimate desire was obedience to the One, and he didn't want it any other way.

Even after Louisa and her father had said their goodbyes to George and started the journey back to Brighton, Papa did not speak. He gazed out the carriage window at the passing homes and quaint countryside, keeping his thoughts to himself. The country lanes wound their way through green hills, and the sound of the horses' hooves was a lullaby to the travelers.

But Louisa didn't have to wait too long to hear Papa's opinion. By breakfast Monday morning, Papa had already composed a lengthy letter to George concerning his preaching methods:

Mr. James Powell to G.M.D.
Brighton, 30th Aug., 1850.

My Dear Sir,

> *Perhaps I ought to apologize for assuming the critic. I only, however, do it on the plea of age, and I then only make these remarks to be received by you if you on consideration think they have any reason in them. I ought perhaps to have commenced with saying how very much I was pleased with your professional services. . . . If in my earlier life I had been asked what I thought of your reading the Scriptures, I should have given an answer of approval, because you avoided monotony by giving the emphasis natural to the various speakers in the narrative parts. But the remarks of my illustrious friend, S. T. Coleridge,[2] modified my opinion. . . . I wish I could give you a tithe of his eloquent words, but his meaning was that in reading the Scriptures, while monotony is avoided, the divine source should never be forgotten, and they should be delivered more as the Oracles of God than the opinions of man. . . .[3]*

Upon receiving Mr. Powell's letter, George informed his betrothed: "Louisa, I think your father approves! I fear I may be getting my hopes up, but I'm optimistic that the Arundel congregation will decide to offer me the position of permanent minister. Do you know what this means, Louisa? I will have a congregation to teach, and we can finally be married, hopefully in the spring!"

"I must get busy, then," thought Louisa. She gathered her sewing basket, filled with needles and strings, buttons and ribbons, and happily busied herself. She was an expert seamstress, so she quickly got to work making shirts and stock-cravats for George,[4] grateful for a distraction from the tedious waiting.

On October 3, George officially received the call to Arundel's Trinity Congregational Church. With gratitude to God, he wrote:

> *The invitation was signed by all of the church members except for five who had not heard me. My professor, Mr. Godwin, told me that the accounts he had heard lately of my acceptableness*

were very gratifying to him. This is something from him, as my sermons have seldom been other than censured by him as unsuitable for the people. I preach for the first time as their pastor next Sunday. . . . In all things I hope God will teach me. To be without him is to be like a little child, just learning to walk, left alone by its mother in Cheapside—and far worse than that faint emblem.[5]

As he had waited for an official call to Arundel, George had also been approached by a congregation in Brighton, where Louisa was staying. This invitation was quite tempting for them both because Brighton was a more well-to-do, better-educated society. But George's heart had already been bound to the congregation in Arundel.

"I am attracted to their plain ways, Louisa. The people are a simple people—not particularly well informed—mostly tradespeople—and in middling circumstances. They chiefly reside in the town, which has between two and three thousand inhabitants. There are none I could call society for me—but with my books now and the beautiful earth, and added to these soon, I hope, my wife—and above all that, God to care for me—in whom I and all things are—I do not much fear the want of congenial society."[6]

Speaking of the simple people in his congregation made George think of his home and of the lovely people he had left behind in Huntly. He longed to show Louisa the tall emerald hills with their scraggly, unkempt rocks and the old castle ruins that echoed with memories—all the idyllic pictures of his childhood.

"Louisa, if my father will receive us, let us visit my Scottish home after our wedding. I should, of course, have much pleasure in letting you and my father know and speak to each other, and should like you to see the sky and the hills which first began to mold my spirit. Quietness is always complete in the countryside," he wrote.

"I'd love that," Louisa replied.

George's ordination was scheduled for the end of November, and he requested that the Reverend Caleb Morris perform it. Morris was a valued friend whose brevity, simple eloquence, and spiritual courage made him a non-conformist powerhouse during a time of legalistic Calvinism. However, because of an unexpected ill turn in George's health, the ordainment was postponed until the following June.

Louisa was anxious about the postponement, probably because of her father's opinion that "a suspicion might arise of something wrong in doctrine or character,"[7] but George did not have a strong feeling either way—he felt that the pastoral call itself implied ordination.

That November, the Powells were back at The Limes, and Louisa was preparing for a long-promised visit to her aunts, who were very dear to her.

"Oh, George, I cannot be at your ordination! Papa says I must continue with my plan to visit my aunts in Leamington. He won't let me cancel—I do hope you will understand. Since Papa is being so supportive of us, I don't want to upset him. I leave on November 7 and hope the weather will not impede me, because after we are married it will be difficult to see them," she wrote.

"Don't worry, my dearest Dear. I understand," he reassured her.

On October 29, 1850, he had written to his father:

> *My congregation I think increases, and the week meetings on the whole are better. We have a prayer-meeting every Monday, and a lecture on Thursday, for which I do not make much preparation—but gather up the gleanings of the Sunday. I mean on those same evenings to have Bible classes, one for young men and the other for young women. I shall have plenty to do. . . . I hope to be able to visit a good deal amongst the poor and unwell.*
>
> *I expect the ordination will take place towards the end of November. I don't like it. . . .*
>
> *It will depend on Mr. Powell whether I take a house at once—there happening to be a desirable one vacant now, and houses*

being very scarce in Arundel. He is coming down to me Saturday to stay till Monday. . . .[8]

Before Louisa left to visit her aunts, the family celebrated her birthday on November 5. George could not be there, but for her birthday he had copied in his exquisite penmanship the complete text of Tennyson's *In Memoriam*. Although an unusual gift, the words were touching and perfect.

*'Tis better to have loved and lost
Than never to have loved at all.*

*Oh, yet we trust that somehow good
Will be the final goal of ill.*

One of Louisa's favorite lines was:

*Strong Son of God, immortal Love,
Whom we, that have not seen thy face,
By faith, and faith alone, embrace,
Believing where we cannot prove*

George held Tennyson in high regard and spoke of how "he has written *the* poem of the hoping doubters, *the* poem of our age, the grand minor organ-fugue of *In Memoriam*. It is the cry of the bereaved Psyche into the dark infinite after the vanished Love."[9]

On November 7, Louisa kept the promise she had made to her aunts and boarded the early morning train for Leamington. Fog hung heavy at the station and faded into the distance as the train pulled away. Louisa settled herself comfortably in her compartment. She had brought a book of Ruskin that George had sent her, and more importantly, a letter from George that had arrived just as she was leaving The Limes. Carefully, she opened the letter, not wanting to tear any precious piece of paper that might contain his lovely handwriting.

The letter was unusually brief, only six lines, but the words were filled with urgency. George had a broken blood vessel and was hemorrhaging from his lungs.

Louisa disembarked at Bletchley and took the next train back to London. She would have traveled across the London Bridge and continued to Arundel, but lacking adequate funds, she returned home to The Limes in the late afternoon.

"My sweet George," she sobbed. "Father in heaven, I cannot bear to lose my humble, valiant, frail-yet-strong poetic prophet, whose eyes see beyond our earthly views and whose ears hear in the silence. Oh, God, please spare this man of Yours."

Louisa's carriage drew as close to the door of The Limes as possible, and she stepped out into the chill winter air. The frost-bound garden beyond the path shared her gloom and made her long for her mother, with her warmth and tenderness, her kind patience and love that never failed.

Slowly, Louisa entered the house, ascended the stairs, and opened the door to her father's study.

Taking her in his comforting arms, he said, "I fear this might be a sign that you are never to marry George MacDonald."

"No, Papa!" she exclaimed. "It is a sign that I must marry him at once and nurse him!"

Mr. Powell left the room, thanking God for his courageous child, and then returned to let her know that she should forego her visit to her aunts and leave immediately for Arundel.

Soon after this decision, reassuring news arrived that kept her at home. George was improving, being kept motionless on his back with leeches on his chest.[10] Louisa's family decided it was neither proper nor possible for her to go to George, so he was left in the capable hands of Mrs. New.[11] Louisa's brother, Alex, took pity on her and went to Arundel for the weekend to check on George. The news and letters he brought back encouraged Louisa, and Louisa's own letters to George give a glimpse of God's mercies and graces, and of her growth in faith and confidence during a difficult time.

Miss Louisa Powell to G.M.D.
The Limes
Nov. 7, 1850

How dear of you to write; but you must not do it if it is at all likely to hurt you one bit. Mrs. New or somebody would send me a report. God keep you and both of us in willingness for His goodwill. . . . Papa has been so very kind to me. I know he loves you. He says he will find a corner somewhere when you are quite better enough to come. [The house was then very full of guests.] Good night, my best and dearest. . . . I should like to be an angel or fairy just to see how you are sleeping. But He is keeping you and I will praise Him. . . .

Nov. 8th, 1850

. . . I suppose you feel weak after the leeches, but I hope they will have had the desired effect by this time. Do not think that you must write to me; I should not be frightened if you think it better to let someone else. Alex will write for you while he is with you. . . . I hope, dearest, you will try and keep your thoughts and mind very peaceful. You have all the love you could wish, but till you are a little stronger, only think of it as a very commonplace sort of thing, and only just exactly what you have a right to. Think no more of me than as a good little girl that will be quite pleased when God makes you better enough to come. . . . I must tell you that I feel quite well today. I walked down to Hackney before breakfast with your letter. . . . Dear Papa sent me his love last night and said that he loved me very much, and that he loved you very much. This was precious to me.[12]

The doctor's final diagnosis was tuberculosis, a disease that typically took lives very rapidly. Poor Louisa could do nothing but wait and pray. Because the air in both London and Arundel was unsuitable for someone in his condition to convalesce, George went to stay with his paternal aunt, Mary Spence, at Newport on the Isle of Wight.

"Do not worry about me, Louisa, I am only allowing myself to write, and eat (despite the cod-liver oil the doctor makes me take), and to gently exercise. Dear Aunt Mary is good to me—she is conscientious about my care and makes sure that I receive the treatment and rest I need. I am already feeling better, and I have even begun writing a lengthy poem!"

It was indeed a lengthy poem, and his extended recuperation allowed him ample time to work and rework it. When he was finally satisfied, he gave it the title *Within and Without* and lovingly dedicated it to Louisa. Scattered throughout the poem are glimpses of how his mind and heart pondered as he convalesced alone in his room.

> *AND do not fear to hope. Can poet's brain*
> *More than the Father's heart rich good invent?*
> *Each time we smell the autumn's dying scent,*
> *We know the primrose time will come again;*
> *Not more we hope, nor less would soothe our pain.*
> *Be bounteous in thy faith, for not mis-spent*
> *Is confidence unto the Father lent:*
> *Thy need is sown and rooted for his rain.*
> *His thoughts are as thine own; nor are his ways*
> *Other than thine, but by pure opulence*
> *Of beauty infinite and love immense.*
> *Work on. One day, beyond all thoughts of praise,*
> *A sunny joy will crown thee with its rays;*
> *Nor other than thy need, thy recompense.*

George and Louisa could have despaired at his grave diagnosis, but throughout his life George never feared death, and he never believed in fate or misfortune or "anything to which men give the name" that "is merely the shadow-side of a good."[13]

His faith and surety were a buttress for Louisa. She followed his example, never faltering in her faith in the Unseen. "Together we will trust in His sovereignty, Louisa," George encouraged her. "Since a man is bound no farther to himself than to do wisely, chance is only to trouble them that stand upon chance. The roots of the seen remain unseen." His unwavering faith pointed Louisa past her fears and to her Savior.[14]

To her surprise, Louisa was also supported by her father, who, after receiving the news of George's bleak prognosis, could have reconsidered his blessing of the couple's engagement, but did not.

"Thank you for believing in us, Papa. Your trust means the world to me. I know you were concerned this was a sign I should never marry George, and I realize this situation must be difficult for you as well. I do so lean on your encouragement," Louisa told him.

Incredibly, during the years of illness and poverty his daughter would later face, James Powell always knew he had made the right decision in supporting her marriage to George.

While the lamplighter awakened the streetlights and stars began winking in the dark, Mr. Powell went to his study, looked about his sanctuary of books and memorabilia, sat at his desk, and with pen in hand composed a letter to George that the young couple treasured forever:

> *Mr. James Powell to G.M.D.*
> *The Limes,*
> *22nd Decr., 1850*
> *Sunday Afternoon*
>
> *My dear Sir,*
>
> *After dinner today I turned to the fire with a rather heavy heart—the recollection of the many, many Sabbath afternoons when I had playfully asked leave of my dear companion to quit the table and go to the fire, forced a tear from my eye and a pang into my heart. But I did not, when I took up my pen, intend to name this, but to tell you that after a glass of wine, we took up your 116 Psalm and sung it in the four parts.*
>
> *I want a bar or two of suitable interlude between each verse, and if you could write music as well as you can poetry I should send*

> it to you to compose it; but we have talked of sending it to Rome—to ask Novello to do it. He is there to spend the reminder of his days. I have not yet seen Alfred N., his son, but I do intend to take it to him that it may be published. . . .
>
> When you return home—for so I suppose I may call Arundel—I shall be happy to run down any Saturday with Louisa—returning on Monday—if you will get us a couple of beds and a sitting-room for two nights. . . .[15]

When the letter arrived, Aunt Mary cautiously brought it to the sickroom and gave it to George, who propped himself up against the pillows and began to read. The curtains were drawn open and light shone in, illuminating the letter before him. Crumbs of sunshine danced in the air, mimicking George's heart as he received his future father-in-law's hopeful words.

"Recovery will be much easier now," he thought.

Christmas arrived at The Limes, and the Powells did their best to keep their spirits light and festive. The siblings enjoyed decorating the Christmas tree with dried fruit, candles, cookies, nuts, and strings of red cranberries. They had always enjoyed a lavish and extravagant Christmas dinner of roasted goose, beef, potatoes, pies, Yorkshire pudding, and plum pudding. Though Mama was gone, she would have wanted them to continue her legacy and make family the center of the holiday. Her chair loomed, a constant shadow watching them sadly as they made the necessary preparations for their first Christmas without her.

Mustering up what fortitude they could, they continued Mama's traditions of feasts, decorations, gifts, and parlor games, always aware of her chair, forlorn and abandoned. Snowflakes peeked in the windows and lifted their spirits, reminding them of the lovely sights, sounds, and scents of Advent. Pine and holly, plum pudding and choice meats, candles and moonlit snow were the cures Louisa's heart needed. Oh, how Louisa wished George could have shared in the festivities and seen how she wanted to celebrate when they could finally start a family of their own!

By mid-January 1851, George was declared well and able to return to the pulpit. After reassuring Louisa that he was fit enough, and reluctantly agreeing to faithfully take his cod-liver oil and limit his preaching to "twenty minutes or so—and never mean to exceed half an hour after this," he resumed his duties at Arundel and allowed his thoughts to turn to marriage and his beloved Louisa.

There is this difference between the growth of some human beings and that of others: in the one case it is a continuous dying, in the other a continuous resurrection.
George MacDonald, *The Princess and Curdie*

CHAPTER 6

BY AND BY BECOMING THOROUGHLY ONE

It is by loving, and not by being loved, that one can come nearest the soul of another; yea, that, where two love, it is the loving of each other, that originates and perfects and assures their blessedness.
George MacDonald, *Phantastes*

George and Louisa were wed on the misty Saturday morning of March 8, 1851. The air was a brisk fifty degrees, and the New River rippled toward Finsbury Park and the Woodberry Wetlands, guiding the wedding carriage to Hackney's Gravel Pit Chapel, where a lovely spire pointed heavenward and quaint gothic windows filtered the light. All the planning and preparation was complete. After a bit of lively discussion, the couple had finally agreed on who would officiate. George had wanted Caleb Morris, his free-thinking pastor friend, but Louisa was not enthused.

"I think I should like Caleb Morris better than anyone except Mr. Scott," he told her.

"But George, don't you remember? He did not endear himself to me when we first met. He's so awkward. Also, he's fat and rosy and not at all what I had always imagined for our wedding."

They finally agreed to be married by the Reverend John Davies at the chapel where Louisa and her siblings had been baptized. Solemn sweetness ruled the wondrous occasion. Louisa, radiant in white, stood demurely beside George, who wore a white satin waistcoat embroidered with sprigs of flowers, which was lent to him by a friend.

Louisa's father did not attend the wedding, but he did send a beautiful white scarf for Louisa to wear beforehand, with the excuse that he had important business in Bristol that would make it impossible to be present. Everyone knew this was just an excuse to cover his fear of being unable to control his emotions without his beloved wife on whom to lean. Unbeknownst to Mr. Powell, his gift became an amusing addition to the solemn occasion when Louisa noticed the shop tag was still attached to the corner of the scarf. It took all her strength not to giggle at this comic revelation.

Even without Mr. Powell present, George's longed-for vision of life with Louisa became reality as Rev. Davies pronounced them man and wife. Earlier, George had penned:

> *I have a feeling as if you were married, and a vision of dark haired children being made happy and the blue eyes and dark eyes playing together beneath the care of blue eyes and dark eyes. I have a vision of the sun-shine of youth adorning more sober middle age, a vision of husband and wife in the unselfishness of their hearts giving up and living for each other's happiness. I see you Louisa at the head of that beautiful family.*[1]

And Louisa's earlier vision about their future began to materialize as well:

> *... I had such a very beautiful dream last night, dear. I dreamt I had a vision, it was so beautiful! I think it was at sunset. I was looking earnestly at the clouds when one thick volume of pink and white cloud had two faces; the cloud was all the shape and colour to show them. I looked at them for a long time not knowing who it was, but soon discovered your face, only grown into a beautiful old man with the most glorified and perfectly beautiful expression upon it. The other for some time I thought was Mama, but upon looking and thinking, hoped it was I, with long white hair. I held a book out of which you were reading. You had your arm round my neck. Was it very conceited of me to imagine that I should ever grow into anything like Mama? Of course my features never can. I dreamt that, after looking for some time, the cloud melted away: then someone told me it was a vision sent to me that I might not fear present evil to either of us. Perhaps this is hardly worth telling you about; but I do not know when I have had any so beautiful a*

> *dream, or any that has made a strong an impression on my waking thoughts. . . .*[2]

But according to their son Greville, Louisa did come to resemble her mother and in old age became "the most beautiful among sisters much handsomer in youth."

The following morning, George was to preach at Rugby en route to Leamington where Louisa's aunts had graciously lent their home to the honeymooners. As they happily unpacked their luggage Saturday evening, they found that the bottle of cod-liver oil he had so carefully packed was broken, its contents splattered all over his Sunday trousers. They chose to find humor in the mishap and remembered it fondly whenever they spoke of their honeymoon.

That evening, George gave Louisa the wedding present he had carefully written for her during his long convalescence. It was a strange, tender, and prophetic poem:

Love me, Beloved

Love me, beloved; for thou mayest lie
Dead in my sight, 'neath the same blue sky;
Love me, O love me, and let me know
The love that within thee moves to and fro;
That many a form of thy love may be
Gathered around thy memory.

Love me beloved; for I may lie
Dead in thy sight, 'neath the same blue sky;
The more thou hast loved me, the less thy pain,
The stronger thy hope till we meet again;
And forth on the pathway we do not know,
With a load of love, my soul would go.

Love me, beloved; for one must lie
Motionless, lifeless, beneath the sky;
The pale stiff lips return no kiss
To the lips that never brought love amiss;
And the dark brown earth be heaped above

By and By Becoming Thoroughly One

The head that lay on the bosom of love.

*Love me, beloved; for both must lie
Under the earth and beneath the sky;
The world be the same when we are gone;
The leaves and the waters all sound on;
The spring comes forth, and the wild flowers live,
Gifs for the poor man's love to give;
The sea, the lordly, the gentle sea,
Tell the same tales to others than thee;
And joys, that flush with an inward morn,
Irradiate hearts that are yet unborn;
A youthful race call our earth their own,
And gaze on its wonders from thought's high throne;
Embraced by fair Nature, the youth will embrace
The maid beside him, his queen of the race;
When thou and I shall have passed away
Like the foam flake thou lookedst on yesterday.*

*Love me, beloved; for both must tread
On the threshold of Hades, the house of the dead;
Where now but in thinkings strange we roam,
We shall live and think, and shall be at home;
The sights and the sounds of the spirit land
No stranger to us than the white sea-sand,
Than the voice of the waves, and the eye of the moon,
Than the crowded street in the sunlit noon.
I pray thee to love me, belov'd of my heart;
If we love not truly, at death we part;
And how would it be with our souls to find
That love, like a body, was left behind!*

*Love me, beloved; Hades and Death
Shall vanish away like a frosty breath;
These hands, that now are at home in thine,
Shall clasp thee again if thou still art mine;
And thou shalt be mine, my spirit's bride,
In the ceaseless flow of eternity's tide,*

> *If the truest love that thy heart can know*
> *Meet the truest love that from mine can flow.*
> *Pray God, beloved, for thee and me,*
> *That our souls may be wedded eternally.*[3]

Louisa treasured his gift until her days ceased to flow. "George is right," she thought to herself. "We love, not this and that about each other, but each the very other—a love as essential to reality, to truth, to religion, as the love of the very God. Where such love is, let the differences of taste, the unfitnesses of temperament be what they may, the two of us must by and by be thoroughly one."[4]

Their home, leased by Louisa's father and furnished to the smallest detail as his wedding gift to them, awaited their return. After their honeymoon, they settled in and busied themselves with making a home. Their days were happy, filled with things to do among the congregation. The congregants were simple people, eager and grateful. Most were country folk who welcomed George and were ready to learn from him.

"Each day they astound me, Louisa. They adhere to the elemental virtues, which among people belonging to the soil are less likely to be hid under a bushel of worldliness," George shared when he returned home one afternoon. "Today, on Arundel's bridge, I met Old Roger. You know how much I love bridges, Louisa. Old Roger was there, and he actually likened my pulpit to the masthead of a ship and said, 'I love a parson, Sir. He's got a good telescope, and he gits to the masthead, and he looks out. And he sings out, "Land ahead!" or "Breakers ahead!" and gives directions accordin' to what he sees.'"

"Why, Darling, I think that is the best metaphor for you that I have ever heard," Louisa replied. She in turn shared with him her day and detailed her delight in nature, of course. "What a lovely, sunny, breezy Sunday afternoon this has been! The street is so still, and our tree whispered most sweetly to me all about you and about Him who cares for both of us. The river is full, and the lights and shadows in the meadows beyond were beautiful."

George, touched by her descriptions, reached for her and smiled.

It was impossible for the people of Arundel not to love their new minister. Louisa shared tenderly and wisely in his work, and her swift, sound sympathy brought her into the favor of all. Being George's helpmate in the pastorate came naturally to her.

There was one man in particular, a Mr. Alpheus Smith, who, despite his own poverty, would minister to the newlyweds by sending them all sorts of delicacies that he never afforded himself—jellies, cream-custards, cold chicken. He never included a note for acknowledgement, and he was especially generous when George was ill.

"The poor understand me, Louisa, just as they understand the Master, but it is evident by the behavior of the more wealthy here that the purse-proud resent my plain speaking. Oh well—riches indubitably favor stupidity, and poverty seems to favor mental and moral development."

"Yes, you have always said that one may readily conclude how poorly God thinks of riches when we see the sort of people he sends them to!" Louisa reminded him.

But despite the behavior of the wealthier class, the young couple were blissfully happy. Louisa never wanted to forget their wonderful days and decided to keep an album to help her remember them. She adorned seventeen thin quarto cards, pasted to a linen strip and stitched and bound between boards, with ferns, ivy, autumn leaves, and her own watercolor illustrations. George added to the album by transcribing sonnets and other poems in his exquisite handwriting. The album was a witness to the couple's great love. The title page stated simply:

POEMS
By G.E.M.

Lighter and sweeter
Let your song be;
And for sorrow—oh, cheat her
With melody!

Because George was now well and able to serve his congregation, he was finally ordained. In June, Mr. Godwin, one of his Highbury professors, proudly presided over the ordination of the Reverend George MacDonald. Louisa's sister, Charlotte, was invited to help entertain Mr. Godwin, a childless widower. They were married two years later by George himself.

After the ordination, George and Louisa entered an even more strenuous period of life. They had frequent visitors, especially Louisa's sisters. Even George's brothers, Alec and John, came to stay. Upon returning home they told their father, "We are greatly delighted with Arundel and with the minister's wife thereof. He is so fortunate, and so blessed."

George was still not well enough to return to all his usual activities, and Arundel's climate didn't help his frail clay tabernacle. But he continued to enjoy his work and writing poetry, and Louisa relished every moment with him in their sweet little home. She loved visiting and entertaining George's congregants, especially the young people, and they loved her as well. Occasionally, George and Louisa were able to visit London for a day, and this refreshed their spirits. They always made sure to see Louisa's family, as well as George's closest friend, Greville Matheson.

George and Louisa had a lovely first year together and settled down into blissful contentment. Each Monday they took long walks in the country, a sacred activity they looked forward to after the concentrated duties of Sunday. After being cooped up in church, George needed to wander free with Louisa, to revel with her in the enchantment of the countryside. Louisa was incandescently happy, and as the new year loomed, she was expecting the greatest gift from God: a wee bairn.

He (God) can be revealed only to the child; perfectly, to the pure child only. All the discipline of the world is to make men children, that God may be revealed to them.
George MacDonald, *The Hope of the Gospel*

CHAPTER 7

FOR RICHER, FOR POORER, IN SICKNESS AND IN HEALTH

Fair freshness of the God-breathed spirit air,
Pass through my soul, and make it strong to love;
Wither with gracious cold what demons dare
Shoot from my hell into my world above;
Let them drop down, like leaves the sun doth sear,
And flutter far into the inane and bare,
Leaving my middle-earth calm, wise, and clear.
George MacDonald, *Diary of an Old Soul*, May 12

Christmas came with goodwill to all men, bringing reflections of the One who was born to be the glory of Israel and a light to the Gentiles. Joy and singing rang through the newlyweds' little nest as Louisa continued her beloved Mama's Christmas traditions.

"Happy Christmas, my Love," said George, eyes misty with gratefulness. "The Word was made flesh and dwelt among us, here in our sweet cottage and in our hearts," he pondered aloud, as though he were seeing a starlit sky full of angels singing and guiding him and Louisa to the manger where their Savior lay.

Christmas carols sounded through their home, lovely and true, as though the stars themselves were joining in praise to the Creator. A child was born, and all the earth was filled with His glory.

The MacDonalds stayed warm in their cottage, awaiting the arrival of their firstborn. A smattering of snow dusted the cobbled streets outside, and candles warmed the windows and welcomed guests. Louisa kept herself occupied by playing the piano her father had purchased—it was probably the wedding gift she used and prized most. Christmas melodies and the Songs of Novalis—music she had composed to George's poems—were often at her fingertips, and she enjoyed singing along while she played. Her mezzo-soprano voice echoed through their home and brought peaceful repose to the anxious mother- and father-to-be.

During the long winter evenings, Louisa also kept busy with her needlework as she prepared for her child's imminent arrival and marveled that she and George had found a quiet rhythm of grace by which they lived and loved together. They had decided from the beginning that they must work diligently, every day, to write their love story well. There was no rushing or worrying. Their home, though full of constant activity, was also a place of peace. They shared an earnest sense of life's daily duties and applied courtesy and kindness, genuine interest and concern, in every interaction with each other. They did everything, whether great or small, in the same spirit and with the same degree of faith because this was the will of God for them. No task was too little or too immense to be undertaken at the command of their Savior—they knew that the Lord prepares each of His children for His work and places before each the duty he or she has been called to do.

It was a cold winter night, January 4, 1852, when the first of the Master's miracles arrived. The new parents named her Lilia Scott and could not imagine anything more amazing than the creation of their child. Lilia Scott's two grandfathers were probably the most excited to welcome the healthy, bouncy, beautiful girl. Light and delicate, this tiny glow of warmth from the Father, this flame aspiring, was George and Louisa's bonnie wee babe, Lilia.

"She is much larger than I expected and seems to have a good pair of lungs," George remarked with awe.

Louisa was just relieved that her sweet girl was healthy. The sorrow her mother had faced when four of her babies died in infancy was a memory Louisa could not forget.

Overcome with emotion, George penned a poem about their beautiful daughter and Louisa's great gift to him:

For Richer, for Poorer, in Sickness and in Health

A Mother's Hymn

My child is lying on my knees;
The signs of Heaven she reads:
My face is all the Heaven she sees,
Is all the Heaven she needs.
And she is well, yea bathed in bliss,
If Heaven lies in my face;
Behind it all is tenderness
And truthfulness and grace.
I also am a child, and I
Am ignorant and weak;
I gaze upon the starry sky
And then I must not speak.
For all behind the starry sky,
Behind the world so broad,
Behind men's hearts and soul doth lie
The Infinite of God.
If I, so often full of doubt,
So true to her can be,
Thou who dost see all round about,
Art very true to me.
And so I sit in thy wide space
My child upon my knee;
She looketh up into my face,
And I look up to Thee.[1]

When Lilia was just two months old, George's brother Alec came to live with them. Alec was a quiet, straightforward businessman who had fallen in love with Miss Hannah Robertson, the daughter of a distinguished surgeon who attended the same chapel as Alec in Manchester. Hannah, however, did not share Alec's feelings, and her rejection caused him to spiral into deep anguish and disappointment. It could have been a coincidence, but Alec's health soon deteriorated, and he began to spit up blood just as George had two years earlier.

Alec came to Arundel in March to be nursed by Louisa.

Taking him into her heart and her keeping, she cared for him carefully. Sadly, his condition did not improve, and he decided to return to his childhood home in Huntly to be near his family. His parting was difficult for both Louisa and George—they knew in their hearts they would likely never see him again. Yet Louisa's kindness and care were not forgotten. All had been done that could be done for dear Alec, and all would be well.

That October, Louisa received a letter from Alec in which he graciously thanked her for her care and medical attention. Carefully, she opened the letter and read Alec's words for George to hear:

> *You were very very kind to me at Arundel. I have not forgotten it in the least, although I have said so little about it. Tell me about Lily—dear little creature! I think I should be able to carry her about a good deal now. I should like to hear her call me Uncle.*
>
> *Alec*[2]

"It is an almost unbelievably humbling thing to give all that you are able to give and then leave the rest to God, Louisa," George said, hoping to comfort her when they received word that Alec's health had deteriorated even further. "There is great joy, but great suffering too, in caring for another, and only a woman of strength and stout-heartedness can endure without breaking." He didn't know then that they would need to draw upon his prophetic words when faced with the future sorrow of losing their own children.

Alec died in his father's arms the following April. Tears fell on the parchment as Louisa wrote a sweet letter to George's stepmother, trying to find the right words to comfort and sustain her. George, who always had the right words at hand, penned a perfect message that strengthened his parents and also himself:

G.M.D. to his Father
Arundel,
April 5, 1853.

> Let the body go beautiful to the grave—entire as the seed of a new body, which keeps the beauty of the old, and only parts with the weakness and imperfection. Surely God that clothes the fields now with the wild flowers risen fresh from their winter-graves, will keep Alec's beauty in His remembrance and not let a manifestation of Himself, as every human form is, so full of the true, simple, noble and pure, be forgotten.[3]

Of all his siblings, George was closest to his brothers, Alec and John. Alec's death was particularly difficult for John, a dreamer, poet, and philosopher. George and John's shared passion for poetry helped them heal from the loss of their brother and brought them even closer together.

After Alec had left for Huntly, George became increasingly aware that things were not as they seemed in his church. As Louisa visited and ministered to congregants, she could sense their unease. Apparently, some of the more affluent members of the congregation were quite unhappy that their new pastor insisted Christians must exhibit the attributes the Bible commends as "fruits of the Spirit." George expected those who claimed to be followers of Christ to actively show compassion and care for all the citizens of Arundel and to stop seeking worldly ambitions.

"God is our Heavenly Fire. His love is a burning fire and His intention is to save us from our sins, not just from hell," he reminded his congregation, which only made the wealthy members more uneasy. They were also uncomfortable with his conviction regarding the universal presence of sacramental grace. Because his positions were difficult to oppose openly, they demanded that he no longer focus his teachings on the quality of their lives and concentrate instead on more abstract topics. They enjoyed their assumed assurance that they were among God's elect, and they did not wish to be challenged to grow in His grace.

"My dearest Dear," George sighed to Louisa, "I firmly believe people have hitherto been a great deal too much taken up about doctrine and far too little about practice. Doctrine, as used in the Bible, means teaching of duty, not theory."

Louisa looked around their comfortable home, her eyes resting on each item she had carefully placed in their sweet abode. Although she had taken great care to prepare their home for the arrival of another baby, deep in her heart she knew their plans would rapidly change. The congregation was rumbling with dissent.

"My most immediate concern, my dear Bear," she said, "is that our landlord, Deacon Hounsom, is unhappy with us too. But if he wishes us to move, that would probably be a good thing. Our family is growing, and we do need more space."

Her suspicions were more than accurate, for soon the ruling objectors pressured George to look for another pastorate, not just another dwelling. Using the MacDonalds' need for a larger house as a pretense, the deacons formally visited George at the end of June. They apologized for their unpleasant decision and informed him that due to deficient funds, the church could only afford to pay him half his salary.

"I am sorry enough to hear it," George replied, "but if it must be, why, I suppose we must try to live on less."

"Oh, but . . . er . . . we thought . . ." stammered Deacon Hounsom, "er . . . we thought you would take it . . . er . . . as a kindly hint, so to speak . . ."

"Of what?" asked George.

"That your preaching is not acceptable, and that you should resign," was the reply.

"I will not be moved," George told Louisa. "So many in our congregation have told me that they are deeply touched by my preaching. I believe God wants us to be willing to make sacrifices, so I will inform them that we will accept their decision and try to live on less."

In July, George was asked to exchange pulpits with a minister in Worthing, Chichester, or Brighton. Because the Brighton minister was George's friend and was experiencing similar troubles with his congregation, he and George decided to switch places. While George preached in Brighton, Louisa stayed home to care for Lily and continued to serve and entertain the Arundel congregation.

"I do believe this is a gift handed to you from God," she told George before he left. "I'm sure He knows you need a respite from the murmurings here. I promise to write frequently and let you know how we're faring and what your little Lily is up to."

He was reluctant to leave them, but Louisa knew he needed to get away.

Her clever, encouraging letters began to arrive as soon as he was settled.

"The other evening Mr. Champion came for dinner. When he said grace, Lily must have been a bit too buoyant and he began with 'O indulgent Parient!' and he asked Him 'that our *h*absent Pastor may be given *h*energy from on 'igh to preach the gospel and all of us grace to perceive our sinful *h*errors!'[4] His accent was hysterical, George! I was able to avoid his sermon, which I've been told had twenty-five headings! But the dear man, he does have such troubles with his children's health and his wife's confinement."

Louisa tried to keep her husband's spirits up by sharing daily musings and tidbits about his little girl. "I cannot write better with Baby in my lap trying to choke herself with the sealing-wax. She is a wonderful baby, though her little white-speckled gum troubles her sorely, if I may judge from her little squeaks and most queer grimaces."

Of course, Louisa shared all the pastoral gossip too, including the time Old Roger stopped by in his smock with a gift of golden gooseberries, and after she gave him the remains of the cold mutton, he "cleaned it to the bone" and put it in his pocket, saying, "the missus will get summut out of he yet."

Another letter described the visit of little Mary Ann, who brought a present of home-brewed beer. Louisa wrote that the dear girl called the beer "very strong and good for nursing" and that "she was looking out of my bedroom window and exclaimed, 'O, what a beautiful garden!' Whereupon I gave her plenty of carnations and went into the garden to get her some jasmine, roses, etc., which delighted her immensely. She kept saying, 'I shan't know what to do with myself if I have such a lot of flowers! Oh, what will my mother say to such a beautiful nosegay!'"

The pastoral duties at Brighton were a short respite for George. He preached, thought of his little family, and waited on God to direct their path. In Arundel, Louisa struggled to pay for her family's needs and realized she must do more than write letters if she wanted to help her husband. Determined to add to George's meager salary, she offered to take three or four little girls into her home and give them "a good English education, with music and the rudiments of French, Italian and German." She posted an advertisement in *The Patriot,* but no pupils came.

While George was absent, the Arundel church held a meeting. The following day, Mr. Bull visited Louisa and informed her of what had been said and decided.

In defense of George he had told the attendees, "I am most unhappy with your treatment of Reverend MacDonald. In the interest of unity, we should put our objections in writing and stop the backbiting."

The group agreed on a statement that expressed their respect but also warned that unless George altered his preaching, harsh consequences would follow. Though Mr. Bull tried to console and encourage Louisa, she knew the suspicions and gossip would continue.

When George finished his post at Brighton and returned home, he was greeted at the door by his smiling, very pregnant wife and his excited toddler, who flung herself at his legs. He had hoped that time away would bring healing and peace to his wayward congregation, but it was evident that his absence had not improved the situation.

"Louisa, this is so disheartening. I fear that my first and perhaps last pastorate is coming to an untimely end," he confided. But despite the disunity among the elders, one by one, his congregants began to tell him how much they appreciated his teachings. It was obvious to both George and

Louisa that the unhappiness lay with only a few unteachable members.

Praying and persisting in the work set before them, George and Louisa agreed that he should continue to labor, to remain faithful to his calling, in the hope of helping his flock. Still, Louisa was heartbroken as she watched her husband struggle and suffer at the hands of petty, bitter people.

"Oh how I wish he could pastor a flock of happy, obedient sheep," she thought while rocking sweet Lilia.

"Louisa, if God ever puts the means at any time in my power, I mean to take another mode of helping men, and no longer stand in this position toward them, in which they regard me more as their servant than as Christ's. Of course, till then, He means me to labor as I am, and I am more than content, I hope," George told her.

But though the love of so many in their congregation was unwavering, dissent increased until it eventually accomplished its destructive work. Disappointed and grieving, George confided to his bride, "Chiefest of all the Christian blessings is peace, Louisa, and chiefest of all terrors is schism. If I remain, there will be a split in the church. I must resign."

She agreed that this was best, but her heart ached for him. She had watched him pray, study, serve, and pour his heart and life into his congregation, and she would miss their friends terribly. "Heaven does grow out of pain endured," she reminded herself.

In May, George resigned.

As much as Louisa wished they could leave immediately and begin anew, she had to remain in Arundel because their next bundle of joy was due in July. With her encouragement, George decided to leave for Manchester to seek counsel and to network with men whom he trusted. He would take a trip to London first because he had been asked to officiate the wedding of his sister Charlotte and his former professor, Rev. J. H. Godwin.

"I do not wish to leave you, Love. My guilt is great. I am leaving you alone to face those who rejected us."

"Don't worry, dearest Dear," she reassured him. "Your

'second wife' Angela will stay with me until the baby arrives. And you must remember that where you are will always be home. My life is centered on you. Sometimes I feel like a little planet that revolves around you, my sun."

Louisa didn't mind staying in Arundel a bit longer, for her father's disappointment in George's resignation would have been difficult to bear. Carefully, she packed the suitcases while George bundled up Lilia, who would go with him.

Standing at the window, Louisa watched their carriage leave for London. Poor George would have to face both his future brother-in-law and Louisa's father.

Just after George left Arundel, a letter arrived from Godwin, which Louisa forwarded to her husband with the words, "Here is a stiff letter from Brother His Holiness!" Godwin clearly didn't think George had done enough to please his congregation, but the professor must have respected his former pupil, and perhaps his eyes had been opened by the time they met to plan for the wedding.

After the wedding festivities had finished, George sent reassurance to his wife: "It is all over now and they are gone. Everything has gone very well—no drawback. We are going to the Forest where we went last time to tea. Lily has been very good. She looked so sweet in her pretty white dress and bonnet they got for her. . . . She had a little champagne, a little raspberry ice and some grapes."

Relieved, Louisa gently folded his letter and smiled. George seemed happy, even around her father at The Limes. While she missed him, she had her own important event to look forward to.

Mary Josephine, their second miracle from the Master, arrived on July 23, 1853. Louisa's sister Annie was a great help during the birth and after, and again Louisa was amazed that her baby was strong and well. Her arms and heart brimmed with blessings. Softly, she turned her head so her cheek could rest against Mary's feathery hair.

"Yes, dear Lord," she prayed, "even in the midst of poverty and uncertainty, how can I not have hope when You grant such lovely wee blessings?"

For Richer, for Poorer, in Sickness and in Health

When I can no more stir my soul to move,
And life is but the ashes of a fire;
When I can but remember that my heart
Once used to live and love, long and aspire,—
O, be thou then the first, the one thou art;
Be thou the calling, before all answering love,
And in me wake hope, fear, boundless desire.
George MacDonald, *Diary of an Old Soul*, January 10

CHAPTER 8

SALTED WITH FIRE

In the great glow of that great love, this death
Would melt away like a fantastic cloud;
I should no more shrink from it than from the breath
That makes in frosty air a nimbus-shroud;
Thou, Love, hast conquered death, and I aloud
Should triumph over him, with thy saintly crowd,
That where the Lamb goes ever followeth.
George MacDonald, *Diary of an Old Soul*, April 30

One of the most difficult things for a woman is to watch her husband suffer and be unable to bear his cross for him. It was clear to Louisa that her and George's families, especially Papa and George's father, were disappointed in George's resignation from Trinity Congregational Church. Mr. Powell became distinctly less cordial toward George, and even Mr. Godwin suggested that if George had just preached what the people wanted, all would be well.

"I cannot do that," George told Louisa when he returned from London. "I am convinced that the Church is in such sad shape because theologians have minimized the teachings of Christ. We must each continuously ponder the Gospel—the story of Jesus."

"Yes," she agreed, "Christ is the center of my life. Learning of Him is the plumb line for my spiritual growth. I know you're right in the middle of God's will in this, and I trust you."

"Preaching is my work, and preach I will, somehow or other," he stated. "That which is gradually bringing to my mind a great eternal peace and hope I will try to give to others—but it is and must be different from what I'd expected. We will find something more."

The next day he kissed wee Mary as she snuggled in Louisa's arms, lifted his sweet Lily and kissed her too, then pulled Louisa to him and gave them all a big bear hug. They

Salted with Fire

made their way to the front door and felt the sweet, still summer air.

"We must thank God for making the world so beautiful," George reminded his family.

Louisa watched as he left, then she quietly shut the door.

As he set out for Manchester, George was hopeful that he would find the next steps of his ministry there, but he returned from the trip without having made progress.

While walking early one morning, he found encouragement in the form of a lark's nest, the symbol of daybreak and abundance. He reminded Louisa of this symbolism by quoting Shakespeare's "Sonnet 29": "Like to the lark at break of day arising / From sullen earth, sings hymns at heaven's gate . . ."

Hopeful, yet still unable to secure lodgings in Manchester and also lacking the funds to do so, they packed their furnishings and shipped them by barge to London with a note enclosed.

"Thank you, Papa, for being willing to receive and store our belongings in your warehouse," Louisa wrote.

"It breaks my heart, but I know I must sell my piano," she told George, and sighed. "We need the funds, and Papa has said he will buy another when we are settled."

"I promise you, my Love, we will get another," George said, squeezing her shoulders. "Besides, I'll miss the courage, purity, love, and joy that flow through my soul when I hear you play."

When they arrived at Manchester, they had no choice but to live apart, taking advantage of their relatives' hospitality. Louisa chose to stay with the girls at The Limes, but after a few weeks she took them to Liverpool and stayed with her brother Alex and his wife Helen.

Beneath the shadow of her family's circumstances, she braced herself. "We must be content to move on," she told herself.

Louisa was learning through the gentle assurances of her Savior that He would meet every need and that she could put her trust in Him.

"Our needs have always been met one way or another, at

just the right time," she reminded herself. "My trust and hope are not in having a home of my own but in my loving Savior and in my husband, who refuses to compromise his personal integrity for monetary gain. It's like George always says: 'Jesus lived a grand simple life in poverty and love. Why should not I?'"

If George had not been a man of godly character and intent, Louisa's path would have been much harder. But he was, so Louisa chose to follow her husband and trust her Savior.

Throughout the fall, George was able to work among the Congregationalists by filling vacant pulpits. This did not pay much. "We are going through the hard time now, without which never man was worth much in himself," he told Louisa. "May He keep me from being a time server, and so I and mine will pass through the world honorable and receive the well done at the end."[1]

Their days apart wore on, and they longed to be together. Louisa was being refined by these trials, and George's encouraging letters were her balm of Gilead:

> *It is a very good thing for us to be parted sometimes. It makes us think, both more truly about each other, and, [because] less interrupted, about our God. . . . We must seek Him.*[2]

Endurance. Trust. Obedience. These are always required when passing through the flames of refinement, and they're the only way to spiritual maturity.

"Do I trust God?" Louisa would ask herself.

"Will I obey Him, no matter what?"

Knowing that George was leading her through the refining fire made the path easier to follow. He was her lighthouse in the storm.

But George's inability to provide for his growing family, and his longing for Louisa, made him depressed. He also feared that his frail lungs, which were always a hindrance, would become a lifelong issue. He was determined to emerge from these trials by finding a home where his family could be together again.

Louisa prayed constantly, especially when she saw the discouragement in his letters:

> *If we could just get enough food to keep* us *alive and the children quite happy, I would rather be half-starved together, than well-fed asunder.... It is rather a sad time for us to begin house-keeping with our little means.... But if we are doing right, it is all the same to the rich God whether we begin with ten pounds or a thousand.* Appearances *are nothing, if* realities *are on our side.*[3]

Finally, the MacDonalds were offered a delightful home, on a temporary basis but rent free, through George's former professor, A. J. Scott. Mr. Scott's wife had two sisters, and one owned Alderley Cross, a farmhouse at Alderley, about fifteen miles from Manchester. After she and George and their daughters moved in, Louisa set about finding a more permanent home.

"Good news, Louisa," George announced one day, taking her in his arms. "An old friend from my Highbury days needs lodging and is willing to pay room and board, and my father sent word that a cask of provisions is on its way from The Farm in Huntly."

"I have encouraging news, too, George," Louisa replied. "Once we find a permanent home, Papa has agreed to cover the rest of our lodging fees until we are self-sufficient, and while you were out applying to positions, I placed another advertisement to take in pupils, and this time one has signed up!"

God also provided the perfect home at No. 3 Camp Terrace in Lower Broughton.

"It's wonderful, dear Bear," Louisa told George. "Large and in some respects handsome, quite respectable and open, but not so fashionable as it once was."

With enough room on the main floor, the home was suitable for lectures and preaching. This was the beginning of George's career in public speaking. And as Louisa grew busy with her daughters and with tutoring, she realized she would need to employ a young woman to help out around the house.

"But she has joints like a Dutch doll and a brain like a Dutch cheese," George teased after observing their hired helper.

Green Grosvenor Park and the River Irwell were within walking distance, and the MacDonalds enjoyed watching Lower Broughton's frequent rowing, racing, swimming, and fishing events. They regularly spotted grey herons, cormorants, mute swans, kingfishers, and many species of goose and duck along the river. Even in the winter they could watch ducks diving in the freezing water, and they especially enjoyed seeing tufted ducks—all black except for their lovely white flanks, blue-grey bills, and golden-yellow eyes—take shelter along the river's banks. The *wit-oo* sound of the male ducks' courtship whistles thrilled Louisa and her daughters during their daily walks.

Finally! All was well and the family wanted for nothing. They were together again in a home of their own.

One morning, George admitted to Louisa, "Your silly Bear was possessed by an angry evil thought yesterday and went out of the room to get rid of it. As I came upstairs to my study, the moon shone bright in the high heavens and the conviction arose within me that God cares for His children. 'Has He really,' I thought, 'put that shining thing up there to light up this round earth, and will He not minister to my wants?' By the way, I think I want to grow a beard."

"Thank goodness his beard grows full and fluffy and not thin and scruffy," thought Louisa.

Beards were not looked on favorably in Victorian England, so naturally George's father reacted to his son's new facial hair with irked amusement. George defended his beard, asserting, "I feel nearer to nature—yes, seriously, nearer to God's intent when He made man in His own image." With that, George never needed to shave again.

The beard also added to George's confidence and conviction that he only needed God's approval, not man's. And Louisa didn't mind it at all. "You look like one of the great prophets of old. Besides, your doctor suggested that a full complement of whiskers might help protect your nasal passages from abrupt changes in air temperature and reduce the risk of hemorrhage. So now you really are my fuzzy, burly Bear."

Money trickled in through George's lectures and the stories and poems he had contributed to *The Christian Spectator*. Louisa quite enjoyed evenings because she loved listening to his lectures, given on the main floor of their home. He spoke of physics and literature, awakening his attendees' interest. He also took in several small boys to tutor, and Louisa was glad to see him busy and happy again. Plus, they needed the income as their family continued to grow.

Caroline Grace MacDonald, the third of the Master's miracles, joined her sisters on September 16, 1854. Again, Louisa was relieved to have a healthy, strong baby, their sweet lady of grace.

Louisa was indeed blessed—she had a home, three lovely girls, and a committed, upright husband. She drew peace and assurance from the fact that her children would be led by a man of impeccable character. What more could any mother want?

An example of George's character is evident in a letter he wrote to a friend from their old church in Arundel who needed his advice on certain personal matters. George's counsel was sure and true:

> *Keep your heart and conscience and hands clean, dear friend, and be ready to lose all, wife and life, rather than act ignobly, unrighteously in the smallest matter—you will not misunderstand me. It is an easy thing to be as honest as society requires of one, but it is not easy to be pure, to be in what are counted better things thoroughly, divinely upright—May God teach me in this.*[4]

When the new year arrived, Longman, a London publisher, agreed to release George's first book, *Within and Without*, a verse drama that revolves around the spiritual quest of its protagonist, Julian. George dedicated it to his beloved Louisa, and the book actually contains his life story and hints at the way his love for God and his love for his wife came together in perfect harmony. It received many enthusiastic reviews.

Even Mr. Powell liked it. George discovered this a few days after publication when he decided to take Lilia to The Limes: "We crept silently into the room to find your father weeping over my book, Louisa! I think he finally recognizes me as a poet, and hopefully he will become more understanding of our difficult circumstances."

For Louisa, this was an answer to prayer. She loved her father and wished he could see her husband's brilliance. Leaving and cleaving were not easy, especially because her and George's parents had openly voiced disapproval. But Louisa had given her heart to George, and they now belonged to each other. She would continue to pray that her father would grow to see George the way she did.

The success of George's book was the encouragement they so desperately needed. To celebrate, they decided to take a holiday. George had always longed to take his family to meet his father and see his childhood home, The Farm in Huntly— "The Land of Dreams," he often called it. But this required that they leave the three little ones with Louisa's family, and things were still strained with Mr. Powell. As it would have been too costly for Louisa and the girls to go with George, Louisa decided that George needed to get away and that she would remain with the children.

It was certainly providential that George was going home. He had learned that his younger sister, Bella, who was only fourteen years old, had developed a lung disease and was spitting up blood. The news came at a terrible time—Louisa had been trying to persuade Bella to come to England and live with them so she could attend the Ladies' College in Manchester. Louisa wanted Bella to have this rare opportunity because Louisa and her sisters had not been allowed to attend college.

"Her condition is grave," the doctor informed Bella's worried family.

"You must go to your sister!" Louisa urged George. "But don't forget that you should have perfect rest and recreation on this holiday, and please remember how your irrepressible intellectual energy is always in conflict with your frail health." Constantly vigilant, Louisa watched over George in every way—she took care of his health, his happiness, and especially his spiritual needs.

Louisa's vigilance, their son Greville later recalled, "is a very notable point in my parents' life. Always as keen and instant, whatever her own ailing or weariness of heart, it becomes more and more needed.... May we realize [her] indefatigable zeal. If such devotion be quite ordinary, it is not therefore less sublime."[5]

On July 1, George left for Huntly. The following day, Louisa wrote to him and expressed her usual encouragement. Most notable, besides her concern and care for him, were her lack of resentment at having to stay behind and her willingness to be vulnerable. There was no guile, no pretense between them.

> *Mrs. G.M.D. to her Husband*
> *Camp Terrace,*
> *July 2nd, 1855.*
>
> *... And I delight in the thought that you are so far on your road to home and your father. If it is such an evening as this in Edinburgh you will enjoy a night's sojourn in that princely city, though you be ever so tired—which you certainly will be by this time, half-past seven. I wonder how the hard-boiled eggs fared? Were you very weary? Such lots of little questions I should ask were I at your side—where I enjoyed being so much this tearful morning. Oh, how the whole world cried as I walked home! So I thought I would try and look for the bright pieces of this "mysterious dispensation." I could not find any bright, but I saw the calm and felt content, only anxious for fear I should not do all and become all that seemed pointed out to me. ...*
>
> *What would I not have given to have seen the beautiful Father*

meet the lovely Son! How happy and how sad you are by this time. . . . Mrs. Andrew says that, as everyone has to eat a peck of dirt, so she believes everyone has got to get through a peck of disagreeables in life; and she thinks our peck must be nearly out. . . . I am so anxiously waiting for your first letter, and still more for the first from Huntly. I wonder what your impression is of the dear invalid? I suppose you would scarcely have known her. But you will, I know, love, tell me all you can. Oh, this is my happiness—to know that you love me so truly in spite of my plainness and ignorance *and temper. God help me! May I send my love to your loves? . . .*[6]

George's visit to Huntly, the first since his wedding, was full of sadness—he could see that Bella was dying. Mindful of Louisa's sacrifice and love, he wrote to her daily, keeping her abreast of everything. As usual, he and Louisa shared with each other their observations of nature, God's majestic artwork.

G.M.D. *to his Wife.*
[July 4th, 1855.]

I am seated alone, a few miles on my way to Huntly. I have passed in the distance the stone crown which tops the square tower of my old college, and the pagoda-looking towers of the old cathedral—and beyond lies the sea. . . . When I get nearer home I shall want to be looking out, and not to write. It would be pleasant to point out to you the old places where your husband wandered and grew, and partly became the man you love now, notwithstanding his faults—which I hope will always be growing less. . . .

I shall feel something like the Ancient Mariner. "Is this the kirk? Is this the mill! Is this my own countree?" A girls' school is crowding into the carriages—not mine; and a country girl has flashed a look of you on me, darling, and it makes my two weary eyes rather dim when I write about it to you. We are passing through a bleak country now. Now we are at the town

> *of Inverury, 20 miles from home by the old road—how far by this I don't know. The country folks stare rather at me, and the louts laugh—my red cap and hairy face afford them amusement. It is a beautiful bright morning with a pale blue sky, and white clouds sleeping in light, and a triumphant God-like sun. . . . I seem to see better in this clear air and plentifulness of light than I have seen for a long time. I hardly wish to put my spectacles on. . . .*[7]

Each morning, Louisa would hurry to the steps to find the day's paper. Ignoring the front page, she would turn to the literary review section to see if any critic had mentioned George's book. She did her best to update him on any appreciative reviews of *Within and Without*, and even passed on an "insulting one." Naturally, unfavorable reviews vexed her, but she tried to be fair, get over her indignation, and let the criticisms go. In addition to sending encouraging reviews, Louisa made sure her letters were frequent and full of minute details and descriptions of the natural world. Words were all she and George could give each other while apart and proved their devout love and commitment.

> *G.M.D. to his Wife*
> *Huntly,*
> *July 5th, 1855*
>
> *. . . I have brought out a table and chair from the house and am sitting under the overhanging boughs of a small tree which was just planted when I visited home last. It is evening, and the birds are singing, and this afternoon I have been walking through one of the fields with my father, so full of the flowers of which I send you some; and down in the nursery lies my poor thin sister, very quiet—or rather sits, for she sits in bed with her knees up and her head leaning upon them—so thin is she! . . .*
>
> *Dear love, I can hardly bear your not being here. . . . It comes so often when I see beautiful things. There is not much beauty*

> here but much to my heart: and there would be to yours, and you would love my home, with its rough stones nearly covered with ivy.[8]

Although Louisa didn't want to worry him, George eventually learned that the children were ill and that the family's meager funds were weighing heavily on his wife. "Hopefully the funds from my book will arrive soon," he wrote to encourage her.

Louisa's sister Flora invited her and the children to stay for the month of July. Apprehensive, Louisa accepted the invitation and left for Liverpool to visit Flora and Mr. Sing, Flora's new, wealthy husband.

As Louisa entered the Sings' home, she couldn't help but notice the lavish furnishings and how they compared to her threadbare furniture at home. "I must remember this feeling," she told herself, "and when I return home I will kneel and thank God that my home will never cause another woman to stumble by wishing she had nicer things."

"George," she informed him, "Everyone is so kind to us here, but I do find it difficult to see my younger sister's luxurious home compared to what you have to put up with at ours. I know it shouldn't bother me so, but you do work so much harder and have so few comforts, so fragile in health and just now being acknowledged to be a great poet—it's hard to bear. The most difficult is how Flora patronizes me. I must learn to take people as I find them and not be impatient with them for not being what I want them to be."

Upon reading that little Mary was teased horribly by her cousin James and had retaliated by biting him, George wrote, "Poor little Elfie, what could she do but bite? It is the only gift she has in self-defense!"

But Louisa did not want George to think he needed to return home because of her troubles. "Do not come back for me a day sooner than you need, if you are well and enjoying yourself, which I know you are intensely. I shall have had a nice change here and shall be better when I go back. . . ." she wrote in response.

What Louisa found most difficult to bear were her siblings'

prideful scolding and judgements. Her sisters, assuming Louisa needed to learn "prudence and economy," would sometimes gossip about her daughters' socks, darned and darned again, the neatly mended embroidery, and the wrinkled shoulder-ribbons that could not be smoothed back after years of use.

Sometimes the criticisms deflated her. "My Husband," she wrote in early August, "Today I was almost mad with weariness, children and jam-making all day long, when Charles and Ellen Coleman visited today. I was drained—everything looked so impossible—so unlike the beauty and life there is in flowers. Ellen looked like a flower, and I like a potato rind."

That Louisa felt "like a potato rind" was not surprising—she was expecting her fourth child. She desperately needed rest, and financial strain, her daughters' illnesses, and pregnancy had all taken their toll. Thankfully, George soon returned home from Scotland. With him he brought a young girl named Elsie Gordon whom his stepmother had insisted he employ as help to Louisa. Elsie settled happily into the MacDonalds' family life and was a near-perfect blessing—a much better help than the girl they had formerly employed.

"I'm so happy you're home, but I'm even happier you were able to spend so much time with your father and say goodbye to sweet Bella," Louisa told George as she sank into his arms. He had needed time with his father—time for their long and loving talks, time full of family lore and the ancient traditions of the Scottish Highlands. He came home full to the brim with ideas, ideas that flowed like rich milk and wild honey, for future novels that would speak of the wisdom and austerity of his ancestors.

Bella died on August 24. The sweet words George penned to his grieving mother touched Louisa's motherly heart as well:

> . . . *Bella has only gone nearer to One who loves her more dearly and tenderly than you do. Or if you even think that she has gone to Alec, who has been waiting for her, it seems no such dreadful thing. God will let him take care of her till you go. I*

> *feel that if I had been in the spirit world before she came, I should have taken her to my heart so warmly that my little sister would soon have felt at home in the new place. We must weep often in this world, but there are very different kinds of tears. Bella will be kept quite safe for you there, and you will never be separated from her in heart. Schiller says—'Death cannot be an evil because it is universal.' God would not let it be the law of His Universe if it were what it looks to us. And dear mother, who could wish an easier, quieter, simpler death than my dear sister's? I should like to wither away out of the world like the flowers that they may come again. . . .*[9]

George began to work again, mainly giving lectures. Fortunately, he soon found a congregation in Bolton, Greater Manchester, that was enthusiastic about his ministry and whose members unanimously invited him to preach. Louisa was overjoyed, especially at the respect with which they treated her husband. After so many disappointments, it was good to be truly welcomed.

Another blessing came in the form of Annabella Milbanke—Lady Byron—the former wife of the famous poet. She told George that his book had placed a powerful hold on her, and she decided to turn her admiration into philanthropy and help the MacDonalds financially. This was an answer to their prayers, and it turned out that Lady Byron needed George and Louisa just as much as they needed her. George became Lady Byron's spiritual mentor and Louisa her lifelong friend.

Unfortunately, these blessings were soon overshadowed when George became severely ill and began hemorrhaging from his lungs. He hovered close to death for several days while doctors desperately tried to stop the bleeding. Forced to stay completely still, he lay quietly in bed with heavy bags of ice on his chest.

Would Louisa lose George, too? Alone in the garden, where hyacinths bloomed against the rough stone wall, God revealed once again that He was there. She would never be alone.

With only a few weeks remaining till the birth of her baby, and George close to death, Louisa needed help and support. "Please come. I need you," she begged her sister Annie, who rushed to her side along with Mrs. Scott's two sisters, the Miss Kerrs, who would sit at George's bedside and read or sing to him for hours.

"I've never known any patient who, fully aware that he might be dying, looked death in the face with such perfect equanimity," Doctor Harrison told Louisa. As difficult as this was to hear, it also strengthened Louisa and gave her peace.

"It was clearly God's sovereignty and perfect timing that brought Lady Byron to us," thought Louisa. Louisa's father and brother-in-law also subsidized her and George's housing expenses, and numerous gifts arrived from unexpected quarters. The Bolton congregation sent a quarter's salary in advance with word that "we are willing to wait any time for you." These graces sent Louisa's anxieties fleeing.

Because it was Christmastime, goodwill poured over the MacDonald home like lovely cream over plum pudding, even as George lay near death.

"We have never known such kindnesses from our friends, some of whom I had never known to be friends before," Louisa told her convalescing husband.

"The Lord means for us to be free from all anxiety, Louisa," he responded, "and if by this time we have not learned to cast all our care on Him who cares for us, I think we are getting the chance to learn it now. I see more and more that nothing will do for anybody in our circumstances but an absolute, enthusiastic confidence in God."

She marveled that even while facing possible death, he led his family with such spiritual truths.

Two weeks later, on January 20, 1856, their beautiful son was born. They named him Greville Matheson MacDonald, after George's oldest and dearest friend.

"I am too tired with writing notes to do more than tell you that I have a son at last," George hurriedly scribbled to his father. "Before ten last night he arrived. Louisa behaved so courageously. He is a great boy—might be three months old they say!"

"Is it not strange that this infant, this tiny, eternal being, is heir of the whole world and those mysteries which only God can reveal?" Louisa asked before bending down to place a gentle kiss on Greville's brow.

With courage, Louisa had already faced so much uncertainty—death, poverty, homelessness, disease—and she would still need courage to face each new year and every adventure that followed.

Lord, in my silver is much metal base,
Else should my being by this time have shown
Thee thy own self therein. Therefore do I
Wake in the furnace. I know thou sittest by,
Refining—look, keep looking in to try
Thy silver; Master, look and see thy face,
Else here I lie for ever, blank as any stone.
George MacDonald, *Diary of an Old Soul,* October 8

CHAPTER 9

THE CHALICE AND THE PATEN: PARENTING, POVERTY, AND PILGRIMAGE

She was a mother. One who is mother only to her own children is not a mother; she is only a woman who has borne children. But here was one of God's mothers.
George MacDonald, *Sir Gibbie*

Upstairs in the front bedroom that overlooked the cobbled streets below, one could usually find Louisa singing to, nursing, and rocking her babies. It didn't matter where they lived—she always made sure she had her trusty rocking chair so her little ones could look into her vivid blue eyes while snuggling into her warm, welcoming lap of safety and love.

In the springtime she could watch her older children playing on the cool grass, looking for wood violets, or picking up milk churns beneath the lilac bushes while the neighbor's dog barked from behind the gate. Summertime brought streets so thick with dust one could hardly hear the clattering hooves of horses as they trotted down the lane, driven by upright men with top hats tilted for shade. Louisa enjoyed watching her children climb trees and chase each other during the long summer days, and fall brought the loveliest foliage for her to contemplate as she rocked her babies while her other children hunted for nuts and colorful leaves. When winter blew in, Louisa greeted the snow from the warmth of her room, watching as it renewed and cleansed everything and gave her children a frosty, sparkling playground.

Absent were the diversions of modern technology, and the children were happier for this. They found sufficient entertainment in simple, free things, and a sense of safety and stability accompanied them through each day. Louisa always made sure their garden had all the stimuli and entertainment a child could need—grass, trees, flowers, vegetables, and a view of the village cathedral beyond the gate.

Every morning, Miss Elsie's lilting voice could be heard floating up the stairwell: "Breakfast is on!" The children would traipse down the stairs to find a simple breakfast, usually porridge and cream, and their father waiting with a smile. Before eight o'clock every morning, George would lead the family in prayer and read a chapter from the Scriptures, only to repeat this again in the evening, always accompanied by Louisa's piano-playing and hearty singing. If Louisa wasn't busy rocking a baby, she could be found hard at work mending her family's numerous bits of clothing, which were always in need of it. Humility and simplicity were residing guests in their home.

Louisa was forever grateful that George had brought Elsie with him when he returned from Scotland, for without her help, she would certainly have been overwhelmed. Elsie was a gem, and her cheerful assistance was invaluable. She didn't mind the drudgery of housework and was probably the happiest person in Manchester. She adored and protected the MacDonald children and was intuitively aware of each child's needs.

"Something extraordinarily sweet has entered our lives," Louisa would say about her.

When the weather was right, Louisa and Elsie would often take the children out to see the world God had made. "How very important it is for us to point out that God cares as much for us as he does for the lilies," Louisa would tell the children.

The children would bring crumbs to feed the swans, as happy as if God were busy making all these lovely parts of nature grow right before their eyes. Pointing out each created thing, they would marvel at what God had made.

"Look, Elsie! Look at the birds everywhere! Look at the plain brown birds! And the ducks! Aren't they silly? Look at their muddy mouths," they'd shout, pointing and giggling.

"Remember what your father always says, children, that the sparrow and the rook are just as respectable as the egg-laying fowl or the dirt-gobbling duck!" Louisa would remind them.

These daily jaunts helped Louisa keep her hopes up and

her heart light amid the uncertainty of motherhood. In Victorian England, motherhood—within marriage—was considered a woman's crowning achievement, the zenith of a woman's spiritual and emotional journey. Queen Victoria was the model for family-centered femininity. During the nineteenth century, motherhood was idealized in popular magazines. It was considered a holy passion, one in which all others would be absorbed and lost—a sacred flame on the altar of the heart—because only heaven knows what a woman suffers in bearing and raising children.

Victorian motherhood was made to sound sweet and heavenly, and for most upper-class women in England, it was at least easy. The difficulties of child-rearing were erased by nannies, governesses, and cooks, because a certain distance was required between parents and their children. Often, children only spent a few hours of the day with their mother and father.

But for Louisa, motherhood was not merely lovely thoughts and kind words. It was not an achievement or requirement she had to fulfill in order to be accepted by Victorian society. For Louisa, motherhood was the sweetest of all gifts granted to her by her Savior, and she received it humbly with a willing, grateful heart.

Each child was one of the Master's miracles. Louisa understood the suffering of childbirth, having watched her mother bear and lose babies and suffer physically afterward. But Louisa never let herself fear—she welcomed every pregnancy, every miracle. She considered herself a chalice, a vessel to be filled to the brim with God's Spirit, to cooperate with her husband and with God, to be poured out for her family. And George was her paten, the plate that supported and upheld the chalice. George's role was a solemn responsibility, and Louisa would need him to continue in it because they would be blessed with seven more miracles between 1857 and 1867. All said, they welcomed eleven children in fifteen years.

"We're on the wrong side of a dozen!" George often teased her.

When others heard him say this, they thought he meant he had thirteen children, as though that number would have pushed the family to "the wrong side." But George and Louisa didn't stop at eleven. They later took in two girls, Honey and Joan Desaint, whose consumptive mother, abandoned by her French husband, lived with them and was cared for by Louisa. When the mother died in 1881, Louisa and George adopted the two girls. In addition, while living at The Retreat, where they moved in 1867, the MacDonalds welcomed a young, very ill boy from extreme poverty. With the help of her daughter Winifred, Louisa taught and guided the boy until he was accepted to the College of Organists. George and Louisa loved and educated all three adopted children as if they were their very own. They even had the privilege of raising their granddaughter, Octavia Grace, when their third daughter, Caroline Grace, died suddenly. Never on the wrong side of a dozen, but always on the right side of heaven, their home overflowed with the Master's miracles.

Children were never a burden to Louisa. She adhered to the Biblical truth that Christianity is defined by caring for the widow and the orphan. Period. "Whenever a child is placed in our midst, we must receive them as though we are receiving Jesus Himself, and if we have a fault, let it be that our generosity outruns our means," Louisa often declared. George agreed.

Before the birth of each much-prayed-for child, Louisa could be found in her rocker, her nimble fingers carefully stitching clothes for her new bundle of joy.

"Someday soon you will have another brother or sister, but right now he or she is growing inside me," she would say to her wondering children.

George would set up the cradle while Louisa arranged a lovely white layette. For diapers and diaper liners, she would have her children cut squares from old pajamas and soft, discarded clothing. At night, Louisa would often take a howling child into her arms, pressing them to her heart to soothe them back to sleep. The stars would shine, the wind would whisper against the window, the chair would rock, and the child would snuggle up against Louisa to find comfort and rest.

"Little wonder is it that I have always adored my mother. I still do so," Greville later reminisced.

Louisa pondered much during these times of waiting. Within her heart were the fear of God, the awe of being chosen to receive a gift, and the humility of knowing her own inadequacy. She resolved that "Right here, right now, right where I am, not somewhere else, is where I will learn best about spiritual maturity. Maturity starts with the willingness to give of oneself."

"But it's such a daunting and eternal task, my dear Bear," she had said to George when she felt her first child moving within.

"Then we must have a foolproof plan," he replied. "We need to start with God to understand the meaning of motherhood and fatherhood. He is the Creator of all things visible and invisible, magnificent and trivial—of every little detail. He desires to be in charge of the everyday, seemingly meaningless things we are given to do as parents."

"Well then, let's draw up our plan. We won't be effective parents unless we agree on how we will shape and mold our children and give saints back to God. We certainly agree that in no other sphere does failure have more dire consequences. Children are a gift, a blessing, a heritage from the Lord—never a penalty," Louisa declared.

And so, early in the evening as the sun slid down to rest behind pillowy clouds, they sat at the kitchen table, the kerosene lamp warming the room and the child in Louisa's womb kicking like a kaleidoscope of butterflies, and wrote their parenting plan. They knew it must be one based on conviction and to which they could adhere without difficulty.

"We will parent with intent and purpose," they said as they smiled at each other, their eyes full of hope.

First, they planned to strive for a peaceful home. "Peace is only possible if we have orderliness," they agreed, "because God is a God of order and peace."

"Next, we will prioritize our children's education based on

each child's gifts, passions, and abilities," George declared. "We'll need to find the golden threads carefully woven within each child by our Creator," Louisa chimed in, "and favor the development of each child in the direction of his or her own bent."

"We will teach each child that God has given them gifts that must be recognized, cultivated, and used to glorify Him alone," George said. "And as difficult as discipline is to administer, if we want to have a peaceful home, we must require immediate obedience. We will teach them that trusting and obeying their parents is the most important method God will use to prepare them for a godly life. We will never give in to disobedience and never threaten what we are not prepared to carry out."

"Oh! And we'll teach them that delayed obedience is disobedience," Louisa reminded him. "We mustn't be hard on quarrelling, but we should be mindful of tempers and greed and spite, as well as of fretting and grumbling. It's important that we always let them come to us, always hear what they have to say, give only justice, and model fair play. We'll never sneer at them, lose our temper, or use their feelings as tools."

"And because I'm a minister, the spiritual life of each of our children will be of utmost importance. They must strive to be pure and blameless in every situation as much as they are able," George said with conviction. "We must be careful to respect the spiritual person of His child, and approach it with reverence, for it too looks the Father in the face and has an audience with Him into which no earthly parent can enter even if he dared to desire it. We must instill no religious doctrine apart from its duty."[1]

"And, as their mother, I think we should demonstrate through our own lives the importance of industry and productivity—and be careful to teach them that God's will is found in being willing to do the next thing in front of you, no matter how trivial," Louisa said. "We must discourage emulation and insist on duty."

"But we must also teach them about quietness before God," added George, "and that work is not always required of a man. There is such a thing as a sacred idleness, the cultivation of which is now fearfully neglected."[2]

"We can't forget to keep things happy at home, and fun, too!" Louisa said. "We have so many lovely ways to enjoy God together through the gifts of music, humor, nature, and literature."

"Yes," he agreed, "Let's work hard to make sure our home will always be a place of hope for others, whether through lectures, music, plays, books, food, nursing the sick, or welcoming a lost child."[3]

"No matter what," said Louisa with conviction.[3] "And one other thing, the most important thing: we must teach them altruism. We must keep our door open to the poor, the needy, the sick, and the lonely, no matter our finances. We must trust God in all circumstances. I am convicted on this point, my Bear. I was reading Isaiah 58 this morning and it is haunting me."

Opening her Bible, she began to read: "Is not this the fast that I choose. . . . Is it not to share your bread with the hungry and bring the homeless poor into your house; when you see the naked, to cover him, and not to hide yourself from your own flesh? Then shall your light break forth like the dawn, and your healing shall spring up speedily; your righteousness shall go before you; the glory of the Lord shall be your rear guard. Then you shall call, and the Lord will answer; you shall cry, and He will say, 'Here I am.'"[4]

"Yes," agreed George. "Amen. And we should never wish our children to do what we would not do ourselves if we were in their positions. We must accept righteous sacrifices and help our children accept them, too."

So they shouldered the plow together through frequent life-threatening illnesses, ever-precarious financial situations, necessary times of separation, and constant changes of residence.

"Picture the yoke, Louisa," George often said. "It is the only way to true rest. Christ said we must first take His yoke upon us, and our yoke is good because it's built for two."

Greville described his parents' guidance amid frequent illness and poverty:

> *For two years he [George] had by teaching subsisted precariously, heroic alike in industry and ailing, while my mother tended and taught her children, superintended cooking, kept the house and its furniture spotless, yet always the lover and support of her husband. Strong in her family were a passionate love of music and a quite singular dramatic gift. Her pure and rich mezzo-soprano voice had been finely trained, and its tenderness did much, I think, to encourage her husband's genius.*[5]

He also fondly recalled his mother's listening ear that brought him to a relationship with his Savior when he was a teenager:

> *I once chanced to go with my mother to hear the Elijah Oratorio at the Albert Hall and Antoinette Sterling's rendering of "O Rest in the Lord." As soon as we reached home, I begged a word with my mother. Though tired from the great music and the slow omnibus journey, she sat up with me till 2 a.m., I mostly on the floor, before I could tell her all my sins. But I went to be in blissful rest from my flagellation; . . . On the following morning my father's only reference to the incident was the warmest embrace I ever remember from him—but, yes, there was one other like it—whilst his eyes shone like stars in a rain-washed sky. Thereafter the whole world became new to me; had not the Kingdom of Heaven come right into its very duties? . . . It has never been to me otherwise than a world of potential, inspired beauty, with its eternally renewing hope. The transformation of my world was not, I think, wholly subjective; it came chiefly, I believe, from the discovery of my mother's and father's love for me . . . from those particular sins which my mother exorcised once and for all when she held me to her heart and wiped all tears from my eyes.*[6]

> *We had no secrets, though sometimes [Mother] was inexorably difficult when I tried to justify things that she could not approve.*

> *Yet how devotedly watchful she was! Her love was always ready to counteract my spiritual loneliness, and always hungry to forgive.*[7]

But life with the MacDonalds was not all duty and striving—they took extra care to have happy times. The family loved playing games, and George was often found in the midst of the activities. Shouts of laughter could be heard in the house whenever the children played tag; what's the time, Mr. Wolf?; kerby; hopscotch; or rounders in the street below. Music, drama, charades, and traipsing through the woods were frequent pastimes in the burgeoning family.

Their yard would swarm with children waiting for a first glimpse of the festivities Louisa prepared for her kids' frequent parties. George and Louisa's close friends would arrive with their excited children freshly clothed in pinafores and corduroy and anxious for the games to begin. Guests gratefully inhaled the wonderful fragrances of spiced goodies, scones, and "nice fish and homely fare," as Louisa liked to call her cooking, and wondered what fun had been planned for them this time.

One of those children, Johnston Forbes-Robertson, later recalled attending a party at the MacDonalds' home:

> *In my early life my father and mother had very dear friends in George MacDonald and his brilliant and witty wife, and the numerous children of both families saw much of each other. Many children's parties were given, and a child with us all was the loveable George MacDonald, who entered into our games with a naïve enthusiasm, to the joy of us youngsters. I remember well that Arthur Hughes, the painter, in the same spirit often helped to entertain at these children's gatherings. MacDonald was a saintly character and literally worshipped by his friends. He brought with him sunlight and hope wherever he went, and was untiring in his good works. No adverse circumstances seemed to touch him one jot, and of those he must have had a full share, for he brought up a large family solely on his pen,*

and with such love and care that all took on something of his disposition.⁸

The MacDonalds also enjoyed giving each other nicknames. Lilia was Goose or Goosie; Mary was often called My Blackbird, Elfie, or Molly; Caroline was Gracie; Maurice was Bogie; Irene was Goblin; George became Greatheart; and Louisa was lovingly called Mother Heart. Each child treasured their terms of endearment, and their funny names accompanied them into adulthood. Their nicknames became plumb lines, bringing them back to their foundation and reminding them of their parents' unconditional love. Louisa even named the family's homes, usually including "Courage" somewhere in the title, a quite fitting addition in light of all the family faced together.

The children's education was a difficult priority, but George and Louisa achieved it. Both parents, when available, taught their children. Louisa taught reading, writing, and music and always stressed the importance of gathering manna from above through education. George gave lessons in Latin, Euclid, science, and math. His familiarity with the writings of William Law, Henry More, George Fox, Blake, Swedenborg, Shakespeare, and Dante, as well as his fluency in French, German, Italian, Greek, and Latin, made him the best of all tutors.

Greville later recalled what home education had been like for him and his siblings:

> *My father in the education of his children, put duty before everything. In spite of his militant repudiation of Calvinism, he upheld passive obedience as essential in training the young. He would tell us we had to accept this or that on trust before we could understand it, this being the surest way to apprehending it when we were older. Yet he was wonderfully patient with me, though I was indubitably much slower than my sisters, and no sternness ever qualified his tenderness in any sickness or repentance. So far as was possible, he never refused me anything I asked. I remember his saying that his own father, poor though*

> he was, had never denied him anything, and that he hoped his own children would be able to say as much of him.
>
> Lessons were given by my mother in any accidentally spare hours; and, over against my stupidity, she would tell of my precocity in beguiling her sex, even while I could not realize that c-a-t must never spell dog. For, she long afterwards told me, once when she was in despair over such elementals, I set a period to my lesson by irrelevantly pleading, 'Mama, what pretty brown eyes you've got'! The discovery, bringing me instant proofs of her love for me, was of more importance to both of us than any claims of a disciplinary alphabet. Never but once in my long life have I met eyes so compelling of loyalty and love as that beloved woman's.[9]

Believing that the awakening of his children's imaginations was more important than academic grammar or coded moralities, George encouraged the reading of fairy tales, often writing them himself, with Louisa reading them aloud to the children.

When one considers all that George and Louisa endured during their many years of bearing and raising children, of poverty and grave illnesses that often led to frequent changes of residence, one can only conclude that God was in the midst of them, using all things to teach them strength, courage, and perseverance.

MacDonald Family Births and Residences

1851	George and Louisa marry March 8 in Hackney
1852	Lilia Scott born January 4
1853	Mary Josephine born July 23
	Move to Manchester
1854	Move to Alderley Cross, then to No. 3 Camp Terrace in Lower Broughton
	Caroline Grace born September 16
1856	Greville Matheson born January 20
	George, Louisa, and Mary leave for Algiers in November for health

1857	Return to London in May
	Irene born August 31
	Move to Huntly Cottage, Hastings
1858	Winifred Louisa born November 6
1859	Move to 18 Queen Square, Bloomsbury
1860	Ronald born October 27
	Move to Tudor Lodge, Regent Park
1862	Move to Earls Terrace, Kensington
	Robert Falconer born July 15
1864	Maurice born February 7
1865	Bernard Powell born September 28
1867	George MacKay born January 23
	Move to The Retreat, Upper Mall, Hammersmith
1870	Secure auxiliary residence at Hastings
1872	In September, arrive in America for nine-month lecture tour
1875	Move to Great Tangley Manor at Wonersh
	Move to Corage at Boscombe, Bournemouth
1879	Move to Villa Barratta at Portofino
1880	Move to Bordighera
	Build home: Casa Coraggio
1900	Move to St. George's Wood

(This list does not include the four other children who were raised by the MacDonalds.)

George and Louisa's children were certainly raised in unusual ways and amid trying circumstances. But Greville's memoir explains how the difficult years benefited him and his siblings:

> ... *the mutual dependence, the unfettered affection, the enduring service, of children to parents and to one another! ... In those Victorian days the family life was an asset in the nation's ethical efficiency. [My parents' letters] suggest, not only the devotion found among large groups of relatives and closely bonded friends, but that there was, throughout, in actual operation, an unexpressed awareness of eternal, creating Purpose. With my father and mother it amounted to conviction,*

> and each one of the family would in turn become more or less subject to the idea of a coordinating Destiny in which each was a responsible agent. Schools may awaken a very desirable esprit de corps: consanguinity which was automatically happiness and education, recompense and forgiveness. Moreover, in the large family, along with a desire for sharing the daily duties, the urgency of being loved is discovered—and how love is won through giving. The best education may belong to a home none too well provided with necessities, and where luxuries are rare. Before we stepped from the home door into an uncharted world, we had already learned much of life's significance; how to belong to one another; thence to the world we lived in; and maybe beyond it. Year by year, as we grew older, our love for father and mother grew wiser and stronger.[10]

George and Louisa frequently discussed raising "the wrong side of a dozen" children. Proof of this is found throughout the pages of George's novels and stories. For example, in *The Wise Woman*, he beautifully illustrates the necessity of parenting with a view of eternity and gives the reader a glimpse of his and Louisa's understanding of how important intentional parenting is for raising godly children. The fairy tale describes the foolish, selfish hearts of two girls, which actually represent the foolish, selfish hearts of all humanity. George exposes the parents' blindness to the girls' poor character as the same distorted vision suffered by most parents.

Placing each child in the arms of their Heavenly Father was his and Louisa's goal. "I want my books to show that we don't see ourselves clearly as children and then as parents, and that we certainly don't see our children clearly, either," he told her. "But there is One with clear, pure vision who intervenes and exposes our flaws to reconcile us to each other and to Himself. When He allows temporal hardship and heartbreak, it is to make us 'lovely creatures.'

"I must convince parents to focus on developing diligence, responsibility, loyalty, duty, obedience, and faith—the processes by which we yield to God's transforming power in order to learn the difference between genuine love and selfish neglect or indulgence. It is our testament to the gracious, nurturing care of our Heavenly Father."

As George wrote and taught, Louisa sang and prayed, nursed and loved. She lived by example the things she most wanted her children to learn: to be industrious and willing to do the next thing; to be filled with God's Spirit so they could pour out His love to those around them; to discover their gifts and use them to bless others; to care for the poor; and, most importantly, to always keep their hearts and homes open to any child in need. And, of course, however busy they were, the family always tried to take their daily tramp, making sure to suit their pace to the smallest child.

How little are we our own! Existence is decreed us; love and suffering are appointed us. We may resist, we may modify; but we cannot help loving, and we cannot help dying. . . . Great in goodness, yea absolutely good, God must be, to have a right to make us—to compel our existence, and decree its laws!
George MacDonald, *What's Mine's Mine*

CHAPTER 10

LIMPING TOWARD JERUSALEM

My harvest withers.
Health, my means to live—
All things seem rushing straight into the dark.
But the dark still is God. . . .
. . . Am I not a spark
Of him who is the light?
George MacDonald, *Diary of an Old Soul*, January 15

Winter mornings glistened, welcomed by sunshine that rippled through lace curtains and by a patient wind that guided clouds behind the roofs of the town like an usher in a theater. The MacDonalds woke to wet cobbled streets, shining after the evening rain, and the rattling of carriages.

Mornings were always busy in the MacDonald home. The babbling of children and babies, the hissing of the trusty stove, and the whistle of the tea kettle brought life to each day and joy to Louisa's heart.

"I must remember the sights and sounds of these mornings when the children are grown," she thought to herself.

Upstairs lay her dear George, weak and ailing, and on her lap slept baby Greville, the corners of his lips coated with milk. Louisa was still trying to gain strength after the birth of her fourth child, and this recovery was progressing more slowly than the last.

"If I could only be this content and sure," she mused as she looked at her wee cherub's peaceful face. With no income, and her critically ill husband confined to bed, Louisa could only turn to God and to the next task set before her.

"The unseen blessing in all of this," she said to herself, "is that I have learned to live frugally. Papa would be happily surprised at that. And I must remember that no matter how cheaply we live, there are always those without, and I must try to be aware of the poverty and hardships beyond our door."

This was not a new or difficult task for her—with her compassionate nature, Louisa had always made it her business to know the plights of others.

When Greville was about two weeks old, a mixed blessing arrived in the person of Mrs. A. J. Scott, the wife of George's mentor and friend. She blew in like a mariner and brought the MacDonalds' ship safely to port. She took George to the Scott home at Cheetham Hill to rest in quiet, but Louisa dearly missed him.

"When George is able, I encourage you to consider getting your family away from here, Louisa," advised Mrs. Scott. "You all need to go south, where the air is cleaner and the climate is warmer."

Louisa agreed, but wondered where they could find the means to do so.

G.M.D. to his Wife
[Cheetham Hill,]
Jan. 24, 1856.

Dearest, sweet Wife,

I think I am a little better to-day. I need hardly tell you I enjoy myself. They are all so kind. I was left quite alone, and spent the time meditating in spite of stupidity—and in reading Hoffman's Golden Pot *again. It is delightful. . . . I never saw Mr. Scott so happy, so merry or so loving as last night. He talked a great deal yesterday about Art, and I have some new thoughts about it from him. . . . It was a divine day and I saw things as I had not seen them before. May our Father teach us—for no one, not even Mr. Scott, can teach us but Him. Indeed we have secrets of our own with Him and no one else. Think of and to Him while you lie there. Tell me about little Greville. Is his hoarseness gone? . . . My love to Annie please. To-morrow we will come.*[1]

George's homecoming was sweet. Louisa never forgot greeting him at the carriage and watching him lift his beloved, worn cap to her. It was a perfect moment.

He recovered in time to travel with his family to London and on to The Limes, where Louisa's sister Phoebe was to be married. They left on February 19, and neither George nor Louisa had much strength. The streets sloped gently before them, and their children sat beside them. The smell of horses and straw permeated the cab as their carriage rattled along narrow cobbled lanes, passing exciting shops and shuffling pedestrians. Sunlight conquered the fog, and the sparkling air revived George and Louisa while their observant, vivacious children pushed their faces to the windows to watch the passing sights, spellbound.

At The Limes, they were warmly welcomed by Annie, who was now the home's mistress and happy to be hostess to them. The wedding was held the next day, and although it was a beautiful ceremony, both George and Louisa were exhausted afterward.

"I must get you to Dr. Wilkinson," Louisa informed her husband. George consented. The doctor declared his lungs "mischief free" and prescribed six months of complete rest.

After relaying George's diagnosis to her sister, Louisa sighed, then quietly went to see the children, who were playing in her childhood nursery.

"Let's go to the park," Annie proposed, attempting to cheer them up. She wanted them to see the newly opened Victoria Park in East London. "I hear it's beautiful. The Crown Estate purchased more than two hundred acres—they took Bonner's Fields and tore down Bishop Bonner's Palace. The park rests between the Regent's and Hertford Union canals. There's a lovely pond for the children and green grass everywhere you look!"

Louisa agreed, and the party took Sewardstone Road to the park's main entrance. Trees shadowed the sprawling greens, which looked perfect for family picnics. Louisa liked the rolling landscape dotted with trees, curving thickets, and flower beds. "It's certainly not flat and dull," she thought. Silent swans, grey herons, mallards, Egyptian geese, and mandarin ducks dominated the water, while mistle thrush and green woodpeckers darted from branch to bush. The children were anxious to feed the ducks and rushed to the bank, where tall nightshades with lovely white petals lined the edges of the water.

"There's a gate named after Edmund Bonner that we must find when the children are ready," Annie informed George and Louisa.

Noticing a child nearby, Louisa nudged her husband. "George, look at the poor boy over there," she said, and without hesitation she gave the child her last sixpence so he could buy a kite. This small act was, like so many of her larger deeds, little short of divine in its hastiness. The event changed her worried heart, and she later put it down as a small story, which George added to his book *Adela Cathcart*.[2]

> Describing their journey to Victoria Park, Louisa wrote:
> *I had been ill, and my husband was ill, and we had nothing to do, and we did not know what would become of us. . . . I knew that all was for the best, as my good husband was always telling me; but my eyes were dim and my heart was troubled, and I could not feel sure that God cared quite so much for us as he did for the lilies. . . . The very colors of the flowers, the blue of the sky, the sleep of the water, seemed to push us out of the happy world that God had made. And yet the children, two of them [they were now out of the carriage and feeding the swans], seemed as happy as if God were busy making the things before their eyes, and holding out each thing as he made it, for them to look at. . . .[3]*

The family remained at The Limes until early March, which gave Louisa's father time to get to know his grandchildren.

"I certainly will miss you," Mr. Powell said as he held Louisa's hands in his own. His eyes misted as he spoke of each wee one.

"I have grown mightily fond and proud of my little grandchildren, the little white Lily with her wondering grey eyes, her sensitive nostrils, her rare sweet smile and that captivating, quick-blossoming of her roses; the little dark-haired elfish Mary with her blackbird's voice and a sweetness more instant than Lily's; the solemn less pretty Gracie, but with her mother's wonderful eyes; and the great greedy baby, his brown eyes all for his mother."[4]

Mr. Powell's lovely grandchildren were so much like his own children that he became once again less standoffish, less rigid. With them he was able to become something more than the reluctant upholder of duty. He knew it was imperative that George move to a warmer climate, so he provided the finances and made it possible.

"You must leave as soon as you can. You should probably take Lily and the baby, but leave Gracie and Elfie here with us. Annie and I will gladly look after them," Mr. Powell insisted.

Early in March, George, Louisa, Lily, and Greville left for Kingswear, a lovely village in the English county of Devon that sits on the east bank at the mouth of the tidal River Dart, opposite Dartmouth. They were able to travel by train, making the last part of their journey aboard the Paignton and Dartmouth Steam Railway, which dropped them off in the village. Louisa could see why Mrs. Scott had recommended Kingswear, with its small tourist shops, a castle overlooking the sea, and the Church of St Thomas of Canterbury elevated above the river. The church was the first thing the MacDonalds saw when they disembarked the train, and its tower welcomed them with the peal of its three bells.

They found simple lodgings on the hillside but had barely settled in when George began hemorrhaging again.

"I think I nearly killed myself racing down those dark steps," Louisa told the doctor when he arrived, then paused to catch her breath. "I was trying to get to the vicar's house for help, and he graciously sent his daughter to fetch you."

The Reverend John Smart, his wife, and his swift-footed daughter had sent for help immediately and comforted Louisa while she waited. Their frequent kindnesses forever endeared them to her. From that time on, Mr. and Mrs. Smart continuously gave of their best to the MacDonalds.

"Isn't it amazing, my dear Bear, how God once again has used our need to bring us such wonderful friends?" Louisa asked her husband.

"The clergyman and all his family are such simple, good people. I want to go to church next Sunday if I am able," he replied.

But a stiff breeze gusted against the surface of the river, and a cold east wind was always blowing, causing the Dartmouth shopkeepers on the opposite bank to shutter their windows. This wind was rough on George's lungs and delayed his recovery.

"I do enjoy looking out from the window, through the mouth of the River Dart, much like Jonah might look through the jaws of the whale, into the great Atlantic," he said with a smile.[5]

Soon they found a lovely cottage called Little Ravenswell. The home was just beginning to show off a wealth of apple blossoms that peeked in the drawing-room window. A quaint garden cascaded down to a low seawall that guarded the home from the waves of the great estuary. In the evenings, the MacDonalds enjoyed watching the low moon bounce splashes of light off the tops of the waves. George spent as much time as possible on the water and found the sea air especially beneficial. He also used this time of rest to copy his collection of poems into a pretty volume, written in his exquisite penmanship. He dated it "Kingswear, Lynmouth, Lynton," because their cottage was close to where Louisa had spent such precious days with her mother eight years before. He gave the book to Louisa.

But despite the sunny shelter of the cottage, with its primroses peeping up in the quiet woods and the crags along the sea, George's progress was painfully slow. And so the plan to visit Huntly finally arranged itself, and they set out for Lynmouth, a stop along the way.

G.M.D. to his Father.
Lynmouth, Devonshire.

> *We came here yesterday by steamer from Kingswear. . . . This is a most romantic country; crowded hills, with wood climbing up to the tops of some from the bottom of the valleys—while others are as bare as any in Scotland; brawling, rocky streams—of which one, the Lynn, at the mouth of which we are situated, runs into the sea direct. . . . We have left warm friends behind us in the clergyman of Kingswear and his family. You should have seen him pulling us and all our luggage in his boat to the steamer, like a ferryman! . . . We shall be here a week at least—after which Louisa will go to Manchester and I by sea to Aberdeen on our way to you. . . .*[6]

With their plan in place, Louisa carefully settled George on the ship, waved goodbye as he stood on the deck, bundled up in a scarf that nearly covered his face, and watched him sail away.

"Off to Manchester to get the children," she said, bracing herself.

As soon as she was able, she and her brood joined George at Huntly, and she finally met her beloved father-in-law in person. George beamed with delight and pride as he introduced Louisa and presented their four children to his parents. At last, George's father and stepmother discovered for themselves what George had always told them: that God had given him a tender wife of inestimable worth.

They spent three lovely months at Huntly. It was the perfect place for George and Louisa to find refuge and a new depth of peace. It was like quenching thirst with a drink of ice-cold water. The girls grew plump on porridge, scones, eggs, and cream, and baby Greville grew to love the rich milk from the family's cow. But George, while he flourished in spirit, did not gain much physical strength, so their family and friends again urged them to winter in the south.

The most adamant was Lady Byron who, although she had not yet met George, felt a deep sense of debt to *Within and Without* and through faithful correspondence had formed an intimate friendship with both George and Louisa. It was probably through her relationship with A. J. Scott that she learned about their empty pockets and George's failing health. At any rate, she covered their travel expenses, introduced them to her close friends, and ordered them to leave Scotland and go to Algiers on the Mediterranean Sea.

"It's the best place for you to hibernate this winter. A change of scenery and society will help you immensely, and I daresay the dry air and sun will fully heal your lungs."

Lady Byron was a purposeful woman of moral strength who had suffered greatly during her marriage to her famous husband. She had hoped that by marrying Lord Byron, she could help him reform his immoral ways and benefit the world by using his magnificent talent for moral and spiritual enlightenment. But he did not keep his promise to improve himself, and she separated from him after a year of marriage. She spent her days seeking ways to be of service without Lord Byron and found delight in helping George in any way he would allow, with the hope that he could continue his writing.

"I'm not the only one financing your holiday," she revealed. "A. J. Scott has been able to raise considerable support."

To George and Louisa, all these gifts were tangible expressions of God's grace and tender care.

After saying goodbye to The Farm and George's beloved Huntly in September 1856, they traveled to London to put all the details together. When they reached London, they checked in with George's publisher, then continued to The Limes. They were disappointed to learn that they couldn't visit Lady Byron to finally meet and thank her, for her own poor health had required her to leave London.

Next they left Lily with Mrs. Godwin, and Grace and baby Greville at The Limes. Because Mary was weak and hadn't fared well in Huntly, they decided to bring her to Algiers.

"She is perhaps the sweetest, least exacting of our children, and gives us the least trouble," Louisa confided to George.

Louisa knew she would miss her babies terribly, but she took courage and accompanied her ailing husband to Africa. It was a long and arduous journey, and they were relieved when they finally arrived in Algiers. George penned a beautiful description of this new and different country to his father, knowing he would want to hear every detail:

G.M.D. to his Father.
Algiers,
Friday, Nov. 28, 1856

*... Under the windows of the hotel there are trees with many yellow oranges. Before us lies the bay of Algiers, filled with the blue Mediterranean—for it is bluer than other seas, or rather more habitually blue.... Oh the multitude of costumes! I have been able to classify them only partially as yet. I will not try to describe them, but my delight in color is gratified here. I have, however, with my Rob Roy plaid and Glengarry bonnet, added one to the multitude of costumes, and seem to amuse some of the people as much as they amuse me. The town is full of French soldiers in all variety of uniforms; and what with their infernal drums and trumpets, and the noise of French and Arabic and the wagons and horses with bells—and, beautiful in themselves, the fountains before the door, we long for quiet.... We cannot lead a hotel-life long, for our money would soon be gone....
The town is built on the hillside, covering no great extent, but very closely built—so closely that a peep of the blue sky is something. The lower part of the town is French, though tinctured with Arabesque; but above, you might fancy—what with narrow passages, the only streets, what with arched ways, and houses projecting till the walls touch, and a constant succession on either hand of courts with Moorish arches, and stairs up and down—that you were in the time of the pirates! Even now the succession of strange countenances is startling—Arabs, Jews, French-Moorish women, all in white, of whom nothing is visible but the eyes, and perhaps the bare feet....
Some that we suppose Turks, and Armenians or Persians—multitudes of donkeys and mules; oxen yoked by the horns; beautiful Arab horses, very small and elegant, mostly white; and yesterday we saw one camel walking along with an Arab or somebody on his hump.... There does not seem nearly the*

misery that we see in London or any of our large towns.

> The countenance and forms of the Aborigines seem much more noble than those of their conquerors. Prominent regular features, dark eyes, slender limbs (the bare legs, bronzed and smooth, would need two to make an English footman's), long, swinging gait—are contrasted with the more common features and most insignificant persons of by far the greater part of the French soldiery. The French are, however, very pleasant people to have to do with. . . .[7]

Before the year ended and 1857 made its entrance, George and Louisa found an apartment in an old Moorish house on a hillside. Lovely green olive groves surrounded their dwelling, which was located near Saint Eugene, a western suburb of the city. They occupied the ground floor, while an archdeacon and his family lived on the floor above. Three windows of various small sizes climbed up the wall, and yellow, green, blue, and black tiles covered the walls in varied patterns. Outside, the roof was vaulted with crossing arches.

From the windows, the MacDonalds looked out on the Mediterranean, with its infinite shades of color and wild, crashing waves. If they stood in their doorway and looked eastward, they could see the snowcapped peaks of the Lesser Atlas range watching them from across the bay.

"The olive trees are lovely, but these walls are chilly and damp from lack of sun. Still, I won't complain—the piano hiding in the recess beckons me," Louisa told George.

The archdeacon and his family were kind neighbors, and they and the MacDonalds became fast friends. Other friends soon followed: Mr. Leigh Smith, who later represented Norwich in the House of Commons; his three daughters, one of whom founded Girton College, the first women's college in Cambridge, and became close friends with novelist George Eliot; and Miss Anna Leigh Smith, whose frail health had brought her family to Algiers and who became a lifelong friend of the MacDonalds. Their brother, Captain Leigh Smith, the renowned Arctic explorer, was in Algiers as well.

The Oliphant family and their daughter, Mrs. Ormond, often joined the group of friends.

"Did you know the Leigh Smiths are cousins of Florence Nightingale? They certainly challenge me with their intellectually emancipated conversations. We're blessed with wonderful friendships, George," Louisa said. "I'm so glad we share this together."

Because the friends made up a small group of English people living far from home, they frequently spent the evenings at one another's apartments for tea and conversation, sometimes traveled together to Marseille to shop, and occasionally enjoyed a picnic expedition in the desert. Each would bring what they could to share, and Mrs. Oliphant's large teapot and six silver teaspoons were frequently requested. These delightful get-togethers were good for George.

"The George MacDonalds we see almost daily," Mrs. Ormond wrote in her diary. "His conversation is clever, and when for the time his writing is cast aside, he is like a merry schoolboy enjoying his recreation hour, unsophisticated, genial and good hearted."[8]

Louisa was delighted to see her husband's gaiety, and it was good for her to be able to open her heart and their apartment to these new, dear friends. "But I do miss my babies," she often thought to herself.

Louisa loved when George would venture out into the Algerian streets wearing his Rob Roy plaid kilt and Glengarry bonnet.

"I must add to all the vibrant colors here," he told her with a wink.

Writing to her sister Caroline, Louisa described their activities:

> *We gave a soiree the other night, and with flowers made the room look quite pretty—great boughs of lovely scented acacia and lots of hawthorn and dear dark rich roses and wild pimpernels, large dark blue ones, and though they were all*

*people with lots of money, I think they enjoyed themselves without wine or delicacies.*⁹

While she was glad George was feeling better, the climate of Algiers did not suit Louisa. The hot, dusty sirocco wind that blew across the Mediterranean from North Africa induced malaise and melancholy that were made worse by Louisa's longing for her children. But she chose to join George in simple pleasures and find joy in Mary's sweet chatter and singing. Mary, ever cheerful and patient, never complained, even though she had developed an eye infection.

From November 1856 to the end of April 1857, the MacDonalds remained in Algiers, but severe bronchitis attacks continued to plague George. He stayed quite busy writing when he was able, and he tired of being an invalid.

"Louisa, I need to go home. Indeed, I would rather die trying to support you and the children than live as we are doing now," he revealed to her. "I can't avoid the fact that my ailment is chronic, and I must learn how to manage with it."

So they returned home to London, to their children, and to their uncertain future. Louisa's mind swirled with questions.

How long would her George remain with her?

How would she go on without him if God should take him home?

How could she best care for him and ease his discomfort?

"I need You, and I need courage," she prayed.

What though things change and pass, nor come again!
Thou, the life-heart of all things, changest never.
The sun shines on; the fair clouds turn to rain,
And glad the earth with many a spring and river.
The hearts that answer change with chill and shiver,
That mourn the past, sad-sick, with hopeless pain,
They know not thee, our changeless heart and brain.
George MacDonald, *Diary of an Old Soul*, October 29

CHAPTER 11

ADESTE FIDELES

There breathes not a breath of the morning air,
But the Spirit of Love is moving there;
Not a trembling leaf on the shadowy tree
Mingles with thousands in harmony;
But the spirit of God doth make the sound,
And the thoughts of the insect that creepeth around.
George MacDonald, "Lessons for a Child" from *Poetical Works*

Home!

They were finally home!

As the family sat in the fire-lit drawing room, drinking tea and eating delicious scones slathered in jam and clotted cream, Louisa sighed the sigh of a mother reunited with her children. Beside her sat her Bear, greatly enjoying his scones. George, being Scottish, would have eaten scones with every meal, but here in England, they were only allowed at teatime.

"I think George is right about scones," Louisa mused. "I could eat these all day!"

"Did you know," Louisa told her sister Annie, "that the night we returned, little Greville howled every time I tried to put him in his cot? He finally went to sleep on my shoulder. Oh, how I missed him, and even though I was so fatigued, his naughtiness made me happy that I was loved and needed. And I am so glad to be back with Mary—we need to get help for her eyes. We call her our little Elfie when she's good and Kelpie when she's naughty, but since her poor eye affliction, she's perpetually Elfie."

"Today George is going to Longman to present the poems he wrote while in Algiers. They've promised to publish them by the end of June," she continued. "I'll get the children out of your hair and go outside for the day. I know you don't mind all of us staying here at The Limes, and you've been so good to take care of my children, but we do need to find a home of our own again. You know what they say: 'Guests are like fish—after three days they stink!'"

"I know you feel like you're in the way, but really, it's fine," Annie assured her. "Besides, you're due to have another little one soon, and you cannot leave until I get to see your sweet baby and make sure you've recovered. And Papa loves having his grandchildren about—he needs their merry repartee!"

Still, Louisa felt out of place and longed to nest in her own home.

"I'm sure being pregnant doesn't help me quiet my emotions and attitude. Perhaps I should bring my children outside on this lovely summer day and try to brighten my spirits," she thought, attempting to dismiss her depression. "I must remember what my dearest Dear frequently says: 'We must be saved from ourselves by very unpleasant things and have no choice whether it shall be by toothache or living on other people's means.' Yes, adversities will keep us from pride, and I do need to be saved from myself."

Nature, that was what Louisa needed. She lifted the latch of the beautiful wrought-iron gate and entered her father's rose garden.

"Thank you, God, for this wonderful place and for the children who bless me every day and teach me who I am," she prayed. Sheltered by the garden wall, she was safe from the wind that made the petals of her father's tea roses sway like fairy wings. The branches of an oak tree peeked over at her from the other side of the wall.

"I house the robin, the hedge sparrows, and the willow wrens—they are all safe in my branches. How much more are you sheltered and protected by our Heavenly Father?" the oak seemed to whisper to her heart.

At summer's end, on August 31, another beautiful baby girl was born to George and Louisa. This new Master's miracle, Irene, made them a family of seven. As always, God provided a nest for His sparrows, and they were able to move to a place of their own in October. Lady Byron was the carrier of God's providence.

"I hope it is no disgrace for me to be rich, as it is not for you to be poor," Lady Byron told George when he visited her

Adeste Fideles

a few days before Irene was born. "If I can do anything for you, you must understand, Mr. MacDonald, that it is rather for the public than yourself." George needed to hear these words, to understand that Lady Byron was motivated not by charity but by helping others to grow from his writings, as she had.[1]

A few days later, Lady Byron's check arrived along with a promise of more at Christmas. Although their benefactor was not in favor of the idea, the MacDonalds decided to find a home in Hastings, a seaside town in the southern county of East Sussex, which they believed would have a better climate for George. They found a dwelling on the Tackleway named Providence House. It was a simple home with thirteen rooms, large enough to accommodate one or two pupils if any decided to room with them. They renamed it Huntly Cottage and set to work making it their home.

"With this large drawing room, it will be the perfect place for me to lecture and teach," George said approvingly.

Huntly Cottage was built on a hillside, and the drawing room had a bay window that stretched across the width of the home and gave a splendid view of the town and the valley below. The cottage was not located in the fashionable part of town, but it was quaint, and Louisa enjoyed setting up her nest. The family could see the steeples of St Clements and All Saints from their window, and the Hastings Castle ruins clung to the crest of Castle Hill above and to the west of the house. The townsfolk were proud to say it was the first castle built by William the Conqueror, and its jutting, crumbling remains presided over the old fishing settlement and the sea below.

Their furniture finally arrived, a bit tattered from storage and transport. The cayenne pepper they'd carefully applied had done a good job of keeping moths away but did not help George's asthma. But oh, how wonderful it was to be together in their own house, where Louisa was once again free to work her magic and make it homey. "And just in time for Christmas!" she said with glee.

Everyone got busy decorating the Christmas tree and making dresses, puddings, caps, and goodies while George hung Christmas pictures on the nursery walls for the children to find in the morning.

"You know, children," said Louisa with a gleam in her eye, "at midnight on Christmas Eve all the animals kneel down to worship the newborn King—wherever they are, all over the world—while the water is turned to wine. That is why you can never enter a stable at midnight—it's set aside for God's creatures to be with Him."

The best way to describe the MacDonalds' first Hastings Christmas is through the manuscript that Louisa compiled and gave to her father for his seventy-seventh birthday. It contains contributions from all of Louisa's siblings—essays on "Happiness" and "The New Year," Alex's story of a schoolboy incident, and various other stories.

Louisa carefully copied everyone's Christmas descriptions into a leather portfolio daintily embossed with a basket of flowers, on which was written, "Dear Papa from your Children's Thoughts." Then she decorated the book with lovely brushstrokes and separated the pages with two silk tassels.

Louisa's contribution to the manuscript is the most detailed description of life in the MacDonald home. Her writing gives a glimpse of her heart for her family and for the children of Hastings, and of her focus on her own little ones' spiritual growth:

> Christmas Day, 1857. *Poor little Elfie's eyes are quite shut. She is very patient, and listens quite quietly to all the talk about the presents and the company expected. Husband and I walked to St. Leonards-on-Sea to see the doctor. A beautiful Christ's Day it was. On our return we found our first guest, little Annie—she owns no other name, her very existence being ignored by her parents—joining our little ones in games of scampering and taking in turns to lead about the poor little blind girl, who looked most pathetic with her outstretched hands feeling everything. Her little new black frock and scarlet jacket with its little gold buttons could only be felt, stroking its soft texture and feeling the buttons. After a short early dinner the*

thirteen poor children came in, with clean frocks and bright faces, to see the Christmas tree. Husband told them the story of the Ugly Duckling. The big ones enjoyed the history, the little ones wondering at everything they saw from the big tree and the big gentleman and his books down to the little baby—though all of them had "got one at home too." . . .

Then all had some toy or book, or pair of warm mitts from the tree, which, however, was not lighted yet. Then they all went into another room, where they ate a cake or a bun, and husband talked to them again and told them the true story of the day— about the good Christ-child. They were all so modest and happy—even the aristocracy of our company, the carpenter's children.

Then they went away glad enough with half a Clapton orange each. At five o'clock we lighted the tree in the middle of the tea table, at the top of which was the day's luxury, the Plum Pudding. . . . How happy everyone looked! The big ones, none of them thinking of themselves, but all pleasing the little ones; and thus came in their own pleasure. A teetotum, Sarah's present for Greville, which had been hanging and twirling on the tree all tea-time, was now brought down, and reels of cotton, 1d. candlesticks, nuts, figs, oranges were numbered and gambled for. The little brooches on the tree for Aunties were to be sent on New Year's Eve.

Then followed the mysterious bran-cake which had been the cause of much wondering anticipation all day. The poor Elf had been all the while feeling everything and getting the little gifts described to her, but never able to open her eyes. Once she said, "I suppose God doesn't wish me to see tonight." The delight of diving the hand into the "soft bran" as Elfie called it, and pulling out a treasure for somebody was something delicious. I wish the senders of the bran-cake could have seen the faces, and heard the exclamations! A history of Punch and Judy was one of the presents the tree afforded Papa, and great glee was there over the display of his elocutionary talents in giving it to our party. I like just to note our pleasure that Sarah and Elizabeth were kindly recognized from Clapton as part of our household, just as we like to do here.

Sunday, December 27th. *A beautiful holyday! Husband and I and all the children down on the beach. All at once a little whisper from Elfie—"Mama, I can see a little!" Then, in a few minutes she bounded away from me, jumping over the breakers—it being low-water. Then the exclamations, "Oh, there is my darling baby, how sweet she looks! Papa! Mama!" scampering to our sides. We were as glad and light-hearted as she: the lost sight was found again!*

In the evening talking to them both delighted me, Mary with her loving assurance about God being so kind. "I should like to see God so much and tell him how glad I am he lets me see again!" and Lily with her puzzled anxious looks about almost all I told her. Her tears came fast in her distress at Jesus lying asleep when they were all so frightened in the boat in the storm, but Mary was sure he had not forgotten them, though he was asleep.

December 30th. *Today comes news of the little new cousin's birth. Mary jumped about the room and danced with delight. Her face got so red. "I'm so glad for we often wanted a baby and a nurse when I was at Auntie's. Mama, I daresay God knewed Auntie wanted a baby—p'raps she asked God to give her one, so he made her a little girl. I wonder where he gets our bones from. I wonder how he puts our feet on. Mine are so nicely put on."*[2]

George was gifted at telling fairy or goblin or brownie stories, and he remembered an inexhaustible list of them. But everyone agreed that the person who made Christmas special in their new home, amid trying circumstances, was Louisa, as Greville later recalled:

That the inspiring spirit of these festivities was my mother is obvious enough, a spirit we shall often see in like

> *transformations of forbidding circumstances. If "more are the children of the desolate than the children of the married wife," then my mother usurped the privilege of the former in addition to her own. I can conceive of no more perfect counterpart to my father's faith than these practical works of my mother, so literally creative, "as the clay is in the potter's hand."*[3]

New Year's 1858 arrived, and the family settled into a peaceful rhythm. George spent the days in his study working on his first fairy tale, *Phantastes*, while Louisa spent her days cuddling, nursing, disciplining, and admonishing her little congregation. Their orderly home did not go unnoticed, as Mrs. Blythe Matthews later recounted after a visit:

> *I was delightfully received by a strikingly handsome young man and a most kind lady, who made me feel at once at home. There were five children at that time, all beautifully behaved and going about the house without troubling anyone. On getting better acquainted with the family, I was much struck by the way in which they carried on their lives with one another. At a certain time in the afternoon you would, on going upstairs to the drawing-room, see on the floor several bundles—each one containing a child! On being spoken to they said, so happily and peacefully, 'We are resting,' that the intruder felt she must immediately disappear. No nurse was with them. One word from the father or mother was sufficient to bring instant attention. . . . In the evenings, when the children were all in bed, Mr. MacDonald would still be writing in his study—* Phantastes, *it was—and Mrs. MacDonald would go down and sit with her husband, when he would read to her with what he had been writing; and I would hear them discussing it on their return to the drawing-room. To hear him read Browning's* Saul *with his gracious and wonderful power was a thing I shall never forget. Mrs. MacDonald's energy and courage were untiring and her capabilities very unusual.*[4]

The new year arrived much like Hamlet's "cock that is the trumpet to the morn," heralding a triumphal beginning. The beautiful shapes made by snow crystals on the windows, the dusting on the church spires and the boughs of the trees, and the white blankets on every ledge and rooftop bore witness to the Creator of light. The children were glad when they saw that it could snow in Hastings. Safe in their home, they grew in grace. They were fed on fairies and imaginative freedom balanced by consistent discipline. Above all, they were taught that they must seek to learn and to become men and women defined by their deeds, not by their perceptions.

"Children, put to task what you learn so you will obtain true moral worth. And most importantly, remember that self-denial is not life-denying but actually self-forgetting—and is the only way to spiritual freedom," Louisa often reminded them.

In the early spring, their tranquil home suddenly became a hospital to George's brother John, whose lungs were diseased and whose health was rapidly deteriorating. George and Louisa were shocked by his appearance—he was weak, coughed continuously, was seized with horrible chest pains, and had little appetite.

Louisa immediately went to work, feeding John rich gravy soups and fowl. She and George had made a friend in Hastings, Dr. Hale, who prescribed absolute rest for the remainder of the year and refused to charge them anything for his services.

Once John's health improved, he journeyed with George to London and then alone to Huntly to be with his family.

"I fear he will not make it through the winter," George told Louisa, "but we must leave him to the Father of Fathers."

George's fear was realized when John died on July 7 at the age of twenty-eight. He was laid to rest beside his brother Alec and his sister Bella in the Drumblade churchyard.

A few days after the burial, George's father was walking at dusk. Looking toward the moor, he saw a figure coming toward him and stepped back within his farm's gate.

"The person walked past the gate, but then turned around and looked right at me," he told his wife. "I recognized the figure as John, my son. He was wearing his customary plaid over his shoulder. I tried to run to him, but my age and lameness hindered me. Then he disappeared at the bend of the road. I ran back home as quickly as my old legs could muster to tell you. He looked me in the eyes and beckoned me."

Though George's father was never the sort to look for supernatural manifestations or believe in the Celtic gift of second sight, the experience shook him. "I'm certain it was John. He returned home and was sending for me."

Just a few weeks later, George's father died of a massive heart attack. George's tower of strength, his beloved father, was gone, along with his two dearest brothers and his sister Bella. Upon hearing the news, George rushed to Huntly to be with his mother.

Louisa, of course, worried about her Bear traveling again, but she knew how great a loss he had suffered and bravely stayed behind, keeping the fires of her home aglow.

Once again, they loved and wrote to and prayed for each other from afar.

> *G.M.D. to his Wife.*
> *[Huntly, August 26, 1858,]*
> *Sunday night.*
>
> *I know that I have uttered your own thoughts, dear Louisa, when I offered Mother and my two sisters our home to live with us. My mother seems a little more cheerful today. Charles and I went to see some poor people this afternoon. It is very pleasant to hear how they all talk about my father. . . .*
>
> *. . . I do love you, and am so grateful for the love you give me. I think God will show himself very kind somehow or other to us both—not that I deserve it, but you do. . . . Do not think I am unhappy. I am glad my father has got through. I love him more than ever. I am cheerful and hopeful. My love to Lily. Tell her I will pull her tooth out for her if she likes. My love to them all and to you, good, kind, beautiful wife.*[5]

When George returned home, he brought with him his father's favorite chair. "This will be the perfect place for you to sit and write," Louisa told him. She placed it in his study by his desk. The beloved chair supported him through each day, absorbed his sorrows, and upheld him as he wrote. Later, the chair was passed on to his son Greville, who sat in it while he wrote the biography of his parents.

George finished his book, *Phantastes: A Faerie Romance for Men and Women,* and it was published on October 28. The book is a spiritual pilgrimage from the physical world of impoverishing possessions to the fairy kingdom of heaven:

> *Surely Thy ships will bring to my poor shore*
> *Of gold and peacocks such a shining store*
> *As will laugh all the dreams to holy scorn*
> *Of love and sorrow that were ever born.*[6]

But critics did not understand the message, and the book was not well received. George was disheartened.

The most critical review was printed in the *Athenæum* on November 6: "Any one after reading it might set up a confusedly-furnished second-hand symbol-shop.... Either from weakness or willfulness, the author of this book slides off the edge of earth to join the phantom company. He seems to have lost all hold of reality ..."

"They do not give my book a chance, Louisa—they don't see that its aim is to compel us to adventure toward the celestial purpose of our daily existence," George lamented. "Without the thatched cottage no cathedral had ever soared; without folk-song no oratorio; without ballad no ode or sonnet."[7]

But God used George's magnificent fantasy to find and redeem a man who would become one of the greatest apologists of the twentieth century. When young Clive Staples Lewis, an avowed atheist, picked up a copy of *Phantastes* while waiting for his train to arrive on March 4, 1916, it changed his life forever. He later recalled:

> *A young man who wishes to remain a sound Atheist cannot be too careful of his reading. . . . That night my imagination was, in a certain sense, baptized; the rest of me, not unnaturally, took longer. I had not the faintest notion what I had let myself in for by buying* Phantastes.[8]

Lewis began wrestling with God until he finally conceded and embraced his Creator and Savior. He later confessed that he had never written a book in which he did not quote George MacDonald. His admiration for George led him to compile a spiritual collection of the minister's works, titled *George MacDonald: An Anthology*.

On November 6, 1858, ten days after *Phantastes* was published, Winifred Louisa was born.

"Oh, George!" exclaimed Louisa. "This fifth daughter of yours certainly is unusually pretty and well-behaved."

"This is a very great day indeed," he said with wonder. "Each time a child is born to us, I am struck with awe that the Miracle Maker has created from our love—such a complete and exquisite and perfect gift. Today the whole world seems to shine with clear light."

With every morn my life afresh must break
The crust of self, gathered about me fresh.
George MacDonald, *Diary of an Old Soul*, October 10

CHAPTER 12

FAITHFUL FOREVER FRIENDS

Long-suffering women, true in heart and life;
Women that make man proud for very love
Of their humility, and of his pride
Ashamed.
George MacDonald, *Within and Without*

Hastings is lovely in the springtime. Louisa would take her little brood of chicks for picnics along the beautiful cliff-tops and by the bay below. They would carefully traverse the steep, stony paths down to the sea and run across the sand, giggling and squirming when the water lapped at their feet. Gulls circled above and sand martins darted along the shore. Sometimes the children would watch fishing ships sail away into the open sea or carefully return to anchor in port. Other times, they would find seabirds nesting their chicks, and they always marveled when the first butterflies and bumblebees emerged and began to feed on early pussy willows. Lambs were born on the marsh, and their bleats duetted with the croaks of marsh frogs.

The seaside was a magical place for the children. They especially loved to find hairy brown-tail moth caterpillars in the bushes. The caterpillars' silky white cocoons tempted the children, but Louisa had to remind them not to touch the webs, for they always irritated the children's fragile skin. "Leave them for the cuckoos to eat!" she'd call across the sand.

Although George's book had not been received as enthusiastically as he had hoped, he started receiving invitations to give lectures, and his spirits brightened, which always encouraged Louisa. The lectures and his professorship at Bedford College brought in a bit of money, but George often lectured for free, and his position as a professor took him away from his family and only paid thirty to fifty guineas a year. As a result, writing became his chief means of supporting his family.

"Louisa, bring the children and join me," he encouraged her. "You can stay at The Limes and dally around London."

Louisa loved this idea. The children would enjoy traipsing in the gardens and riding horses with their grandfather. And Louisa had missed the scents of Papa's roses, of the mignonette and scarlet anemones, of the yellow lichen clinging to the stones. "We will come," she wrote to George.

Once they had arrived and settled in at The Limes, Lady Byron would sometimes send her carriage to fetch them for lunch or tea. Louisa came to love the kind yet stern woman. If it were not for Lady Byron's generosity, after all, the MacDonalds may not have survived those years.

But Lady Byron needed them too. She was older and her health was fading. Her friendship with the MacDonalds comforted her, and their genuine care for her well-being, as well as the spiritual insight she gleaned from George, sustained her. Lady Byron never spoke of her pain, but she was able to confide in George and Louisa, sharing of the sorrow she had endured during her marriage. The couple kept her confidence for the rest of their lives.

In between George's lectures, the family would return to their cottage at Hastings, but the demand for his speeches increased and he was also offered a real teaching position at Bedford College in July. This was the boost his confidence needed.

"You must come back to London," Lady Byron advised him. "I hope to secure the house of my friends the de Morgans for you to live in."

It seemed like a good idea, what with the increasing work available for George in the city. So once again Louisa packed up her home and children and moved with George to London. But when they arrived, they found that the de Morgans' home was no longer available.

"We've been through this before," she told her husband. "We'll manage."

It really is remarkable that Louisa didn't let any home or location own her. She chose her role as a wife and mother—

to support and care for her husband and children—over her preferences about where to live.

Fortunately, the MacDonalds found an available house at 18 Queen Square in Bloomsbury and were able to stay there for six months. It was a lovely place, and Greville and the girls thought the square was delightful.

"Look at the girls, George," Louisa pointed out one day. "Aren't they adorable running and curtseying around the statue of Queen Anne? And Greville follows the gardener all around. His favorite thing is to pick up the dead leaves and help the gardener put them in the bonfire."

"Yes, dearest Dear, this is the perfect place for us, and it will give us time to find a suitable home."

They did find a suitable home, Tudor Lodge, a Victorian Gothic house at the end of Albert Street in Camden. It had been built by the historical painter Charles Lucy, who made sure it was artistic.

"It's perfect," said George excitedly. "It has so much character and will be a great inspiration for my novels. Look at the angels propped up on the sills of the cathedral windows, and that studio out back will be quite suitable for me to lecture in."

"I do so like the unfinished cast of the Madonna left in the wall of the entrance hall. She'll help me watch over our little brood," Louisa said, smiling. "And I love the weeping ash that garlands the garden, and all the marigolds and wildflowers everywhere. The rooms are small, but I think it will be a happy and romantic house."

The red brick home had limestone mullioned windows and a little garden in the front that greeted each visitor. For Louisa, a garden was always a necessity, and the larger garden behind Tudor Lodge gave her room to plan and grow. Once again, Louisa worked her magic and made the new abode a comfortable home for her continuously growing family.

After they had settled in at Tudor Lodge, George's sister Louise joined them to finish her education at Bedford College. His position at the college had facilitated this opportunity for her, and her arrival was a blessing to Louisa because Louise was a great help in the home.

The family's move was solidified when George placed his desk and his beloved father's chair in the center of the room where he planned to write and lecture. The children found this large studio a curious place with its giant oil painting of King Charles that had been left behind by Mr. Lucy, the Elgin Marble casts of the Parthenon frieze along the opposite wall, and sunlight filtering in through the north-facing skylight. It was a magical place.

Because the studio was so large, it was also the perfect place for Louisa to give parties for the children. They loved to act out the fairy tales and stories she would read to them and then transpose into plays for future performances.

"Imagination is the key to their academic success later on," she told Louise as the two women planned the next party. "Fairy tales teach them courage and give them that intangible rainbow clue to the miracles of God."

Years later, Greville fondly recalled the impact of these fairy tales:

> *I am increasingly sure that fairy-tale is a necessary corrective to the inevitably mechanical of much school education. It is a wild flower for the child adventurer to clutch at and gather for his joy: from its free, untutored glory all literature has grown. Fairy-tale is always pointing the conflict between good and evil, and the stubborn facts of hard-heartedness and greed. As the child is father of the man, so is fairy-tale greater than its intellectual offspring, more significant of the spiritual, passionate consanguinity of weed and rose, tiger and lamb, dragon and saint, that binds all creatures into a destined harmony.*[1]

"Mama, can we perform *The Story of the Three Bears* again, and will Daddy cover himself with a skin rug and pretend to be a bear for us? He does growl so well!" one child asked.

"But I like it when he is the Prince transformed into a Beast!" interjected another child.

"Remember how that story made one of you cry when the Beast became human again?" asked Lilia.

"It's because Bob the Beast of unkempt fur is the one he loved," said another with a giggle.

"Mama, you make the Grimm brothers' stories so dear to us that we can't help but hunger for their incessant repetition, and we do so love when you make the little dramas out of Hans Christian Andersen for us to act!" Lilia said as she hugged her mother and gathered the others together.

"My favorite thing is making the chairs into horses by turning them upside down, and making the coal scuttle into a dragon, and making Winifred be the captive princess who is waiting for us to deliver her," added Greville.

The Elgin Marble casts were the perfect place for Louisa to put candles at Christmastime. The children remembered the illuminated frieze when they were older as they reminisced about their mother's artistry in entertaining. Most of all, they had enjoyed singing Christmas carols.

> *Still more is the sweetness of these memories that holds. Nothing could outweigh our Christmas carols; even now, in spite of deaf ears' refusals, I can never forget them. The same spirit of fairy-tale ruled these ancient songs. Their simple belief in God, their trust in Nature's ministrations put to shame all our endeavors to teach the ethics of religion. Where in Church doctrine can we find anything so inspiring, at once realistic and symbolic, as The Holly and The Ivy? Even as I write its title, back come to me in longing delight the jolly old carol's words:*
>
> > *'O, the rising of the sun*
> > *The running of the deer,*
> > *The playing of the merry organ,*
> > *Sweet singing the choir!'*
>
> *Just as the child knows if his porridge is well cooked and loves his milk creamy, so does he know the worth of those old, ever young things. In a word he must have freedom to run and dance and sing, if he is to find his life.*[2]

Now that they were settled, the MacDonalds knew they needed to decide where to worship, and they chose to attend St Peter on Vere Street. Dirtied by fog and dust, it stood just off Oxford Street and welcomed parishioners rain or shine. Frederick Denison Maurice was the newly appointed pastor. George cherished sitting at the feet of a man he held in high esteem and finally decided to join the Church of England.

William Cowper, the stepson of Lord Palmerston, was responsible for F. D. Maurice's appointment as the preacher at St Peter in 1860. Mr. Cowper and his wife later became Lord and Lady Mount Temple; they were zealously religious and became close friends of the MacDonalds. They also shared George's controversial views.

While George continued to lecture, teach, and write, Louisa remained a busy bird, flitting about, taking care of her babies and her Bear, who was always sitting at his desk. Because George had to spend long hours writing, Louisa took over the family correspondence and spent a great deal of time writing to their family and ever-growing circle of friends.

"Your health is so frail—I am determined that you should have as much rest and quiet as possible," Louisa would remind George when he tried to do too much. "Your intellectual pursuits too often conflict with your health." Her admonition was needed, for George used every available moment to write.

The next book he published was *The Portent*, a spooky Highland tale about second sight and a mysterious sleepwalking lady. The story doesn't contain a didactic element like *Phantastes* does, but its haunting twists and turns are compelling.

"George, what does this story mean?" Louisa asked one day while gently rubbing his shoulders.

"You may make of it what you like. If you see anything in it, take it, and I am glad you have it, but I wrote it for the tale," he answered before gently kissing her hand.[3]

The Portent was first serialized in *The Cornhill Magazine* and then published as a book four years later. Unfortunately, the royalties took a while to arrive.

Then, to the MacDonalds' great sorrow, Lady Byron succumbed to a long illness and died in her sleep on May 16, 1860. They grieved the loss of such a true and godly friend, and sorely missed her tender care, prayers, and wise counsel. And though Lady Byron's frequent, timely financial gifts were not as important to the MacDonalds as her friendship, the loss of income filled their days with anxiety.

"George, I'm so sorry," Louisa said between sobs one evening when he returned to Tudor Lodge. "We needed food and necessities, so I took the omnibus to the shops. I'm not sure how, but when I left the omnibus my purse was gone, and with it our last sovereign. Sweet Lily must know how bad things are, because when I made dinner, she said she didn't have an appetite. Our sweet Goosie-Goose went without and refused to eat."

"Take my hand, Louisa," George said quietly as he reached for her. He led her to the drawing room. "Let's pray."

Outside, the rain fell gently, matching the tears on Louisa's cheeks. She listened to the gentle conversation between her husband and their Heavenly Father.

As they stood watching the evening sky darken, the postman walked up the steps and dropped a letter in the box on the porch. He knocked twice, and the sound shook them from their quiet despair. George dutifully opened the door and checked the postbox.

"Louisa!" he gasped. "Look! It's a letter from Lady Byron's executors with a check enclosed for three hundred pounds!"[4]

"Oh, my darling Bear," she exclaimed, hugging him before softly kissing his cheek. "She continues to bless us, and just in the nick of time."

Besides providing monetary help, Lady Byron had also introduced the MacDonalds to many great intellectuals. Between poverty, George's poor health, and the demands of young children, the family was not easily able to move about in that social world, but George's rising reputation as a writer and a lecturer made them welcome. The Recorder of London, Russell Gurney, introduced them to F. D. Maurice and also to Mrs. Maria Price La Touche, who became a close friend of

Louisa and lovingly called her Mother Brown-Bird. Mrs. La Touche introduced them to John Ruskin, the leading art critic of the Victorian era. The MacDonalds' circle of intimate friends soon grew to include Miss Mulock, the writer Mrs. Oliphant, Charles Kingsley, William Makepeace Thackeray, and the publisher George Murray Smith. Of those "North of the Tweed," as they called their Scottish friends, the most stalwart and reliable were John Stuart Blackie, Alexander Smith, and Norman McLeod.

George Murray Smith greatly encouraged the MacDonalds during their difficult times. He often invited them to dinners, at which they met the famous writers James Greenwood; G. H. Lewes; Leslie Stephen, founder of the *Dictionary of National Biography* and father of Virginia Woolf; Leigh Hunt; James Payn, novelist and *The Cornhill Magazine* editor; and Henry S. King. But George was never comfortable at these gatherings.

"I abhor these literary parties, Louisa. This elite world is one that we care little enough for anyway. They make me feel sick—I cannot help it. I'd take more pleasure smoking a pipe now and then with an old cobbler somewhere about the Theobald's Road than in the evening with the most delightful literary society that London can furnish."[5]

But the MacDonalds' growing circle didn't just include writers, and not all their friends were part of England's most renowned elite. Many of the MacDonalds' acquaintances also had religious and artistic interests. George and Louisa became closest to sculptor Alexander Munro and painter Arthur Hughes. Both men had a deep, abiding, private faith. As George began to write more books, he asked Hughes to be his illustrator, and their words and images partnered perfectly. Munro used five-year-old Greville as his model for the boy-and-dolphin fountain in Hyde Park and was once inspired to make a bronze medallion of George when he saw George's thick, curly hair blowing wildly around his face on a windy day. He made two of these medallions; one is now in the Scottish National Portrait Gallery in Edinburgh and the other is held by King's College, Aberdeen.

Another group of friends was made up of social activists. Barbara Bodichon of Girton introduced George and Louisa to Elizabeth Jesser Reid, the founder and principal of Bedford College, as well as to Dr. Elizabeth Garrett Anderson, Anna Sidgwick, Miss Buss, Miss Beale, and Josephine Butler—all champions of the feminist movement and women's rights.

Dr. Elizabeth Garrett Anderson was a trailblazer: she was the first woman to qualify as a physician and surgeon in Britain, she co-founded the first female-staffed hospital, and she was Britain's first female mayor. She and Josephine Butler, a distinguished Christian writer, were active in the women's suffrage movement and became members of the National Society for Women's Suffrage Central Committee. They were passionate about improving women's education, abolishing child prostitution, and ending the trafficking of young English women and children to the Continent. Along with Barbara Bodichon, they collected fifteen hundred signatures on a petition for women's suffrage in 1866. They encouraged Louisa to sign, and historians believe she did. The petition was presented to the House of Commons by John Stuart Mill, a member of Parliament, marking the start of an era during which bills in favor of women's rights were introduced on an almost annual basis.

The MacDonalds' friendship with these women greatly influenced George in ways that are reflected in his novels and lectures. He created female characters who "resoundingly proclaimed the equality of the sexes . . . with the creation of a truly courageous, non-stereotypical heroine for the first time in a very serious work of fantasy."[6] He often made women the heroes in his books, and even in his sweet fairy tales the women are brave and heroic. In *Adela Cathcart*, he exposes the plight of women in Victorian society; in *The Light Princess*, the princess rescues the prince from the water; and in *The Princess and the Goblin*, Princess Irene rescues Curdie from the mines. And in a lecture on the poetry of John Milton, given to a large audience at Gilcomston Free Church, George spoke up for women by encouraging men to be whole and straightforward: "You will never get the best work from a man, be his intellect what it may be, except that man be pure throughout. It is time that such a doctrine were preached when we are having all contemptible and vile opinions set forth on such things. Why should not a man dare to speak on this point? Why should he not say to women, 'Women, demand more; be more true to yourselves, and men will grant you more.'"[7]

George's novels reveal his love for Louisa and his appreciation for her intellect and spiritual maturity:

> *I watched everything about her; and interpreted it by what I know about women. I believe that many of them go into a consumption just from discontent.... The theological nourishment which is offered them is generally no better than husks. They cannot live upon it, and so die and go home to their Father. And without good spiritual food to keep the spiritual sense healthy and true, they cannot see the things about them as they really are. They cannot find interest in them, because they cannot find their own place amongst them.*[8]

The MacDonald children's favorite new friend was probably the Reverend C. L. Dodgson, also known as Lewis Carroll. Rev. Dodgson had a troublesome stutter that kept him out of the pulpit and led him to the MacDonalds, who were also patients of Dr. James Hunt. Dodgson became one of their most intimate friends and grew in the hearts of the MacDonald children because of his humorous love for them. The children adopted him and called him Uncle Dodgson, and they felt like miracle workers because his stutter disappeared whenever he was around them.

"We love it when he comes to Tudor Lodge," they agreed enthusiastically.

Of course they did. Whenever Uncle Dodgson visited, they crowded around him while he drew silly pictures and amused them with absurd stories. He was a great caricaturist. Their annual trip to the Polytechnic to see the "dissolving views" lantern shows of Christmas fairy tales[9] entranced them, and afterward Uncle Dodgson always took them to the toy shop on Regent Street and let each child choose a gift. Then he treated them to Bath buns and ginger beer. He was a great addition to the MacDonald family and reinforced Louisa's belief that fairy tales encourage children's subconscious and spiritual longings.

"Mama," Greville once exclaimed, running in from the garden, "Uncle Dodgson says I should turn my head into marble, because then it will never suffer from combing all my curls. The brush *does* hinder my ability to learn lessons."

One day, a manuscript arrived from Uncle Dodgson. "He has given me a book to read to you," Louisa told her children. "He wants your honest assessment. If you like it, he's going to publish it. Look—isn't it lovely? Each word is in his impeccable calligraphy, and he even drew all these lovely pictures!"

The children gathered around and listened as she read.

"I wish there were sixty thousand more volumes," said Greville when Louisa had finished. "But I wish the soldiers weren't just a pack of cards," he added, lamenting that officers of the queen should be stout and substantial.

The children's approval gave Uncle Dodgson the courage to find a publisher, and in 1865, *Alice's Adventures in Wonderland* was published.

Perhaps the most important turning point for George's writing came during a dinner with his circle of friends. While at George Smith's home, his attention was drawn to Charles Manby Smith, the gifted journalist, who had just recited a Scottish epitaph.

"What's that, what's that? Say it again, Mr. Smith!" George cried. The journalist complied, the words rolling off his tongue with beauty and life.

> *Here lie I, Martin Elginbrodde;*
> *Hae mercy o' my soul, Lord God;*
> *As I wad do, were I Lord God,*
> *An' ye war Martin Elginbrodde!*

"Louisa!" George exclaimed when he returned home that evening. "Manby Smith has given me the epitaph that's the gem of the whole. I know now how I must write. I have so many stories in my heart from Huntly, and I need to write about the places and the people I grew up loving—I must use their vernacular to tell the story true. My readers need to experience the lovely Scottish brogue and appreciate the Highlanders' colloquialisms. The epitaph compels me to write everything with a didactic message—I must show the true picture of God and purpose of man. Smith told me, 'Mr. MacDonald, if you would but write novels, you would find all the publishers saving up to buy them from you! Nothing but fiction pays,' and Louisa, I think he's right!"

Unfortunately, George's asthma returned, and his doctors decided that the clay in the MacDonalds' yard was the cause. Also, Tudor Lodge had become too small for the growing family. Pregnant again, Louisa knew they needed more room in a more congenial area. She found a larger house at 12 Earls Terrace in Kensington and once again set about establishing a new home for her children and frail husband.

To speed his recovery, George went to stay with Louisa's uncle, Mark Sharman, on his farm in Nottingham. It was the perfect place for George to rest and recover while Louisa organized the move.

"Don't worry, Dear. I know you're reluctant to leave me and the children, but I want you to take Gracie and Goblin with you and enjoy the quiet. You can start writing your novel," Louisa insisted.

When George and his two daughters arrived at Nottingham, Uncle Sharman pulled up to the train station with a quaint dogcart, loaded them in, and drove them to his country home.

"Nobody could be kinder than Uncle is," George wrote to Louisa after arriving. "Since dinner I have been to see the horses and the pigs—both splendid—but each after his kind, as the Bible says. Verily, there is one glory of horses and the other of pigs."

Of course, as an equestrian lover, he preferred the horses.

Nottingham was a wonderful place to rest, and Gracie and Irene enjoyed farm life. They often ventured out past the meadows to the edge of the woods, where ribbons of greenery wove their way through majestic oaks and Sherwood pines. They collected heather, foxglove, moss, and reindeer lichen. Sometimes a friendly hedgehog, fox, or fallow deer would venture to the edge of the meadow. If the girls were quiet, they could hear the green woodpecker's laugh or the tawny owl's haunting call. But their favorite place was the stable, which was filled with splendid riding horses.

"Louisa," George wrote to her, "I am so pleased that the children have inherited my passionate love for horses."

While recuperating, George spent his days writing and his evenings playing whist in the parlor. He developed the Scottish epitaph he had heard Manby Smith recite into *David Elginbrod*, his first successful novel. He modeled the title character on his father, who exemplified integrity and goodness and who was a mirror of the Divine Father. Drawing on his childhood memories, George captured the essence of the Aberdeenshire colloquialism, which endeared the book to his Scottish readers. His descriptions of humble village life, now recognized as an essential element of the Kailyard school of Scottish fiction, idealized his Highlander homeland. Filled with suspense, ghosts, secret passageways, and stolen jewels, *David Elginbrod* is replete with beautiful passages and descriptions of natural scenery. The book's reflections on life and evil are refined, thoughtful, and morally invigorating.

When George's health had improved and Louisa had resettled their household, George, Gracie, and Irene moved to their new home in Kensington. Three important factors had determined the family's choice of 12 Earls Terrace: it was built on gravel soil, which was more suitable for George's lungs than the clay of their last home; it was conveniently located, so his students could come for lectures and classes; and it comfortably accommodated their blossoming family. With a new wee one about to arrive, Louisa welcomed the additional space.

The house stood back a bit from Kensington High Road, and behind the house was the famous Edwardes Square, where many writers and artists lived. Built in the early nineteenth century, Edwardes Square boasts a magical garden with rolling lawns, whispering trees, serpentine paths, and woodland walks. Fortunately for the MacDonalds, the residents of Earls Terrace shared rights to the garden, so the children had free rein to run and play. And it was the perfect setting for George to complete his novel.

"Louisa, can you tell who I have modeled this character after?" George asked with a gleam in his eye.

"Read it to me with your lovely brogue, and I will guess," she answered.

> *He trusts in God so absolutely, that he leaves his salvation to him—utterly, fearlessly; and forgetting it, as being no concern of his, sets himself to do the work that God has given him to do, even as his Lord did before him.... He believes entirely that God loves, yea, is love; and, therefore, that hell itself must be subservient to that love, and but an embodiment of it; that the grand work of Justice is to make way for a Love which will give to every man that which is right and ten times more, even if it should be by means of awful suffering.*[10]

"I believe, dearest Dear, that you have just perfectly described our Reverend Maurice," she guessed correctly. "David Elginbrod is surely the finest character you have ever created, and the passages are so beautiful that it makes me long to return to The Farm and your Highland home."

"I heartily agree," he responded.

"You must dedicate this masterpiece to Lady Byron," Louisa said as she reached for his hand. "What would have become of us without her faithful friendship?"

"The dedication will say, 'With a love stronger than death,'" he decided as he held Louisa's hand and reflected on the powerful grace and goodness Lady Byron had given them.

When the manuscript was finally complete, George submitted *David Elginbrod* to Smith, Elder & Co., a publishing company.

But it was rejected.

Fortunately, a Miss Jessie Ballantyne had visited the MacDonalds and read George's book. Enthralled, she recommended it to her novelist friend Mrs. Craik, who in turn passed it on to her publisher, Hurst and Blackett.

"You would be fools not to publish it," Mrs. Craik boldly advised.

Hurst and Blackett listened and published George's novel in three volumes in 1863. The company paid him ninety pounds. *David Elginbrod* was well received, described by *The Times* as "the work of a man of genius." Nothing could have made Louisa's heart prouder—now others could see the brilliance of her husband, the poet, the preacher, the writer, the Scot.

Between the excitement about *David Elginbrod*'s publication and its subsequent appearance on bookshelves, another MacDonald entered the world. At approximately five thirty in the morning on February 7, 1864, Maurice MacDonald, George and Louisa's ninth miracle from the Master, was born.

"Another little brawly bairn!" George proudly exclaimed as he kissed his wife and swaddled his new son. "I think we should ask our vicar for permission to give our wee child his name, and see if he is willing to be little Maurice's godfather."

The Reverend Maurice was honored by their request and took his role as godfather seriously. Until his death, the vicar faithfully wrote to Maurice, encouraging him to grow in wisdom and stature and grace.

But the many births, the frequent moves, and the constant demands of her growing family caused Louisa's health to decline. Recognizing that she needed time to gain her strength, George took his family to Hastings so Louisa could rest and breathe in the fresh sea air.

Remarkably, despite her poor health, unsinkable Louisa remained willing to bear more of the Master's miracles, should He choose to send them.

"I'm sure it doesn't matter about having so many children—after all, you can't do what you ought for two, so you may as well have eleven or twelve," she kidded George.

Smiling at her sweet baby boy, she marveled that God had

granted her another healthy child. Louisa knew that she could not raise so many children alone—that she must continually look to her Savior for strength and guidance.

"I do not take your sacrifices lightly, my Love. I see. In birthing and nurturing new life, a woman must find joy and purpose in the simple and mundane, and be what babies need most—the hero of their hearts and the keeper of their souls. You are a channel for life, which is neither a common nor an easy task, and I am profoundly grateful," George said, his face solemn. "Bearing a gift, a child, is a holy sacrifice in which women partake as handmaidens of the Lord. I suspect that what men consider the common transactions of life are actually the most sacred channels for the spread of the heavenly leaven."

Her heart—like every heart, if only its fallen sides were cleared away—was an inexhaustible fountain of love: she loved everything she saw.
George MacDonald, *The Day Boy and the Night Girl*

Louisa's parents, James and Phoebe Powell. The captions are handwritten by Irene MacDonald.

Louisa MacDonald in her early thirties, c. 1855.

Faithful Forever Friends

Louisa MacDonald with George MacKay MacDonald, taken by Charles Dodgson c. 1870)

Louisa MacDonald, date unknown

George MacDonald at this writing desk in 1862, age 37, at the time he was just beginning his career as a novelist.

Irene, Lilia, Grace, Winifred, and Louisa MacDonald in bathing hats at Porto Fino, Italy, in 1878-1879.

Faithful Forever Friends

George and Louisa MacDonald and their children in Boscombe, taken c. 1876. Edward (Ted) Hughes is at the right of the picture, next to his fiancé Mary MacDonald (swathed in rugs).

Drawing of Louisa MacDonald by Edward Hughes, August, 1882

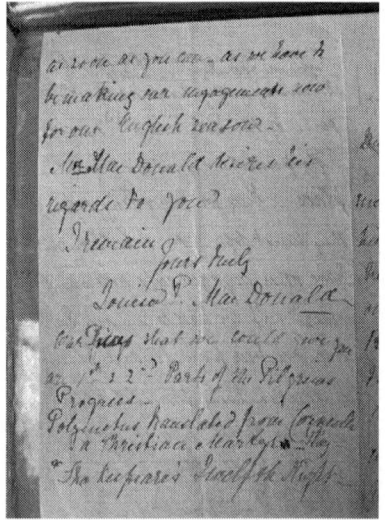

Three pages from a letter written by Louisa MacDonald to unknown recipient discussing possible acting bookings, either parts 1 or 2 of Bunyan's Pilgrims Progress or possibly Shakespeare's Twelfth Night.

Miniature of Louisa MacDonald by unknown artist

George MacDonald, c. 1880

Far Above Rubies: The Life of Louisa MacDonald

Louisa MacDonald, 1885

George and Louisa MacDonald, late 1880s

CHAPTER 13

DO THE NEXT THING

In every heart there is a consciousness of some duty or other required of it: that is the will of God. He who would be saved must get up and do that will—if it be but to sweep a room or make an apology, or pay a debt. It was he who had kept the commandments whom Jesus invited to be his follower in poverty and labour.
George MacDonald, letter to an unknown lady, 1866

Each morning Louisa entered George's study with a tea tray and a smile. She would stoke the fire, cozy the room, and check the light by which her Bear worked. When satisfied, she'd sit beside him.

"Fancy a cuppa?" she'd ask. Sipping his tea, George would nestle in his favorite chair and revel in these sweet, seemingly ordinary moments with his wife.

"Oh, Love, this first sip in the morning, drunk from your lovely teacups, the sunlight casting shadows on the floor, you flitting about like a bird, and the sound of our bonnie bairns above—it's these little things that the big ones are made of," he told her one morning as he watched the fire dance in the hearth.

"I do so love the way you see things the rest of us cannot," she responded.

Giggles echoed from the large, bright nursery above, nourishing Louisa's soul. Her children's joyful noises were like sunbeams during a stormy day. Mama Louisa reigned serenely over her brood, adeptly compartmentalizing their naughty moments by recognizing that those moments were separate from her children's true hearts. Both Louisa and George often read fairy tales to their children. George entertained them with his well-trained voice, while Louisa soothed them with sweet, quiet tones. Listening attentively with hands folded in muslin-draped laps, the children always hoped the fairy tales would give them sweet thoughts for their afternoon rest.

After their quiet time, the children would venture outside,

either to Edwardes Square and their "personal garden"—their secret, mysterious land of play—or to Holland Park, which was within walking distance.

To reach the park, they would take the main entrance from Kensington High Street and enter through the Belgian wrought-iron gates. Then they would traipse into Lady Holland's Dahlia Garden or the Dutch Garden, which were their favorite parts of Holland Park. The bright flowers that lined the borders of the Dahlia Garden were a new fad in England. Lady Holland had first set eyes on dahlias while living in France and Spain. Enthralled, she had seeds sent back to England in 1804 and received credit for permanently introducing the flowers to the country.

Sculptures dotted the park and became magical subjects in the children's imaginations. The children especially loved the giant sculpture of Lord Holland created by George Frederic Watts. They would look for frogs napping on the water lilies that grew in the center stone basin, then follow the north lawn to the woodlands, which led them to the Rose Walk and its fragrant pink Mme Caroline Testout hybrids. In the spring, they would scamper toward the Sun Terrace to see tulips popping up.

This was home. The MacDonalds were together, safe and sound. Could anything be more blissful?

They lived in Kensington for the next seven years—their longest stretch yet in a home—and happy years they were for all. Until then, Louisa had often felt like the biblical Sarah, packing up and moving away from all that she knew, led to trust her Father and be a helpmate to her beloved George. But no matter where she and her family lived, she had learned to delight in God and to remember that her true home was at the seat of His Grace, where her heart's desire, her "bonnie wee bairns," bobbled about her knees and her beloved Bear wrapped her in love. Her family was God's will and purpose for Louisa.

With the success of *David Elginbrod*, his yearly teaching salary, and continuing invitations to lecture, George finally had a steadier income, and this was probably a significant factor in his much-improved health. For Louisa, his healthy countenance was a great relief.

"I have been amazingly well all winter," he assured her. "In fact, I believe I have turned a huge corner—I am past forty and invalidity. I can have a bad cold now without either bronchitis or asthma. I'm amazed at myself."

One of the MacDonalds' close friends, John Ruskin, often spent time at Earls Terrace and frequently urged them to visit the Continent, particularly Switzerland. And so a trip was planned. George, his Highbury friend William Matheson, and his new friend William Sainsbury traveled to the Continent with Ruskin's recommendations as their guide. Their wives did not wish to join them.

"I do think you will enjoy Mr. Sainsbury's company," Louisa encouraged George. "He is a very nice gentleman—although he does enjoy pretending to grumble."

In truth, Louisa would have loved to go with George and see the sights of Europe, but she was in the last months of pregnancy with their tenth child.

"I must remind myself that in acceptance I will find peace. I will be brave," she thought as she waved goodbye to her beloved Bear and prepared to stay home with her nine children.

George wrote to her faithfully and described the sights in stunning detail. She devoured each letter, feeling as though she was seeing Europe with him.

Because repairs were being done at Earls Terrace, Louisa decided to get away, too, and took the children to The Limes to visit her aging father.

"I realize I'm invading this peaceful home with a large tribe of chicks, but they'll behave well, and I'll try my best to help you care for Papa. I know how much you love him, and I also know the burden you carry," she said, trying to encourage her sister Carrie when they arrived. "But my pregnancy may hinder me a bit."

Although she had good intentions, Louisa found the task of caring for both her father and her children to be too much, and she soon left The Limes to visit nearby friends. She tried to keep busy but was always anxious about her adventuresome Bear, especially given his proclivity to seek extreme experiences. She prayed for and wrote to him often, carefully describing her days with the children and their amusing antics, and her anxiety was evident in her letters.

> *I hope you won't try exploring by yourself. . . . I am not afraid of your doing it for the sake of saying you have done wonderful things but I am afraid of your doing it for the sake of getting 'divine air' from 'God's steeples.'*[1]

And Louisa was right to be concerned, because George was excited to climb the cathedral steeple in Antwerp. He had always found heights fascinating.

> *God be praised for that spire [Antwerp Cathedral]. I would go up though my head ached and I seemed worn out. 616 steps, 410 feet! I made the others go. I was on the point of crying several times with delight, only I didn't. But just think of a man being able to sit at a finger-and-pedal board—250 feet from the ground and play any tune he liked on 40 bells yet higher—play to the whole city below! Oh how I should delight to build a cathedral—towers if nothing else. . . .*
>
> *. . . If I hadn't climbed that tower and had a breath of divine air, I should have been ill today. I went up ill and came down well. . . . Oh, for the mountains—God's church towers! But I have nothing in me to-day but weakness and hope. If I am ill again any time, that awful height, though I soon got over the feeling, will haunt me with yawning depth. . . . But I thank God for that tower. . . .*[2]

That summer was extremely hot. This made George's trip, as well as Louisa's pregnancy, quite unpleasant at times.

"I am not impressed with Cologne," George wrote after his party arrived. "The bad smells impress me more than the cathedral, and I am suffering badly from a toothache. Perhaps the best things we have seen since we left home were first the sight of the people pouring out of the cathedral at Antwerp as we entered, and then the congregation remaining afterwards. But someday I must take you here, it is just the place to write a book. Will you come sweet wife? Now onward to Basel and then Strasbourg!"

"Goodness! There is nothing worse than an annoying toothache," Louisa thought, "but I am so very glad he gets to visit those majestic cathedrals."

The ancient, glorious city of Strasbourg did not disappoint the three men. Red stone walls and beautiful stained glass windows graced the cathedral, which was much more fascinating than the cathedral in Cologne.

"The clock in the steeple is full of moving figures and fantasies as big as a house telling everything that a clock could know about!" George wrote to Louisa.

But Switzerland was George's favorite by far. It was beyond what he had imagined.

> *Once today, looking through the mist, I said with just a slight reservation of doubt in my heart, 'There that is as high as I want it to be,' and straightway I saw a higher point grow out of the mist beyond. So I have found it with all the ways of God. And so will you too, dear love.*[3]

The Alps had a mystical influence on George's soul and would bear fruit in his future novels.

"My first sight of the snow-clad Alps from Schaffhausen will always be associated with every just and noble sorrow, joy or affection," he remembered later when he tried to explain the eminent beauty—the magnificence and awe—that mingled with his longing for Louisa, whose own noble sorrow, joy, and affection awaited him at home. Later, while writing *Wilfrid Cumbermede*, he was able to put into words the exaltation he felt when first seeing the Alps:

> *The mist yet rolled thick below, but far away and far up, yet as if close at hand, the clouds were broken into a mighty window through which looked in upon us a huge mountain peak*

> swathed in snow. One great level band of darker cloud crossed its breast, above which rose the peak, triumphant in calmness, and stood unutterably solemn and grand, in clouds as white as its own whiteness. It had been there all the time! . . . With a sudden sweep the clouds curtained the mighty window and the Jungfrau withdrew into its Holy of Holies. . . . But from the mind it glorified it has never vanished. . . . To have beheld a truth is an apotheosis. What the truth was I could not tell; but I had seen something which raised me above my former self and made me long to rise higher yet. . . .[4]

As much as he enjoyed his trip abroad, George was emotionally and physically spent and most ready to return to England, to his Love and his bairns. He came home in August, and Louisa was overjoyed.

"Oh! But I did miss you!" she exclaimed as she greeted him with a hug.

"I wish you could have been with me," he said, looking at her adoringly. "You know, your eyes reach my soul—and probably are the reason I write about eyes and their depths in my novels."

"Your letters were beautiful, and enough for me, my Bear. I felt like I was seeing everything with you."

Upon his return, George heard that the Regius Chair of Rhetoric and Belles Lettres, a professorship at the University of Edinburgh, had become available. Louisa was unexcited about the prospect of another move and was equally concerned that the damp climate of Scotland would be unsuitable for George's weak lungs, but she supported his desire and sent him to Edinburgh to apply for the chair. On the way, he stayed with his friend Thomas Erskine, a famous theologian who possessed a godly spirit. Erskine introduced George to Thomas Carlyle, another man whom George came to hold in high esteem. Both men provided references for him, but he was not chosen for the professorship.

"I must say, I am relieved," Louisa admitted.

"The right man has got the chair," George said, "and failures must be taken in stride. I will allow myself to be disappointed for half an hour or so, to demonstrate to the children how to deal with their own discouragements in the future."

"Besides," Louisa added, "this has been a rough summer of pregnancy. I do apologize for my restlessness and nightly anxieties. I don't know why I wake up so often with worries that always seem to disappear in the morning. I'm simply ashamed of having talked to you with all my insane changes of mood. One night, God spoke to me, and heaven came. Oh, the sweetness of that rest and that sleep in Him! I was overcome with calm and trust in you, as well. I can't tell you what it was like. But I will try your way of making each present time do its duty. I will do the next thing in front of me."

"My darling, I shall love you more than ever. I can hardly be sorry for your sufferings if they made you hear one word from Him which I do think you would hear. Thank you with all my heart for trusting me with your worries in the night," he reassured her lovingly.[5] "Now, do try to sleep and don't go fancying all kinds of things. You will trouble the brain of the little one. Let's concentrate on the wee bairn you're cooking—I hope it will be a girl."

"I know you love sweet girls," Louisa kidded. "And I do hope for a girl too, since the last three have been boys!"

But the Miracle Maker sent another son to join their brood of chickens, as George lovingly referred to his children. Bernard Powell entered the world on September 28, 1865. Now they had ten children.

"Ten!" Louisa sighed with contentment.

Ten to guide. Ten who found joy in birds and beasts, stars and sunshine, flowers and water, wind and snow, and the joys of sleep and play. Louisa's heart was lifted daily by the lovely sights and sounds and scents of her brawny bairns, her blossoming children through whom God revealed His light.

God was also fulfilling George's heart's desire to spread His love through writing. As his popularity grew, George was able to reach others' hearts even without a pulpit. Writing became his primary endeavor because he found it to be the best way to express his Christian convictions. He received more requests to lecture and began speaking at King's College London in 1866. In addition, he was often asked to speak from pulpits on Sundays.

At King's College—the first institution to champion higher education for all—George taught evening classes to working men and women. On Tuesday evenings, he lectured on literature from the time of Gower and Chaucer through 1625, and on Friday evenings his subjects were "Poetry and Poets of the last 100 years," and "Prose Composition and Prosody." The students were enthusiastic and receptive, so he enjoyed teaching them.

His reputation as a talented novelist finally established, George wrote continuously and produced his finest works during the 1860s. *Alec Forbes of Howglen*, *Robert Falconer*, *The Disciple and Other Poems*, *Dealings with the Fairies*, *Annals of a Quiet Neighbourhood*, and *Unspoken Sermons* were all published during the MacDonalds' years at Kensington.

The amazing number of novels George wrote in this short span is proof that his health and energy were much improved. The number also reveals his impeccable work ethic. As always, Louisa was his first reader and critical adviser. He valued her opinions and never published a book without knowing she approved.

But on an early February morning in 1866, sorrow visited the MacDonalds once again.

"My Dear," Louisa informed George when news arrived of the death of their close friend, A. J. Scott, "he's gone."

Mr. Scott had traveled to the continent in the hope that the trip would improve his strength, but he died in Veytaux, Switzerland in January. He had been one of George's dearest friends, so his death was quite a blow.

"I had decided to dedicate *Robert Falconer* to him, and now it is too late to tell him," George said, looking sadly around his study.

"I know you will feel this loss very deeply," Louisa said as she walked around the desk to comfort him.

Robert Falconer was finally published the next year, and in the tribute, George wrote: "To the memory of the man who stands highest in the oratory of my memory, Alexander John Scott, I, daring, presume to dedicate this book."

"That is perfectly put," Louisa said with a smile.

To his children, George dedicated *Dealings with the Fairies*, writing, "Where more is meant than meets the ear," a lovely reminder to them of the hidden spiritual realities that fairy tales can reveal.

Unspoken Sermons contains the messages that were silenced at Arundel. Each chapter is a sermon that brings the reader into the very presence of the Living God. The book reminds the reader that it is not merely what one says and does, but also what one genuinely believes, that will be tested by God's consuming fire.

"I love these sermons," Louisa told George. "They make me want to cry out for the Light—that Light by which all darkness will one day cease. I do so wish that you had been able to speak these truths from your own pulpit, but I suppose this is God's way of making sure that many more will receive His words through you."

"And through you I receive more than I ever dreamed. I marvel that yet again, you are carrying my child," he replied. Louisa's approval mattered most to George. She was his prized gift from God, far above rubies. He could not love her more.

On January 23, 1867, the last of the Master's miracles, George MacKay MacDonald, was born. Although he was the final child Louisa birthed, he would not be the last of the MacDonalds' children—they would add four more in the future.

Lilia, Mary, Caroline, Greville, Irene, Winifred, Ronald, Robert, Maurice, Bernard, and now little George MacKay. Eleven miracles from the Master. Eleven visible, tangible, eternal beings. God's sacred will for Louisa's life. She had been pregnant a total of eight years. "It's hard to imagine," she said, shaking her head in wonder.

Though she was tired, sick, and emotionally spent, unsinkable Louisa nursed baby George, recovered from her ills, oversaw her nearly a dozen chicks, and cared for her frail husband. In addition, she dealt with abject poverty, took on the majority of the responsibility of educating her children, taught drama and music, and protected her husband from the harsh criticism he received when he preached from dissenting congregations' pulpits. It's no wonder George had high praise for Louisa and insisted they hire help to assist her. He knew he could not accomplish anything without her by his side.

Years later, Greville wrote about his mother's profound influence on his father's success:

> *My mother's constant vigilance over my father in his sickness and pleasure, his bodily and spiritual needs, is a very notable point in my parents' life. Always keen and instant, whatever her own ailing or weariness of heart.... We realize [her] indefatigable zeal.*[6]

George often told Louisa, "I could not have accomplished any of this without you, my true Pearl of Great Price." Knowing that her husband adored and appreciated her made it easier for Louisa to find contentment in any circumstance.

By living in the presence of the living One, they had become themselves His presence—dim lanterns through which His light shone steady. Who obeys, shines.
George MacDonald, *The Elect Lady*

CHAPTER 14

THE SOUND OF A FAR-OFF SONG

For freedom is the unclosing of the idea which lies at our root, and is the vital power of our existence. The rose is the freedom of the rose tree.
George MacDonald, *Donal Grant*

Bude is a picturesque coastal town in northeast Cornwall. As a Victorian retreat, it was the perfect place for the MacDonalds to spend the summer of 1867. George and Louisa gathered their flock and journeyed to the sea, where they rented two cottages at the end of the quay that provided exciting views for the children as ships were loaded and unloaded at the wharf. The holiday was necessary. George had been subjected to scorn as a result of his frequent preaching from dissenting pulpits. Always protective of her husband, Louisa found this difficult to bear.

"Mama, can we go to the beach again?" was a refrain often heard at their seaside cottage.

"Of course," was always her reply. Her favorite view was of her children skipping down to the harbor. Sparkling sand made of weathered, bright yellow shells spread before them like dotted swiss, and rocks jutted out of the sea, suggesting past shipwrecks.

Alongside the sea runs the River Neet, across which stretches the famous Nanny Moore's Bridge. At high tide, the southwest wind causes glorious waves to breach the seawall. Dodging in and out of the waves, George carried Maurice and Bernard, one under each arm. Shouts of glee escaped all three.

"The children do so love sea bathing," Louisa told her Bear.

"I'm partial to eating the crab and lobster!" George replied with a wink. "And the church at Kilkhampton has inspired me to write another novel, this one about a seaboard parish."

Carved medieval benches and four engraved columns greeted the MacDonalds as they entered the church. The columns' capitals were decorated with carvings of odd, beastly faces, and the children were mesmerized by the fanciful arabesque designs, heraldic shields, Biblical symbols, and heads of different sorts that greeted them at the end of each bench. It's no wonder George was inspired.

John Ruskin encouraged the MacDonalds to allow his student, social reformer Octavia Hill, to join them at Bude. Octavia was a remarkable woman, the perfect example of altruism, and was strongly committed to alleviating poverty. Ruskin's investment had enabled her to put her theories into practice. She believed in self-reliance and made it a key part of her housing system, designed to encourage tenants to better themselves. In her view, helping the poor required personal, carefully targeted, efficient supervision. Her luminous brown eyes revealed her ardor, and she unconsciously lifted them toward heaven whenever she spoke of important matters. Worn out by her reform labors, she came to Bude for rest.

Octavia was a blessing in disguise—she spent every morning with the children, taking them across the breakwater to the top of Chapel Rock and helping them with their lessons. She was the only one able to help Greville, who had struggled horribly with Latin grammar. He later bragged that, from then on, he was always top of his class in Latin. His family also discovered during this time that he had severe hearing loss, which accounted for his struggles in the classroom.

Books, nature, rhymes, games, and imaginative play made up the children's schoolhouse that summer. Years later, Greville reminisced about the education he and his siblings received:

> *True feeding of the child is more subtle a thing than psychologists can fathom. George MacDonald did fathom it— and in a way that was absolutely matchless. Magic and mystery, nonsense and fun—in no egregious fashions of the day, but in enduring forms of beauty—did more for us than moral precept or standardized education.*[1]

For Louisa, Bude was heaven. The sunsets, the fauna, the water birds that broke up the monotony of the horizon and drew her eyes to the sky—all these refreshed and renewed her.

On misty mornings, the children would warm themselves in front of the kitchen range until they were scolded for being underfoot and hindering breakfast. To the children, the stove was like a big black dragon, but not a mean dragon—a nice one. They could often be found lying flat on their stomachs, devouring what books they were allowed, and Octavia was always nearby, helping Louisa. It was the perfect summer, remembered by Greville as the merriest of his childhood.

> *Those days at Bude remain in my mind as the happiest of all my childhood's holidays; and chiefly because our father, in spite of his indefatigable writing, took more share in our romps and pleasures than I ever remember. Then closer, because lighter-hearted, friendship with some of our parents' friends was possible, and certainly made for our happiness.*[2]

Although George spent an enormous amount of time writing, he also spent time with his children, and they never forgot those moments.

"Papa is a magician!" they told their mother.

"Did you see how the horses reacted to him today? They refused to continue pulling our wagonette home because they were tired, and the driver couldn't get them to budge. Papa took the reins and with one word—no whip—they obeyed!"

"It is because every creature, rich or poor, eloquent or dumb, strives to help your Papa. He was hungry and they fed him, a stranger and they took him home. Remember, he and you are not men and women of the world," Louisa responded as her children's eyes widened with wonder.

Autumn arrived and the family returned to Earls Terrace. They decided they needed more space to accommodate all eleven children, so they moved once again, this time to The Retreat, in Upper Mall, Hammersmith. Later, famous textile designer William Morris renamed the home Kelmscott House. It's a three-story brown-brick home that overlooks the

Thames; its welcoming door features elements of classical architecture. Behind the house, the MacDonalds enjoyed a much-admired garden and a long, welcoming lawn lined with trees, shrubs, and rose beds. Lush, fairy-like ferns thrived in the shady lower garden.

"A roomy old stable. Now we can get a horse!" George gleefully observed as they perused their new abode.

"I love the walnut tree—and is that a tulip tree? I've never seen anything like it," remarked Louisa. "And look over there, Dear, at the wall of shrubbery—the statue of Artemis is leaping. Won't the children be delighted? And I think the ancient elms separating us from the river are charming. This will be the perfect place to entertain."

"But we must set aside a room for a Prophet's Chamber," George requested.

"A Prophet's Chamber?"

"Yes. Remember the wealthy woman who gave Elisha bread in the fourth chapter of Second Kings? She directed her husband to make a little chamber with a bed, a table, a stool, and a candlestick, to be a place of refuge whenever Elisha visited. Prophet's Chambers have been built for traveling teachers and evangelists ever since. I've always wanted a room to set aside as one," he explained.

"The Prophet's Chamber," Louisa said with a smile. "I like that name. And I think it is always good to have a retreat for a clergyman or weary traveler."

The MacDonalds' Prophet's Chamber became the perfect refuge for many. During the holidays, as well as annual Oxford and Cambridge Boat Races, the family welcomed guests. The Retreat allowed George and Louisa to entertain on a much larger scale than ever before. Tennyson himself attended a literary gathering there and with his deep, sad voice read poetry to rich and poor alike.

With so many children, Louisa did not need hired help, and the kids actually enjoyed serving refreshments and meeting laureates and peasants alike. Everyone was invited, everyone was welcome, no matter their social or economic standing.

Once they'd settled in, the MacDonalds immediately began to help Octavia Hill serve the poor. Lilia became Octavia's greatest help and went wherever she was needed.

"Let's invite the tenants to our home," Louisa suggested one day as she thought of others' great needs. "We can feed them and perform a play for them right here."

And so, beginning in 1867, The Retreat hosted annual entertainment for those Octavia was helping. Every year, between thirty and one hundred people attended. The MacDonalds' dearest friends and relatives always joined and lent a hand. In her spare time, Louisa wrote the plays the children acted out, usually fairy tales. She also provided a midday dinner before the play and a tea afterward.

Because fairy tales, especially those by the Brothers Grimm, held the children's imagination, Louisa adapted several into plays. The plays were well received, and she became more ambitious. She adapted *Beauty and the Beast*, Zola's *L'Assommoir*, and Dickens's *The Haunted Man*. To end the evening with fun, the MacDonalds always concluded with games and country dancing.

"Poor old Ruskin," Louisa told George one night. "I believe he went home half dead with unfed fatigue. He seemed shocked by our poorly dressed guests, and I do believe we neglected him in our anxiety to entertain everyone. We must do better next time."

"But he did join in the dancing, and seemed quite happy," George added.

Their friendship with Octavia meant that altruism abounded in their home and among the poor of London. George and Louisa admired the way Octavia worked: she seldom gave money to the poor and instead moved heaven and earth to find them work, winning their respect and conformity.

"It is the consistent giving of work that we are helping her to do," Louisa told her inquiring children.

The MacDonalds supported Octavia's energies and ministered to her. She often spoke of how much she owed to George and especially to *David Elginbrod*, which had influenced her greatly.

"His lectures often nearly bring tears to my eyes by the beauty and truth and suddenness of what he says," she wrote to a friend.[3] Out of appreciation, she asked Madame Bodichon to allow one of the MacDonald daughters to attend Bodichon's art classes without paying additional fees.

Soon, the MacDonalds converted the coach house into a theater, which became the perfect place to perform plays for the community. The boys constructed the stage, and Louisa and the girls sewed the curtains. E. R. Hughes, the nephew of their illustrator friend Arthur Hughes, painted designs on the curtains. The theater had a gas-lit stage where Lilia often played Lady Macbeth and George took the title role. Beloved by her younger siblings, Lilia had grown into a tender, devoted sister and a gifted actress.

Just like Louisa, Lilia mothered everyone. In addition, she had learned to read at an early age, and before eleven years old had an intimate knowledge of Shakespeare, which added to her genius for acting. Thus the coach house became a place for the poor, sent by Octavia, to be accepted and entertained by a troupe of siblings led by Lilia.

The MacDonalds' days were happy, filled with learning and playing. To Louisa's delight, the children showed an aptitude for music. The family's ever-growing circle of friends enjoyed the children's many talents and helped them access musical instruments, one being a handsome grand piano, a gift from Ruskin.

"Our little prodigies clearly get the gift of music from their mother," George mused.

"You know, Gracie plays Beethoven in a way I've never heard before," Louisa told him proudly. "I've been thinking the children should start sharing their gifts with others. Let's reserve Sunday evenings for tea and supper and invite the Mathesons and whoever they would like to bring."

And so it began. The children played and served and rolled up their sleeves afterward, tea towels in hand, for wash-up time. They all did their share: some played the piano well, all sang sweetly, one played the violin, and everyone sang carols at Christmastime. Grace performed Beethoven, Chopin, and Schumann magnificently. At the end of each evening, George concluded with readings from Scripture and literature, then prayer.

The children continually added plays their mother had adapted to their repertoire, including *The Tetterbys* and *The Pilgrim's Progress*. The latter, which was most requested, had always been an important story in the MacDonald home. They often discussed its portrait of a true Christian's spiritual journey, and its vivid descriptions were rich with applicable truth.

"The parlor represents your heart, my dear children," Louisa instructed, "and the dust of sin and inward corruptions collects and settles on the heart that was never sanctified by the sweet grace of the Gospel. The broom taken to the floor is the law, and the sweeper merely spreads the dust around the room with his broom, making it difficult to see clearly. The law is unable to justify or cleanse a man. But when the water, the Gospel, comes and is sprinkled upon the floor, it makes the soul clean. Sin is vanquished and subdued, and the heart is fit for the King of Glory to inhabit."

Within their own parlor stood a seventeenth-century oak cabinet that Louisa had purchased. On the cabinet were two carvings from *The Pilgrim's Progress*. One showed Prudence looking at herself in a hand mirror; the other showed Charity, who would soon be holding another baby in addition to the many who were hanging on her skirt. To the MacDonald children, these carvings represented their mother, who always seemed to find someone needing to be cared for or befriended.

On one occasion, an Oxford graduate came to The Retreat, begging in rags. He stayed for many weeks until George was able to find employment for him on the staff of a London newspaper.

"Mama," Greville shouted from his room, "did you give that man my new coat before he left?"

"Oh, dear," she called up to him. "I believe I must have."

Another man, a drunkard, came to The Retreat to be

reformed, and his fiancée joined him to help Louisa cure him. He recovered and married his fiancée, and they started a family. Even a broken-down horse was mended at The Retreat. All the while, the MacDonald children watched, helped, and wondered at their mother's healing hands and voluminous heart, so perfectly engraved in the panels of the cabinet.

Perhaps Louisa's most significant act of benevolence was taking in a poor, sickly boy named Willie Nicholls. She nursed and loved him and, when he was well enough, educated him. Winifred, an accomplished organist who noticed Willie's aptitude, devotedly taught him to play. Thanks to her guidance, he qualified at the College of Organists and afterward went on to become a professor of singing at the Royal Academy in London.

Because George now had a home large enough for both work and play, he was able to produce several books. In 1868, *Robert Falconer*, *Guild Court*, and *The Seaboard Parish* were all published, and his books were increasing in market value. Proud of their alumni's growing fame, the University of Aberdeen awarded George a doctor of laws degree in consideration of his "high literary eminence as a poet and an author." Louisa was elated.

Around the same time, the Reverend Samuel McComb, DD, of Harvard, heard George speak. McComb later included in his book, *Preaching in Theory and Practice*, an acknowledgment of his lifelong debt to George:

> *George MacDonald, poet, novelist, preacher, affords the most remarkable illustration known to me of this mysterious creative faculty of mind.... In a dimly lighted, ugly, dingy chapel.... As soon as the preacher began his sermon, those things were forgotten.... In simple, beautiful, conversational English ... he poured forth, apparently without effort, a stream of noble thoughts and gracious sentiments which woke responsive echoes in my heart. The audience, gathered from all parts of the metropolis, was held in the hollow of his hand. On the same day I heard Dr. Westcott in Westminster Abbey and Mr. Spurgeon*

> *in his Tabernacle; but good as their sermons were, it was George MacDonald that made an impression that the lapse of years has failed to efface. I have often wondered since what was, from the psychological point of view, the secret of his fascination.*[4]

George was often invited to fill a Sunday pulpit, but he never took a fee, and he also decided that he would neither allow churches to advertise his preaching nor to pass the collection plate.

"Louisa, I feel that it is much like the money changers in the temple," he explained. "It grates painfully on my ears to hear of churches holding services for the sake of reducing debt, and I believe I am often asked to preach for just such a reason."

"I wholeheartedly agree, dearest Bear," she replied. "Debts must be paid, and we will be true to our own, but you should only preach for the sake of helping others become true and trusting."

"Speaking of debts, I realize our large family and the demands of our hospitality can be a strain on you, dear Louisa. Though my novels are commanding better prices, we still seem to be stretched financially."

Finances were tight, but life was amusing and exciting. Meals were erratic, but no one complained, because self-forgetfulness was the rule of the house.

"Remember your father's motto, children. 'God mends all'—it is our faith. The Divine Guide will carry us over any difficulties, each day and always," Louisa often reminded them.

"And Mary, I do appreciate how readily you accept such a giant share of responsibility for your siblings," she added. "You are so kind to manage Bernard so nicely in the mornings." There was nothing sweeter to Louisa than seeing her daughters grow in grace.

"Dear," she told George, "Bernard was such an angel last night. His smile radiated love, and he never cried once. And Mary is so sweet and helpful. I think both Lily's and Mary's prices, if not above rubies yet, exceed garnets, don't you?"[5]

The Retreat fostered grace, and the home's beauty mirrored the gorgeous violets, poppies, daisies, and gentians that lined its flower beds. Louisa spent her days guiding the children in what Greville described as "magic and mystery, nonsense and fun," and "enduring forms of beauty." The children were always imaginative, and they were most honest when they spoke of what they liked or disliked—they had not yet learned the art of belying their true beliefs.

Their thoughts were best displayed at teatime, when they became particularly chatty as they enjoyed clotted cream an inch thick with strawberry jam on top. Louisa enjoyed teatime, especially when George could join them. Though the children didn't realize it, tea with their father was yet another aspect of their education. George's keen sense of logic and his listening ears, penetrating blue eyes, and expressive face encouraged their conversations, all the while teaching them common sense and discernment.

The new year brought with it a new job for George. He resigned his post at King's College in March 1869 and agreed to become the editor of *Good Words for the Young* magazine. He was also invited to give several lectures in Scotland, where he commanded large crowds and was received with enthusiasm. He had finally established a strong reputation in both Scotland and Manchester and lectured in those locations the most. But he was taxing himself to the point that he again fell deathly ill and, refusing to properly rest, began to cough up blood.

"Louisa," he told her, "I am so stubborn and slow to learn that I must quit overtaxing myself, and yet balance the perspective that I must continue to live and serve, and not inflate myself. I have gone through some of the folds of the shadow of death since I saw you, but the light has never ceased to shine."[6]

When he felt up to it, he reminded Louisa of his promise to take her to Switzerland. "I desperately need rest and relaxation, so we should finally go there together," he told her.

"But it's summer now, and didn't you suffer in the stifling heat last time?" Louisa reminded him. "Instead, I think you should accept the invitation to join the yachting trip up the coast of Norway. You will be accompanied by mostly Scottish clergy, and it will be cool and restful." Once again, she willingly sacrificed her pleasure for George's greater good.

Delighted with the sparkling water and the prospect of excitement, George boarded *The Blue Bell* and it set sail. The boat, owned by a wealthy merchant, offered all the luxuries and amenities available to passengers at the time. But George's poor health overtook him, and he spent most of his days in a windowless cabin, unable to view the stunningly beautiful northern coastline.

When Louisa heard of his poor condition, she wrote to him immediately. "I trust you will come home straight from Trondhjem. Ah! do dear—only perhaps you may get better by that time, and then the North Wind might after all comfort you in that long hair."[7]

Sadly, George's condition deteriorated to the point that all he could consume was pale beef tea. When the other passengers learned that the steamer *Norway* was leaving for England, they made arrangements for George to be placed on board. Louisa met him at King's Cross and described the reunion in a letter to his aunt, Mrs. MacColl:

> *I shall never forget what I saw on arriving at the Platform. There was an invalid carriage and in it a man propped up with pillows looking as if he were in the last stage of consumption, with a horrid cough. I could scarcely believe for a minute that it was George. He could hardly raise himself. His eyes were sunken, his cheeks hollow and he was so weak that his voice as hollow as his cheeks could not speak.*[8]

When Louisa finally brought George home, he looked so horrible that his children thought he was dead. Secure in his own bed, he "looked all round the room and cried with thankfulness," Louisa informed his aunt. A small vase filled with his favorite flower, sweet peas, sat on his bedside table.

"Oh it was wonderful to see him sleeping, sleeping on and on like the stillest sleep of an infant. He says tho' it was nearly worth it all—the wonderful effect of the blue sky just above him as they laid him on the floor of his cabin when they took the skylight up—when they lifted him up with cords. It was as if he looked out from his grave the tall mast of the vessel rising from his cabin—that and the blue sky was all he saw then he felt his Resurrection was come but I should like to hear him tell this. It was his one spot of joy," Louisa told his aunt.[9]

Louisa's tender nursing was absolutely essential, for George was nearer to death than he had ever been before.

"You are so dreadfully altered, my dear Bear," she said as she gently wiped his brow, "and you have suffered so. But who shall say these sufferings were not for other people in what you may hereafter write?"

"The way people looked at me as they carried me from the boat, I felt like a hero coming from the wars!" he said, taking a positive outlook. "But alas, I had done nothing for anybody, yet whatever I have learned from this, I will try to pass on in my books."

His recovery was long and slow, and he found it difficult to pick up the task of writing again. To speed his recovery, he and Louisa took a boat trip up the west coast to Scotland, where they briefly visited Huntly. While George and Louisa were gone, Lily graciously cared for her siblings at The Retreat. The visit jump-started George's writing and he produced *Ranald Bannerman's Boyhood*, a thinly disguised account of his own boyhood in Huntly.

Louisa was relieved and immeasurably grateful that God had quite miraculously healed her husband. Still, George was not fully recovered and was plagued with frequent attacks of asthma and bronchitis, so Louisa was exhausted. Hoping the sea air would be restorative for them both, they decided to find more permanent lodgings in Hastings so they could spend winters by the sea and the remainder of the year at The Retreat. Besides, it was only a two-and-a-half-hour train ride from one place to the other.

Nursing was Louisa's gift. She was an especially tender caregiver, and the task certainly required a lot of time, especially as it was not just George who was ill. The

MacDonald children contracted many irksome childhood diseases—mumps, boils, painful sties, debilitating headaches, and all the ailments that are rare today thanks to improved hygiene and advanced medicine—and only Louisa seemed to be able to provide the love and care her children needed. She had the rare capacity to handle such taxing situations.

Hastings did provide rest, and George was again able to write at a rapid pace. *Ronald Bannerman's Boyhood* was followed by *The Miracles of Our Lord*, *At the Back of the North Wind*, *Works of Fancy and Imagination*, *Wilfrid Cumbermede*, *The Vicar's Daughter*, and *The Princess and the Goblin*.

George was not the only author in the family—even Louisa wrote a book, *Chamber Dramas for Children*. It contains several of the plays she had adapted for her children.

But the beginning of the new decade brought grievous changes that would challenge Louisa's faith. On June 20, 1870, her beloved father, James Powell, died at the age of ninety-one. Three months later, her brother Alexander joined him in death. Other loved ones would soon follow.

"Life is propagation," George wrote in *Castle Warlock*. "The perfect thing, from the spirit of God downwards, sends itself onward, not its work only, but its life."[10]

For Louisa, this meant that while her heart secretly hoped her family, by adding to and multiplying itself, would always remain about her, she knew that reality, that cruel and constant guest, brings death as well as birth, and inevitable, inescapable change.

People find this great fault with me—that I turn my stories into sermons. They forget that I have a Master to serve first before I can wait upon the public.
George MacDonald[11]

CHAPTER 15

AMERICA

Lord, loosen in me the hold of visible things;
Help me to walk by faith and not by sight;
I would, through thickest veils and coverings,
See into the chambers of the living light.
Lord, in the land of things that swell and seem,
Help me to walk by the other light supreme,
Which shows thy facts behind man's vaguely hinting dream.
George MacDonald, *Diary of an Old Soul*, September 25

At the pinnacle of his literary success, George's acclaim extended beyond England and across the Atlantic to America. His books were quite popular there, but because copyright laws were not in place, George received little, if any, profit from American sales. While visiting England in 1869, an American, Mr. James T. Fields, suggested that George seriously consider traveling to America for a lecture tour. Lecturing was all the rage in America, and popular European speakers were in great demand. Even Dickens, Thackeray, Tyndall, and Yates had accepted the profitable invitation. After Mr. Fields returned to America, Richard Watson Gilder began corresponding with George on the subject, and in December 1871, George decided to tour America.

"I cannot allow you to travel alone, dearest Bear. I will go with you," Louisa insisted. "I'm sure our families will help with the children. Lilia and Mary are grown women now and have offered to step in."

She walked about the parlor and lit each candle. Their delicate light lifted her heart and removed the temptation to worry about leaving her little ones and missing their birthdays and Christmas. The tapering flames bid her to lift her palms in prayer to the Father of Lights, who vanquishes darkness.

George agreed that it would be best if Louisa accompanied him in case of illness. Greville was to travel with them, while Lilia and Mary, ages twenty and nineteen, respectively, would be left in charge of the younger children.

On the condition that he not lecture more than five nights a week and at a fee of thirty pounds per lecture, everything was settled with Messrs. Redpath & Fall of Boston, the preeminent American lecture bureau. George would tour during the next six or eight winter months. His modesty in refusing to send the agents any press releases or friendly testimonials cost him enormously, and he could and should have been paid much more than he was offered.

But before George and Louisa embarked on their American adventure, they were shocked by the dreadful news that their dearest friend, F. D. Maurice, had died. Then in July, Dr. Norman McLeod, a longtime friend of George, also passed away. So too did Greville Ewing Matheson, George's earliest, most brother-like friend. These were great losses for George and for Louisa, who loved each one of her husband's faithful friends.

September 1872 arrived, leaves fell softly to the earth, and the scents of fall swirled throughout London, signaling that it was time to depart for America. The SS *Malta* was a modest iron passenger-and-cargo ship with a magnificent golden female figurehead adorning its bow. Its serene sails and sensible structure welcomed George, Louisa, sixteen-year-old Greville, and their bright, as-yet-untarnished expectations of the New World.

Louisa, who was prone to seasickness, anticipated a long and difficult voyage, but was pleasantly surprised to learn that their trip to Boston would take a mere twelve days.

"I will muster my pluck and face the sea with a good attitude," she said to herself, "but oh, how time moves slowly in the nausea of sickness." Although the weather was exceptionally fair, she never left her berth.

They reached Boston on September 30, two days earlier than expected, and were greeted at the dock by General Sherwin and James Redpath, who delivered them to the home of James T. Fields and his wife. The MacDonalds were warmly welcomed at 148 Charles Street, where the literary lights were always bright.

Everyone wanted an invitation to the Fields' home, where Charles Dickens had mixed punch and taught guests his favorite parlor games, John Greenleaf Whittier and Harriet Beecher Stowe had vied to tell ghost stories, and Nathaniel Hawthorne had paced his bedroom floor one sad night in the final, unhappy year of his life. In his book *The American Scene*, Henry James even described the Fields' "effaced anonymous door" where he found "merciful refuge." Henry Wadsworth Longfellow was one of the home's most frequent guests, invited often because of his kind and charming personality. Although popular political personalities also frequented the house, the Fields were better known for their mission to bring literature to everyone in America through public lectures.

The house was narrow, three stories tall, and had a long backyard that extended out to the Charles River. The drawing room and library took up the entire second floor and boasted full-length windows that provided memorable views of the sun setting over the river. The home was a lovely place for the MacDonalds to stay. Greville's favorite room was the enormous library because its wall-to-wall bookshelves were filled with first editions and manuscripts. Mr. Fields entertained his guests with endless humorous stories, and Greville enjoyed them most of anyone.

"It seems that all we do here is laugh!" he told everyone.

"The Fields certainly are devoted in their care for us, and Annie is quite beautiful. Her tender stateliness has won my heart, and yours, Greville," Louisa said with a wink.

Once settled, ever-busy Louisa gathered her little ones about her from 3,000 miles away by writing long letters filled with warmth, humor, and details about their Papa's health. Her letters reveal her ability to describe people and places, nature and moments, with wit and kindness. It is no wonder George gave over his correspondence to her. Her first letter to her children reveals her heart best:

> *Mrs. G.M.D. to Mary J.M.D.*
> *Boston,*
> *Thursday morning, Oct. 3rd, 1872.*

America

My Dear Elfie (and all Angels),

I can hardly believe we have been here three days—it seems like nearly as many weeks. Such a sense of newness and strangeness, clearness and brightness, all about and around us! . . . I'll try and fancy what questions you would ask me if I could get home tonight. Well, you'd want to know how I and Papa are—very well, thank you, dear; all of us flourishing apparently, both by the way we walk, talk, look, eat and sleep—though as to the latter I hope to improve in that function as we get used to not having anything substantial to eat after three o'clock, unless you call tea and thin wafer-biscuits and iced water substantialities! They are very *charming people that we are with. You must not think they are not hospitable—quite the contrary—only they cram all their feed into two meals. Such breakfasts! And then dinner. Only we have not learnt to eat so much all at once. They have at eight o'clock breakfast fish and bird and meat and omelets and hominy or porridge and potatoes and beans and other vegetables, and four or five kinds of bread, and tea and coffee and iced water and Vichy water and wine if you like; and then a regular fruit dessert just like dinner with finger glasses and d'oyleys in due form. Mr. Fields is a polished, genial, kind, well-educated man. His wife a nature's lady—refined, delicate, largish and kind. He is, and evidently has been a lion hunter, but it seems to me that this is because of his love of the lions more than for any reflected glory he gets by it. His autographs and letters and books, first editions, authors' own copies, presents of MS. copies, etc., etc., are really things to count oneself rich in possessing; but he only seems to rejoice in them as a schoolboy might dance with joy about his prizes for athletic sports. He is very simple-hearted and clever in his own way. He tells a story "first-rate," and has lots of most excellent ones to tell. . . . She is really great and no end of kind. Her mind seems full of beautiful and best things—verse and prose. . . . I mean to write much more to-day, but the callers and callers and callers—one after another, or rather in twos and threes after each other—have prevented me. Mr. Redpath says that Papa's*

> *popularity goes very much in strata—very much I think as it does at home. Those who care for him, care very much—others can't endure his writings. So they can't tell till they try whether he will take.... The very first person we saw in Mrs. Fields' house was Mrs. B. Stowe!*[1]

In Louisa's next letter, written two days later, she described meeting Emerson and his wife and daughter, who came for lunch; afterward, they went to see Longfellow.

> *He showed us his rooms and his pictures, and we saw one of his daughters. His house was Washington's headquarters—a hundred years old—which here is as wonderful as a three-hundred would be with us.... One amusing chapter in the evening was my talking to a youth, a tremendous big boy with large open eyes who had travelled a good deal and talked charmingly, I thought, for so young and so big a fellow. I thought perhaps he was going into the Navy—thought he would make a jolly captain. I thought I was talking very kindly to him and encouraged him to speak his mind about things. When I heard afterwards he is* the great preacher [Phillips Brooks] *of the town—an episcopalian clergyman, and is run after tremendously, I never was more flabbergasted....*[2]

"I think it is Emerson, though he never spoke to me directly, who remains the most vivid in my mind. He seemed to me like a mountaineer daring to climb into the blue of heaven, and coming down to our level again, to give us news and hope far more lovely than Moses' tablets of stone," Greville later told his parents.[3]

The MacDonalds did not move in the elite circles of London society but, as soon as they arrived in America, were introduced to all the notable New Englanders. One was Oliver Wendell Holmes, the "poet laureate" of Boston. These significant Americans attended George's lectures, which were crammed with people. The crowd would hush as he approached the podium, carrying with him only a small volume of Burns. He never relied on notes, and, as in his books, he always pointed the audience to the ways of Christ.

One reporter wrote, "In the others we have known the force of great minds, but in him the glow of a great soul."

Louisa fell in love with New England and New York. She and George were meeting brilliant, famous authors who recognized and appreciated George's own brilliance. "There is nothing that touches my heart more than seeing my humble dearest Bear overwhelmed by the admiration and applause of these enthusiastic Americans," she told her teenage son. She and George had been married for twenty-one years, but the first ten had been filled with hardship, failure, and ill health. The second ten brought a rise in renown, and now at last Louisa could watch as the whole world began to recognize her talented husband. What a change from the poor tutor who had stepped across her father's threshold and opened heaven's portal to her!

Louisa's greatest challenge was monitoring George's health and stamina. The lecture tour was too heavily scheduled, and Louisa was often forced to forbid him from attending social functions held in his honor. This frequently frustrated his keeper, Mr. Redpath.

"Your father is the bear," she told Greville, "who must dance when his keeper, Mr. Redpath, shakes the chain."

"Did you hear Mr. Fields call Mr. Redpath the 'Drag-on'?" Greville asked his mother, amused.

"Yes." She smiled. "I often seem to incur the wrath of Redpath when I am forced to cancel these numerous appointments. He lacks the ability to consider the effects of long daily journeys and tedious social functions."

"I think it's preposterous that he dislikes Papa accepting invitations to preach," said Greville. "And he cannot understand that Papa preaches without gratuity because he wants the public to hear him freely."

"We must endeavor to discreetly protect your father," Louisa said, and Greville agreed.

Forty engagements filled the MacDonalds' calendar up to Christmas, and they expected Redpath to add more. Before George's first lecture in Cambridgeport, Massachusetts, he and Louisa were presented to most of New England's literary society.

"There are so many kind people who want to meet your father that it's difficult to limit these engagements. Unfortunately, I am having to be the disagreeable one who says 'No' to the Fields," Louisa confided to Greville after cancelling an excursion to the countryside. "He will not be fit for his lecture on Wednesday if he doesn't rest."

"Driving about the country seeing the marvelous colors of the trees is my favorite thing so far," Greville told her. "These trees here—one giant blaze of carmine or blood in color, and the variety of foliage. I especially like the exquisitely graceful form of the American elms and do so wish we had them in England."

They had timed their visit perfectly and would never forget the magnificent colors of New England in the fall.

They were also charmed by New England's agricultural society, sweetness of life, abundant food, simplicity of comfort, and ever-present literary culture.

"These New Englanders resemble more the farmer-class of Scotland in my boyhood days, although there luxury was all unknown and the ghost of John Knox still haunted their outlook," George observed.[4]

Greville later wrote:

> *Farmers lived well upon their produce, worked along with the wives and daughters, whose refinement was evidenced as much in their tasteful dress as in their hospitality and the personal services to their guests and to one another. Their reading was extensive, and their religion, though generous and wide, was still tempered by the puritanism that had brought their forbears across the Atlantic.*[5]

George's lectures included excerpts from *Hamlet*, *King Lear*, and *Macbeth*, and from the writings of Tom Hood, Tennyson, Milton, and the audiences' favorite, Burns.

America

"There has been nothing like this since Dickens," Fields declared after one lecture, his eyes full of tears as he shook George's hand.

"Why didn't you tell me you could do this sort of thing?" Redpath asked, rushing at George after his first lecture. "I could have got three hundred dollars a lecture for you!"

But the one person who was not surprised was Louisa. She had known, from the moment George had first noticed her and had dared to tell her how she stood in his heart, that the world needed his wisdom. She was now perfectly at peace, and later that evening, while lying in bed, she wept a little with joy.

George was not the only one who won the hearts of New England—Louisa did as well.

"Her social charm, her beautiful yet inexpensive dressing, her wonderful eyes—in a land, moreover, where this feature was more generally notable than with us—and the fact that notwithstanding her grace of figure and sprightliness in manner, she was mother of eleven children, a number—'the *wrong* side of a dozen,' my father said—quite as phenomenal in the States then as it would be here now, made her as popular as her husband," Greville later wrote.[6]

"Greville, dear," Louisa would often ask, "please run upstairs and fetch that photo of all of us."

"You send me to get it so often that you ought to just wear it like a sandwich board," he'd reply sarcastically.

New England ladies would look, amazed, from the photo of Louisa's children to the sweet, petite, satirical lady standing before them. They admired her, for it was obvious that Louisa was almost as much responsible for her husband as for her children. As a typical teenage boy, Greville did not find his mother remarkable, but observing the Americans' reactions made him appreciate her more.

"Mama, Papa, I've realized something. By inviting me to come with you to America, you've opened the door for me to see you through the eyes of others and to understand better your courage and devotion—how you are strengthened by your intense love for all and by faith in that 'Law of

Loveliness' John Ruskin talks of, in which our Creator found for you delight and belief. You are the reason we're here. And I begin to see how it's your passion for God, Papa, rather than your logical intellect or superb eloquence, that makes men follow you," Greville admitted.[7]

At the end of October, they visited John Greenleaf Whittier, the famous abolitionist and Quaker poet of Amesbury. Whittier had written a letter to the local press in which he lauded George's great work for the cause of religion and poetry and urged everyone to take advantage of the opportunity to hear him lecture. The MacDonalds stayed at Whittier's home, a sweet country cottage. The poet was "one of the sweetest, most dignified, loving, humble and gentle of men," Louisa later wrote to her children. "After his lecture, the Scots gave your Papa a copy of Whittier's poems. The next morning Mr. Whittier told me, 'Friend George must not be the only one to have a present,' and he gave me a lovely copy of his latest volume."

"What a lovely, holy man, full of fire and the enjoyment of all things good," the MacDonalds agreed as they left Amesbury.

After Amesbury they visited Providence, Rhode Island, before returning to Boston to lecture again. On Saturday evening, November 9, the Fields held a reception for the MacDonalds, but before it had concluded, the party was informed that a fire was raging in the heart of Boston. It came dangerously close to the Fields' home, and the household began packing their valuables.

"Mama, look at the sky!" Greville exclaimed, pointing to the sparks and ash that still floated in the air. "All the smoke is casting a shadow on the moon."

The next morning, Greville explored the burnt ruins of the city, finding it difficult to distinguish one street from another. The fire had consumed nearly one hundred acres, and property worth $50 million had turned to ash and smoke. Mr. Fields was certain that he was ruined.

Monday morning arrived and Mrs. Cunningham of Milton, a dear lady, came to fetch the MacDonalds to bring them to her home. They never forgot how generous she was in heart, hand, and hospitality—she became their lifelong friend.

After George's initial success in Boston, the family was sent to New York, where they stayed with Dr. J. G. Holland, the novelist and editor of *Scribner's Magazine*. He too became a lifelong friend. From New York, the MacDonalds took a carriage lined with gold and brown satin to what Greville called the "white marble palace" of the Lippincotts, in Philadelphia.

"William Penn would be disappointed by the sedate, cold manners here in his city. They seem unable to muster any enthusiasm," Louisa noted, "and the ladies in this house are more splendaciously attired than any I have visited!"

From Philadelphia, they traveled to Scotch Plains, New Jersey, and then to Washington, where the Russell Gurneys welcomed them graciously. From there they visited Baltimore, where Greville admired the extraordinary beauty of every church girl that Sunday. Reluctantly, he left the chapel, and the MacDonalds returned to Washington, where George was afflicted with a severe attack of bronchitis that required him to cancel several lectures. Louisa wrote to Lilia to inform her of George's condition:

Mrs. G.M.D. to Lilia S.M.D.
1512 H. Street, Washington,
Dec. 3rd.

Dearest Lily,

I never saw [your father] more prostrate except, of course, at the time of the Manchester illness. It is very serious this attack for him—we do not know yet whether he will be able to lecture again at all, and if he does he can scarcely make up all he has lost before the close of the lecture season. But if he can but get what will cover the debts that trouble him I do not think we ought to mind about more. . . . We have given up Chicago. . . . But the Life is more than meat or money, and if you get Papa back alive and well we shall not mind that he could not make so many dollars as he intended. "I do so want to see Bobbie and Maurice," and he said it in such a sad tone. He longs to be home, and he seems to have little hope that he will be able to go on lecturing. But I hope—though my heart-strings are very near cracking in ten different places—that we may be able to go on. . . . The dear Gurneys are so dear; Mrs. G. is lovely. . . .

*Your loving
Mother.*

In the following letter from George to Mary, it is obvious that he dearly missed his children. Reading the poem he enclosed, titled "A Song for Both Sides of the Atlantic," one can only wonder if six to eight months seemed like years to him.

G.M.D. to Mary J.M.D.

My Darling Elfie,

. . . I am much better, and have just written these verses to send to my chickens for the Little-Baby time [Christmas Day]. Would we were all the holy babies of our Father in heaven— out and out, I mean. My love to Lily and everyone. I have thought you all over.

*Your loving
Father.*

A Song for Both Sides of the Atlantic.

*Fur-footed, slow, for all thy gracious charms,
We pray thee, dear December, to depart;
We kiss the Child thou bearest in thine arms,
But all the year he dwelleth in our hearts.*

*Young January, with the wrinkled face,
Follow thy sisters on their starry way;
Sweep on, we beg thee, with thy snowy train;
When next thou com'st, we'll give thee leave to stay.*

> *Make, February, few steps o'er the floor,*
> *Nor linger by the hearth when thou should'st cross;*
> *Haste thee, nor turn to courtesy at the door;*
> *Pass through, and make us richer by thy loss.*
>
> *Nor beat thy robes, O March, nor clutch the hair*
> *That hither, thither, all about thee flies;*
> *O let thy dusty winds afar thee bear,*
> *That thy sweet sister come with smile and sighs.*
>
> *And yet we care not whether sigh or smile*
> *Shall, April, on thy fair face win the day;*
> *We love thee, girl, but thou hast not a wile*
> *To move a prayer except—oh, haste away!*
>
> *Come then, dear May; lead o'er the sea-waves dull*
> *The eager ship, the angel of the boon;*
> *And when our arms are as our full hearts full,*
> *Then go or linger, dear and perfect June.*[8]

Throughout George's bout of bronchitis, unsinkable Louisa stayed by his side, ever watchful of his needs.

"Up! Let's be about! We are going for a drive, dear Bear," she told him one afternoon. "I know Dr. Coles wants you to stay in bed, but you have no chance of recovering in the confining, dry, overheated atmosphere of this house. You need God's fresh air and the lovely sights of nature."

Miraculously, by employing faith and resiliency, George recovered quickly. After the drive with Louisa, his stove failed and a mighty storm of wind and sparkling snow roared outside and blew into his room, onto his face, and all around him. He grew calm and peaceful and woke indescribably better the next morning. The fresh air and beautiful scenery had worked their magic, and George was able to resume his lectures. Louisa was relieved beyond words.

Soon they boarded a Pullman car to Elmira, New York, to stay with Mark Twain's mother-in-law, Mrs. Langdon. George became close friends with Mark Twain, and the two were able to see each other several times while the MacDonalds were in New York. They discussed collaborating on a future novel together and securing its copyright on both sides of the Atlantic, but this idea never came to fruition.

"I was not aware of what a deeply religious man Mr. Twain is," Louisa told George and Greville.

"Did you know his father-in-law wants him to write a Life of Christ?" George asked. "He believes Mark's keen observations and knowledge of men might startle readers into a truer faith, and I think I agree."

When Christmas Eve arrived, the weather was cold and dismal, and the MacDonalds had to board a train from Elmira to Jersey City. They would remember the journey as their worst ever. The stoves in the cars couldn't burn when the train wasn't moving swiftly, and its speed was hindered by giant snowdrifts. When the MacDonalds finally arrived, three hours late, they were famished and half-frozen.

"We have arrived so late that no one is here to meet us," Louisa informed the men.

George held on to Greville's arm and struggled to move. Tears rolled down his cheeks, and he had to stop frequently. Fortunately, the inn was just across the road, but the thermometer showed five degrees below zero, and George said the air felt like acid cutting up his lungs.

"Greville, we must get your father out of the cold," said Louisa.

"It is such agony to see him like this, Mama," Greville responded.

When they finally reached the inn, Louisa went to work with her remedies, pouring herself out once again until she had nothing left to give. She took comfort in the fact that she was pouring her strength and prayers into the hollow of God's hands, to be kept for eternity. By morning, George was well enough to travel to Newark to meet Richard Watson Gilder, poet and managing editor of *Scribner's*, and Gilder's mother.

Mr. Gilder made a great impression on Greville, and both the poet and his mother became Greville's dear friends.

Thanks to Mr. Gilder, America discovered that George

MacDonald was more than just an orator; his unusual gifts of confident humility, valor, and simplicity uplifted his audiences and warmed them through and through. "I believe it is due to Mr. Gilder's enthusiasm for your father that so many warm-hearted souls have discovered Christ Himself through your father's lectures," Louisa marveled to her son.

The press validated Louisa's belief in her husband's skill. In one New England religious paper, a critic wrote, "The most engaging of lecturers, his language exact and copious comes from him with the dew of thought upon it, fresh as if just conceived. He walked into our hearts." Another publication proclaimed, "His gesture is, of all Englishmen we have ever listened to, the best, full of ease, grace and nature, while his hands and fingers are full of significance, pointed with meaning and dripping with emotion."

A New York religious publication stated, "There is something indescribable about the man which holds the audience till the last word. It is not eloquence or poetry, nor is there any straining for effect, but it is the man's soul that captivates. You love the man at once.... How could the people help listening to a man who thus brought his tribute to their hearts? It was a unique and characteristic effort, great in its very simplicity and originality, combined with exquisite touches of tenderness and keen searchings of human hearts."[9]

Louisa read these reviews and marveled at the reverence and enthusiasm with which George's audiences received him.

When George had regained his strength, the MacDonalds proceeded with their plans for him to lecture in Chicago. But before they continued their tour, George had an engagement to attend.

"Louisa, I accepted the invitation from the Burns Society in New York. The event will be at Delmonico's," he informed her. "I'm glad that I brought my full dress set—kilt, sword, dirk, and sgian-dubh!" The custom of the Caledonian Society in London had always been that everyone must appear in their native Highlander costume, and George was pleased when the Burns Society told him they believed the same.

"How was the dinner, dear Bear?" Louisa asked when he

returned that evening.

"Well, my Love, I was the only guest not in black tails and white tie! But all went well. When I entered the room in my full regalia, I was greeted with rapturous delight!"

"I wish I could have seen that!" she exclaimed.

Rested and ready to continue, the MacDonalds whirled about the East Coast by train—from Pittsburgh to Cincinnati, and then on to Chicago. They took the northern route through Buffalo to Niagara Falls and Toronto, Canada. After George's lectures in Chicago, they went to Ann Arbor and Montreal, then back to Boston.

Along the way, Louisa wrote frequently, and with vivid details, to her children in England:

> *Niagara was our greatest and only treat of the kind since we came. The standing on the top of that Terrapin Tower and feeling borne up and away from everything and seeing those mighty waves rolling and dashing beneath us, brought the idea of infinity and majesty more intent upon me than anything in my life—anything material, I mean, that ever I saw. I felt as if I might be, and behold yet not be, of the earth or on it. I imagine that I knew more certainly then than ever before what it would be to have a spiritual body and belong to Creation—not merely to this little earth-bit of it.*[10]

As the MacDonalds' tour wound down, their new American friends held a matinee lecture and a dinner, hosted by Mr. Fields, for their benefit. In addition, Mrs. Whitney, a Boston author, inaugurated a "Copyright Testimonial" for George by raising over $1,500 in recognition of the thousands of his books printed in America for which he had not been paid royalties.

These newfound friendships were like manna from heaven. So many of the people the MacDonalds met on their tour would remain their lifelong friends: the Fields, Oliver Wendell Holmes, Richard Gilder, Maria Oakley, George Bacon, the Rev. Whittier, the Russell Gurneys, Longfellow, Mary Mapes Dodge, Harriet Beecher Stowe, Emerson, Dr. Holland, Mrs.

Cunningham, Mrs. Langdon and her son-in-law Mark Twain—and many more.

"The sun seems to shine more brilliantly even in the coldest of winters when you are surrounded by the glow and warmth of true friendship," Louisa reflected.

Although she enjoyed America and was grateful to be with George, she had missed several of her children's birthdays and longed to see their faces again. Her love was miraculous and immeasurable, and no matter how many children she had, it sprung up like living water and grew like a tiny mustard seed.

The letter Louisa sent Maurice for his ninth birthday shows just how much she missed him and desired that he grow in grace and in the knowledge of Christ. At the end of her letter, she mentions his daisies, and he must have been pleased to know that his mother, though thousands of miles away, shared this joy with him. Sadly, Maurice would only live another six years.

Mrs. G.M.D. to Maurice M.D.
Altoona, Pennsylvania,
Feb. 16th, 1873.

My Dearest Maurice,

I was very sorry I couldn't write to you on the 7th of February, my darling, precious little son—you are not forgotten by your Father and Mother. . . . People that love each other can't be very far off each other, though a great big sea comes between the bodies of them. Love joins us, doesn't it, dear boy? When you are thinking about me you have got me, and when I think about you I know you are mine. I know God gave you to me and so you are mine; and I can think of your dear face and the loving little kiss and the loving little way you have of doing things for me; that brings you quite close to my mind, and then my heart holds you very tight when I get hold of you so! . . . But all your life God will be nearer to you than I can ever be, and He can help you more than Papa or I ever can. You are more His even than mine. We may often mistake you, or be so far away from you that we cannot look at you and speak to you just the minute you want something; but God the Great Father will never misunderstand you and He is always near you and helps every time you call to Him. Even when you only wish you could speak to Him, He will help you to speak to Him. And every time you want to do what is right, He is in you making you want it. So, dear darling Boy, you must take care not to send Him away, but ask Him to come into you more and more. . . .

*Your own
Mother.*

I am glad to hear you have had daisies already in your grass. They sell them sometimes in pots here.[11]

George, Louisa, and Greville spent their final days in America at Dr. Holland's home on Park Avenue in New York.

"My Dear, a group of men are here to see you," Louisa announced one day as she entered the room where George was writing. She ushered the visitors in and left the study.

"They have asked me to accept the pastorate of their church on Fifth Avenue," he told her after the men had left.

"Really, George? What an honor."

"But I cannot accept. I have already declined their offer. Louisa, they offered me a stipend of $20,000 per year. I could not possibly accept such a post and such a salary."

"You know, Papa," Greville interjected, "if you had accepted their offer I'd be able to go to Oxford!"

"Son, I do not trust in my riches. I trust in the merits of my Lord and Savior. I trust in His finished work, in the sacrifice He has offered."[12]

As a token of public gratitude, approximately fifty of George's preeminent literary friends invited him to present a farewell lecture. *Hamlet* was the requested subject, and the lecture was held at the huge Association Hall, with all proceeds to be given to George. On May 19, every inch of the hall was packed.

"My dearest Dear," Louisa whispered as they entered the

hall, "even Mark Twain and Bret Harte are here!"

At the conclusion of his lecture, George gave his final farewell:

"For the kindness I have received in America I am very grateful. We came loving you and knowing that we should love you yet more; and instead of being disappointed, our hearts are larger and fuller for the love of so many more friends than we had before. If word of mine could be of any value, the love between the countries will surely be at least a little strengthened by your goodness, which, if only in honesty, but yet more in happiness, we are compelled to carry back with us. Your big hearts, huge in hospitality and welcome, have been very tender with me and mine—so patient with my failures and shortcomings."[13]

On May 24, 1873, the three MacDonalds set sail for their beloved England. Louisa's pen couldn't keep up with her excitement as she wrote to her children:

> *Oh, my boys, my little and big boys, my heart swells so big so big to think of seeing you so soon—it will be very soon after you get this and my dear dear gentle girls. I shall really shall I really have you again. God be praised for the hope even.*

They had made so many dear friends. So many Americans had been touched and changed by George's message.

> *A few days ago Dr. George Macdonald, the most spiritual and poetic novelist of the day, left these shores to return to his native country.... His homely, stirring, beautifully simple words ... have left an echo in the hearts of every one who heard them, which will never quite die out. More than any living man we know of, Dr. Macdonald has the rare power of inspiring his readers and hearers with a personal affection and love for himself. They feel that in him they have a true man, with the brain of a poet and heart of a child; a man who could never be other than simple, and honest, and loveable; with a peculiarly refined and healthy nature, full of sweetness and warmth and light.*[14]

The waves lulled the MacDonalds as they travelled back to England. They would miss their newfound friends, but Louisa couldn't wait to see her children again.

Thy fishes breathe but where thy waters roll;
Thy birds fly but within thy airy sea;
My soul breathes only in thy infinite soul;
I breathe, I think, I love, I live but thee.
Oh breathe, oh think,—O Love, live into me;
Unworthy is my life till all divine,
Till thou see in me only what is thine.
George MacDonald, *Diary of an Old Soul*, January 5

CHAPTER 16

TETHERED TO THE CROSS

A perfect faith would lift us absolutely above fear. It is in the cracks, crannies, and gulfy faults of our belief, the gaps that are not faith, that the snow of apprehension settles, and the ice of unkindness forms.
George MacDonald, *Sir Gibbie*

"They're here! They're here!" shouted the children as they ran down the stairs to jump and dance about George, Louisa, and Greville.

Ten children anxiously awaited their turn to be embraced by Mama and Papa. Everyone agreed that they must never ever be apart again.

Louisa's heart soared as she looked around the sun-filled parlor. She sighed with joyful relief. Her children's laughter and clear, sweet voices were a symphony to her hungry ears. God had used the time of separation to strengthen their family, transforming eddies into a steady channel of love that flowed deep and strong.

The next two years were the happiest the MacDonalds spent at The Retreat. After regaining his physical and mental strength, George published *Gutta Percha Willie* and penned *Malcolm*. He also enjoyed a temporary respite from the debts that often weighed him down.

"Healing is coming to you, bit by bit, my dearest Bear," Louisa encouraged him. "And we must keep strong in our faith about our finances, for as you always say, the morrow will take thought for yesterday even before itself."[1]

Although he was ill more or less from 1874 to 1875, George had enough energy for ambitious literary pursuits. Besides writing *Malcolm* and *Gutta Percha Willie*, he also published *St. George and St. Michael*, *Thomas Wingfold, Curate*, *The Wise Woman* (later titled *The Lost Princess*), and *England's Antiphon*, the last of which was illustrated by Arthur Hughes. In each novel, George successfully combined theology and romance. And he was even well enough to deliver the inaugural address at the Working Women's College.

The family's American friends visited frequently, and while George was reluctant to set his writing aside and devote himself fully to his guests, Louisa welcomed each caller with grace and warmth. The MacDonalds' visitors included Laird Collier and his two sons; Mrs. Whitney and her husband and daughter; Tennyson; Mark Twain; Antoinette Sterling and her future husband; and Mary Mapes Dodge, author of *The Silver Skates*, and her son.

"I'm certainly glad we've experienced American hospitality—otherwise I would have no idea how to make our Yankee guests feel at home!" Louisa told her daughters. "They were quite lavish with us, so we will have to do our best!"

Louisa and her girls rolled up their sleeves and got to work. They polished the silver, dusted and tuned, scrubbed and mended, and gathered goodies from the garden. Louisa enjoyed baking and preparing for each guest. Her daughters learned from her cheerful example and considered work a privilege rather than a burden.

"Always remember that there's no such thing as certain women having the rare gift of hospitality," she'd tell them as they worked alongside one another. "It is not a gift bestowed, but a command from the Lord. Keeping an open heart and an open home is an act of obedience. Who knows, we may even be entertaining angels unaware!"

They carefully prepared evening entertainment and welcomed their guests with music, singing, and Louisa's wonderful dramas.

That winter, a great joy arrived in the form of Mr. Edward "Ted" R. Hughes, who had asked for Mary Josephine's hand in marriage. Ted was Arthur Hughes's nephew, which made the union all the more wonderful. A young artist, Ted was quickly gaining fame for his pure ideals and technical excellence, and he was "an Apollo in looks," affectionate, industrious, and a notable gentleman.

The MacDonalds were thrilled, and Louisa referred to Edward as her twelfth child.

But their joy was quickly interrupted when Mary

contracted scarlet fever, which resulted in rapid weight loss and serious complications in her lungs. Louisa leaned on her Savior and spent every moment caring for Mary.

Weary from the constant demands of nursing her daughter, Louisa confided to George, "I think I now understand why Blake wrote, 'Guide thou my hand which trembles exceedingly upon the Rock of Ages.' And I've been thinking, dear Bear—I'm convinced that living near the river is to blame for your chronic illness and now Mary's scarlet fever. I think we need to find a better place. Also, I think it would be best to arrange for Mary to spend time by the sea—she is so worried and pale and distracted. We must get her well so we can plan her wedding."

"Yes," he agreed. "And I don't believe it would be advisable for me to tour America again next year as planned—not while Mary is so ill. She needs you, and I won't go without you."

In the spring of 1875, Louisa found a suitable home situated between Guildford and Wonersh. Great Tangley Manor was an old, fully furnished Tudor farmhouse that the owner had made available for six months. Louisa and the children moved to Tangley in early April. Once they'd settled in, she wrote to George:

Mrs. G.M.D. to her Husband.
Tangley Manor,
Sunday afternoon, 2 o'clock,
April 17th, 1875.

We have just come in from a morning on the hills through the lanes. We sat down in the sun for more than an hour. I read over one of your sermons given in Renshaw Street, to them—it was so appropriate for the occasion. . . . I never felt more like an old mother hen—all the boys and girls are so good to me and yet so independent and happy. We have been reading the Blithesdale Romance *in the afternoons and evenings, a book easily realized in this house of really seven gables—and so completely shut away from all life but our own. . . . Charming*

> *lanes and sloping hills, and woods—abound all round us—I feel as if it were almost too good to be true that such a place is ours for 6 months. I am always looking at things with your eyes; and I do think, blue as they are, you will see the sky heavenly blue and the air deliciously balmy and quiet. . . .*[2]

"It was built when Shakespeare was a boy—in 1582, Louisa!" George said with delight when he saw the house. "Just look—it has great oak beams within and without."

The majority of the house, as it stood when the MacDonalds arrived, had been built by Richard Cayll. The site has a rich architectural history, and some of the timbers from the Armada fleet were incorporated into the dining room panels. The boys relished the fact that the home was a medieval hall during the thirteenth and fourteenth centuries, and Louisa favored its many gardens. There were kitchen gardens, an alpine garden, an iris garden, a pergola walk, a rock garden, a flower-bordered lake, and her favorite, a court garden featuring an extensive run of wisteria that climbed the western wall of the house. And with stables, cow sheds, piggeries, and barns, the house had endless entertainment for the children.

"Bear, since my Papa died, I do have a small income of my own, and I would like to purchase a horse for you," Louisa said as she and George walked around the stable. It looked quite forlorn without a horse to shelter. "You have always said there is nothing so good for the inside of a man as the outside of a horse."

George assented, and their new mare soon arrived, granting work and play to the boys, who groomed and doted on her. George affectionately named her Kitty. Sometimes the boys would take her to the front lawn, and Louisa would stand at the window to watch them frolic. A few of the MacDonalds' relatives chided them that they could not afford the luxury of a horse. Uncle Joshua Sing was one such relative, but he sent a check to cover the mare's expenses for a year.

"George! Look out there!" Louisa exclaimed, pointing out a large Tudor window. "Out on the lawn—they've brought

Kitty out to gallivant and she has her front hoof up on Greville's shoulder. She sure is an affectionate girl!"

"She'll help them grow into godly men," George said. "Yesterday I walked Kitty up to Blackheath and enjoyed the country for the first time in a long while. It was almost perfect—warm, but not too hot—and there was the loveliest heather I have ever seen, and a thousand dainty interminglings of wildness and culture."[3]

Kitty certainly provided inspiration for the horses that play such a large role in the plot of *St. George and St. Michael*, and for Diamond and Ruby, two characters in *At the Back of the North Wind*.

> *"There are horses in heaven for angels to ride upon, as well as other animals, lions and eagles and bulls, in more important situations. The horses the angels ride, must be angel-horses, else the angels couldn't ride upon them. Well, I'm one of them."*[4]

The children loved their six months at Tangley. Lily even wrote to Mary, who was staying by the sea, and urged her to join them: "Come down! Come down! Come down and see the sun, come and see the moon ... come and see the cows and calves ... come and see the sun set and get strength enough to see it rise. Come and look at the holly hocks and sun flowers. One group of hollyhocks we saw tonight is like nothing but the pink of your dress and the colour your cheeks should be."[5]

When winter came and their lease ended, the MacDonalds decided to move permanently to the seaside town of Bournemouth, on the south coast of England, where Mary had been recuperating. Bournemouth, which overlooks the English Channel, was a popular resort town among those who were ill. The pine trees and sea air were considered beneficial for lung ailments, and the popular pastime of sea bathing was thought to be quite curative. A garden, with paths and walkways, had been constructed along a stream that runs toward the sea. One path, the Invalids' Walk, traversed the town and extended to the ocean.

Because a railway had arrived at Bournemouth five years prior, the MacDonalds' move was quite easy. The train was even able to transport Kitty to a beautiful new stable by the sea.

"Do you know, Louisa, that Kitty neighed at me as soon as I entered the train car?" George asked. "She was so gentle and good that we even let her loose on the platform!"

They found a quaint, newly built home that was hidden among pines. It stood in the most enchanting location—on the edge of a cliff, facing the sea. And Louisa was delighted with her new garden.

"This is the best place to care for Mary," she told George, marveling at God's goodness. "And we must call our new home Corage, after the anagram of your name: Corage! God mend all!" She knew it would take fortitude and endurance to trust God after yet another move.

"Here we will walk slowly and bow often; we will let His light flow through us, just as He flows through the tree branches, giving hints of gladness," she told her worried heart.

Doctors disagreed about Mary's diagnosis. One said she had quinsy, another suggested scarlet fever. Mary's bones ached, her throat was severely inflamed, and every evening, without fail, her fever rose terribly high. Every morning and every evening, Louisa gave Mary rubdowns to lower her temperature. Because Mary was in so much pain, Louisa did even the most miniscule tasks for her. Sweet Mary appreciated this, and she tried to encourage her mother every day by declaring that she was on the mend. But Louisa knew her daughter too well.

"How dreadfully, dreadfully thin she has got, though her face is beginning to look more red, I think," she wrote to Lily.[6]

Corage was a wonderful place for Mary to heal. The wind carried with it the sound of the sea and rustled through the pines. The scent of the trees mingled with the scent of the sea and delighted the MacDonalds.

To the delight of everyone, they acquired two new ponies from Henry Cecil, who had been a teacher at Sheffield

Academy with George's brother John. Henry lived at Boscombe with his consumptive wife, and after she passed away, he gifted her two shaggy Shetland ponies, Zephyr and Zoe, along with their harness and chaise, to the MacDonalds.

The "Z's" were a sweet repose for Louisa, who took them out on errands, though the family chided her for her lack of control over the ponies.

"I know you find it comical to watch them take me about, and it's true, I have no control over them, but I'm convinced they know the rules of the road and always get me where I'm meant to be!" she'd reply.

Mary's health improved for a time, and Ted's occasional visits seemed to revive her. Often, the two could be found in the parlor, Ted playing cello and Mary accompanying him on the piano. But Mary soon withdrew and lost interest in everything.

"Lammie is very cold. She goes out in a seal skin in the sun and still isn't warm," Grace observed. "I am so glad that Papa is a bit better, but oh, why does Mary get worse?"

Although George was writing novels at a rate very few authors could match, his work was continually denigrated by prominent critics who wanted to be entertained rather than enlightened. In addition, British publishers were paying him less than they had been previously, and dishonest American publishers refused to pay him the royalties he deserved. This compounded the family's financial strain.

The cost to raise such a large family—one that included many teenagers with varying needs, a son in medical school, a daughter at the Slade School of Fine Art, and George and Mary with their ever-mounting medical bills—was enormous. Fortunately, Louisa's great-aunt had left her a hundred-pound legacy that helped cover Greville's medical school fees, and an uncle offered him a clerkship in his stockbroking office.

"I hoped in God, and will hope in Him even if that worst of earthly evils, debt, should overwhelm me," George said. "But I will not stray from God's calling to serve the next generation through my books."

"We must remember that every time things are at their

lowest, God intervenes," he and Louisa often reminded each other.

Louisa also created a plan to stabilize their finances. "We've enjoyed putting on plays for years now, and I've even had my little collection of dramas published. I know it's just been a family hobby, but I say we begin presenting our plays to the public."

The girls were thrilled at the prospect and got busy sewing costumes and painting backdrops. The possibility of presenting quality dramas was exciting to everyone—except their society-conscious relatives, a few longtime friends, and Greville. Undaunted, Louisa forged ahead.

"What society may say or do about it, I simply do not care. We are only taking up an art that has been unjustly undervalued and left too much to unfit representations," George told her.

"Why do you allow this, Papa?" Greville asked his father when he was home from college. "I can understand Mama and the girls doing plays, but why must my brothers have their education interrupted? Yes, Lily is a good actress, but the others are not, and besides, it's an embarrassment to me."

"I have my concerns, too," George answered. "But your mother is certain that God has given her this work. She believes this will help relieve my weariness, and I must assent to her interpretation of God's will. This is God's way of humbling me and delivering me of my worldly pride. Your mother is devoted to her family and her darlings' interests—and she is just as concerned about her sons' education."

He paused and looked Greville in the eyes. "You have no concept, my boy, of how deep your mother's love is for you—for you and your brothers and sisters. It's as if you were each her only chick. But I'm glad you confided in me. Remember, it's the shirking of duty, not the betrayal of feeling, that constitutes weakness."

Then Greville remembered the time a few years earlier when his mother had sat on the floor beside him for half the night while he lay in anguish till his sins were confessed, and how she brought the newness of dawn to his soul. He remembered the imperishable joy of a mother's miraculous healing.

The MacDonalds' first public play was *The Tetterbys*, performed at Miss Kingsbury's Convalescent Home in Hastings. It was a success both artistically and financially; the local press praised the "completeness of the production and Mrs. MacDonald's remarkable powers in character delineation." From then on, Louisa's organizational gift was turned to practical use; she was able to relieve George's financial burdens while also devotedly caring for her children.

Louisa also completed her passion project, a dramatization of the second part of *The Pilgrim's Progress*. A memorable moment came on March 8, 1877, George and Louisa's twenty-sixth wedding anniversary, when the family performed the play for the first time at Christchurch, Hampshire. The adaptation became their most successful production. The girls had painted thrilling designs on the large curtain backdrops and proudly called them the "Beulah curtains."

For a number of years, the MacDonalds gave performances throughout London. In the beginning, Ronald played the part of Greatheart in *Pilgrim's Progress*, but once George was persuaded to assume the role for a performance at Grosvenor House in London, the part became his.

"The girls are sewing you a majestic black robe and covering it with gold sequins," Louisa said. "With your blue eyes, flowing beard, and commanding voice, you're the perfect representation of this spiritual masterpiece."[7]

Princess Louise was present at their premiere. Twenty-five years later, when she was introduced to Winifred and learned that she was the daughter of George MacDonald, the princess said, "Oh, I saw him act once! I am right, am I not? He was the author of *Robert Falconer*? I think you would like to know that my mother—Queen Victoria, you know—gave that book to every one of her grandsons."[8]

While Louisa was busy with the plays and the children, George continued to write, despite his frequent ill health. His next novel, *The Marquis of Lossie*, was published in 1877.

The MacDonalds soon became even stronger friends with

the Cowper-Temples, who lived near the family's new home. The Cowper-Temples had decided to open the spacious grounds of their home at Broadlands for religious conferences. George became one of their most persuasive speakers, but this meant he was often gone that summer, so Louisa kept in touch through faithful letters.

> *Mrs. G.M.D. to her Husband at Broadlands.*
> *Corage, Boscombe,*
> *[Aug. 2, 1877]*
>
> *I keep picturing you to myself under the beeches. Comforting and inspiring other people—and I am not to hear your winged words. . . . Our darling little sick lamb is better certainly. . . . The sea and the pines are making such a sweet noise—I am at the open door-window after tea, Mary on the sofa behind it. Ted [Hughes] is mending some braid on her jacket. . . . If it were not for that dreadful fever! and the tearing cough! . . . Lily is well and very beautiful—as nearly perfect a woman as lives anywhere I think "here below."*[9]

Mrs. Georgina Cowper-Temple read the letter and, handing it back to George, exclaimed, "What a wife she is to you!"

Though the families had been friends since the early 1860s, their relationship deepened after the MacDonalds moved to Bournemouth. When the Cowper-Temples became aware of the MacDonalds' dire financial straits in March 1877, Georgina raised for them a large sum of money, the majority of which most likely came from her and her husband. The gift was given with the requirement that the MacDonalds could only use part for daily expenses and must use the rest to finally purchase a home of their own.

George normally refused gifts that he considered handouts, and he always insisted on treating gifts as loans, which he scrupulously repaid. But the Cowper-Temples' gift, given in love, he accepted as a gift from God. His letter to them reveals his humble gratitude:

Sometimes I do not know how to thank God for a special gift, because from him it is all and equally gift. But I can thank him for making me the surer that he is and that he does care for the sparrows. This kindness of yours also is only just like and your goodness to me and mine has been just a part of the Father's and in thanking you I thank him. . . . I would gladly owe no man anything but love. And for this which you and my other friends have given me I do not feel that I owe anything but love. What is given me is mine, and love to boot. If I did not believe in the love, however unmerited, I could not take the money. . . . The portion you allow me to use takes a load off me. It may be good for me however to have a few years in a house we can call our own, and therefore I think that, as God has sent me this towards one, he may be meaning that I shall be able to add to it in the years to come so that I may be able to build or buy someday.[10]

The gift came at the perfect time, for Mary's ill health could no longer be ignored and took precedence over building a home. That autumn, the MacDonalds decided they must use the new funds to take Mary to Italy in the hope that its warmer, more suitable climate would cure her.

Their friends at Broadlands assembled under the beech trees and prayed for Mary, who lay in her bed at Corage.

"Our poor pet Mary," said George with a sigh. "But Love is Lord of all, and all shall be well. I will trust."[11]

My Lord, I find that nothing else will do,
But follow where thou goest, sit at thy feet,
And where I have thee not, still run to meet.
Roses are scentless, hopeless are the morns,
Rest is but weakness, laughter crackling thorns,
If thou, the Truth, do not make them true:
Thou are my life, O Christ, and nothing else will do.
George MacDonald, *Diary of an Old Soul*, February 4

CHAPTER 17

THROUGH THE VALLEY OF SHADOWS

It is not the high summer long that is God's. The winter also is His. And into His winter He came to visit us. And all man's winters are His—the winter of our poverty, the winter of our sorrow, the winter of our unhappiness—even "the winter of our discontent."
George MacDonald, *Adela Cathcart*

Morning's sunlit dew and night's blaze of constellations seeped into Louisa's weary soul. The knowledge that the Almighty, Eternal Lord loved her, loved Mary, and loved her whole family banished doubt and bewilderment, giving her strength to rise each day and obey His commands.

It was a while before the doctor gave Mary permission to travel, but she rallied, and the family quickly made plans to leave England before winter arrived. Lily, Mary, Irene, and Ronald accompanied Louisa to Nervi, Italy, as did Mary's maid and Hatty Russell, their Italian-speaking friend. Hatty's mother lived in Nervi, which was a major reason the MacDonalds chose Italy as the place for Mary to heal.

At the time, Italy was in the throes of various internal revolutions. Victor Emmanuel II, the former King of Sardinia, had made himself King of Italy and was struggling to tie up loose ends after adding Rome to his realm. More prudent travelers would have avoided Italy, but the MacDonalds were not concerned with current events.

"Louisa, I know more of the politics of the kingdom of heaven than I do of the kingdoms of this world," George often said.

Winifred and Greville stayed in England and relished the chance to care for their father, who had moved back to The Retreat to work but was ill once again with bronchitis and pleurisy. Greville, one of only three out of seven candidates who had passed their medical examinations, often came to The Retreat in the evenings to help care for George.

"He is a boy no longer. . . . One thing he sees plainly—the

elevating power of suffering," George wrote to Louisa.

Surrounded by boxes, George and the children who remained in England oversaw preparations for textile designer William Morris to take over The Retreat. Reluctantly, they left their beloved horses; the ponies were housed with the Cowper-Temples, and the mare was sold. They moved all their boxes to the River Villa next door, which they decided to keep for Greville and in which he and one of his school friends would live. Finally, they placed Corage in an agent's care.

The same dauntless resolve that Louisa had often had to muster would conquer the seemingly impassable mountain of sickness that again separated her family. Deep within, she knew joy's light could be found in life's pain.

Louisa and her party crossed the English Channel at Folkstone, then took a train south. Louisa was reluctant to travel in a coupe, a half-compartment at the end of a train, but it was necessary for Mary's comfort.

"You must not mind that," George insisted. "I see more and more how to be able to trust, and I think we shall always find that we can get through."

But they were both concerned they would not be able to afford passage to Italy for him and the remaining children that winter.

Nervi is a charming village near Genoa and Portofino in northwest Italy. When the MacDonalds arrived, the town was surrounded by olive and citrus groves, and beautiful villas stood along its shore. Its climate was favored by those who, like Mary, had pulmonary illnesses. Refreshing winds swirled over the cliffs from which the famous Torro Gropallo overlooked the sea. The winter months were known for being particularly pleasant.

After seeing an advertisement for the Palazzo Cattaneo, Louisa decided to rent the villa for the winter because it was modestly priced. Its spacious citrus gardens gave off glorious scents, and the terraced hillside overlooked the sparkling sea. Mary, who had often longed to travel abroad, found Italy refreshing and restorative, although she did miss Ted Hughes.

George struggled with being separated from Louisa and four of his children. Nothing seemed to be working out with his book publishers, and his health, his finances, and Mary's plight weighed heavily on his heart. He felt like a bruised reed, ready to break. He wrote to Louisa, admitting his spiritual doubts:

> *G.M.D. to his Wife.*
>
> *. . . Never had I so many worldly mosquitoes about me, but they don't get within my curtains much. I grow surer and surer. Winnie nurses me so sweetly . . . and I don't think I shall be long ill. I have seldom been quieter in mind than this day*—*but* I am sometimes hard put to it with the Apollyon of unbelief. . . .[1]

George never worried about sharing his doubts or despair with Louisa. She knew that he never truly doubted the Life and Light that shone behind his sorrows. He penned cries to God in his *Diary of an Old Soul*.

> *Have pity on us for the look of things*
> *When blank denial stares us in the face.*
> *Although the serpent-mask have lied before,*
> *It fascinates the bird that darkling sings,*
> *And numbs the little prayer-bird's beating wings;*[2]

> *Through all the fog, through all earth's wintery sighs,*
> *I scent Thy spring, I feel the eternal air,*
> *Warm, soft, and dewy, filled with flowery eyes,*
> *And gentle, murmuring motions everywhere—*
> *Of life in heart, and tree, and brook, and moss;*
> *Thy breath wakes beauty, love, and bliss, and prayer,*
> *And strength to hang with nails upon thy cross.*[3]

The mild Italian fall was working wonders for Mary, revitalizing both her body and her spirit. Cautiously hopeful, Louisa began considering the possibility of performing her dramas in Italy to help with finances. A large English-speaking community lived in the resort area of Genoa, and they assured her they would welcome her dramatic performances.

"Please pack all of our costumes and backdrops and send them to me," Louisa wrote to Grace. "Our plays could greatly improve our family finances."

"I admit that acting is a great relief to me," George confessed. "It justifies our going to Italy."

After paying all their bills, George was left with fifty pounds—not enough to reunite his family in Italy. At the insistence of the Cowper-Temples, he accepted their gift of two hundred pounds. This gift bolstered his hope that the family would be together in Italy for Christmas.

"I did try to refuse it, Louisa," he explained, "but they wouldn't listen."

Then he surprised her with wonderful news. The previous year, he had been presented to Her Royal Highness Princess Alice, whom he found charming and unpretentious. He believed this introduction was the catalyst for the Queen's decision to give him a Civil List pension, which meant more reliable finances. "The Queen is not as stingy as I had predicted," George told Winnie with a wink.

G.M.D. to his Wife.
Corage,
Nov. 2, 1877.

... We are now getting ready to start, though we cannot be out by your birthday. My love and thanks to you for being what you are and have been to me. May your birthday be hopeful, for hope is sure to come right if only we go on hoping long enough. My love to my Mary on her mother's birthday [November 5th]. I never forget the lark's nest I found the morning she was born. . . . [Here comes a letter] from Lord Beaconsfield's secretary, telling me that the Queen has given me one hundred pounds a year. Isn't it nice? I must send you the news for your birthday. . . . Mrs. Temple thinks it is the Princess Alice's

doing, but Mr. Russell Gurney rather thinks it is Lord Beaconsfield's, moved by late reviews.[4]

Just as they had hoped, George and his chicks left to join Louisa and hers in Italy. Louisa and Ronald met them at the Genoa station and brought them to the villa, where George hurried up the stairs to Mary's room and found her bright in spirit but much thinner than the last time he had seen her.

"I feel just like a badly cut nine-pin," she said with a smile. "When I try to stand up, I tumble over before the ball touches me!"

When George left Mary's room, the others made him close his eyes while they led him through a vast oval hall. They took him to a small private chapel, hidden behind a trellis, lined with crucifixes, with a marble Madonna and altar at the front. Behind a curtain, one of his daughters was playing "Abide with Me."

"I am deeply moved," he told his brood. "We have a little core of rest in the heart of the home—a chamber opening out into the infinite. But we must remember that this chapel fulfills its purpose only if we have a similar chamber within our hearts where the Son of Man reigns."

"This is a wonderful house," George said later, complimenting Louisa on her find. "We look straight south, nearly right down onto the Mediterranean. And look at the marvelous colors! I've been composing a poem about it. How do you like some of these stanzas?

"Few curtains cloud the windows wide,
Few carpets warm the spaces great;
On marble floors the footsteps slide,
Or stalk on tiles and slabs of slate.

"With room enough for day and night,
And some for welcome friends' repose:
Room, room, blest room, in width and height,
For verse to burgeon out of prose.

> "And so the house, with room for guest,
> With lofty hall, and stairways wide,
> With quiet cell for hoping rest,
> Thank God! has all our need supplied."⁵

His study had a window that let him look over the vast dining hall like "a benignant gnome, or evil djinn!"

"And did you know, my Love, that when you play the piano your music drifts up to where I am working in my study? The view is so lovely I must refrain from wasting my days staring out at the Ligurian Sea and the sailing ships that dot the clear waters."

The family was elated to finally be together again. It was a great relief to Louisa, especially, for she had been urging George to make haste because of Mary's declining health. She wanted Ted to come for Christmas, too, and wondered if they should urge him to hurry and marry Mary.

"Wouldn't you have married me if I were dying?" she asked George.

"Of course! But it could be that Ted is shy. And it's up to him to decide."

Although Ted couldn't join them for Christmas, the Russell Gurneys could. To celebrate, the MacDonalds opened a special bottle of wine and offered words of gratitude for all that God had done.

For Christmas that year, George composed a poem for his family and friends.

Written for my Friends, Christmas, 1877, Nervi.

> *They all were looking for a king*
> *To slay their foes, and lift them high:*
> *He came a little baby thing*
> *That made a woman cry.*
>
> *O Son of Man, to right my lot*
> *Nought but thy presence can avail;*
> *Yet on the road thy wheels are not,*

Nor on the sea thy sail.

> *My why or when thou wilt not heed,*
> *But come down thine own secret stair,*
> *That thou may'st answer all my need,*
> *Yea, every by-gone prayer.*[6]

"You've always had a passion for stairways," Louisa said with a smile when she had finished reading the poem.

The Italian coast delighted the MacDonalds. The air was cleaner, the sunsets were stunning, and the solitude permeated their lives.

"These sunsets are different from English or American or even Algerian sunsets," George said, looking out to sea. "Their prevailing characteristic is the soft blending of dull, tender colors, as if every hue were wrapped up in its own twilight—a twilight made of thoughts of other colors—like the hues of a Roman scarf."

"I wish I could memorize each sunset," Louisa replied, knowing that they both feared the approaching sunset of Mary's life.

By this point, Mary was merely skin and bones. Thankfully, Ted came to Nervi in early January, which temporarily revived her. She suffered meekly, and all the while her family felt the weight of her decline.

"The sweetness of her spirit never seems to fail," Ronald observed.

Indeed, her spirit continued to touch each soul, and it never diminished as her life slowly ebbed away. On April 27, 1878, Mary Josephine died at Nervi, three months before her twenty-fifth birthday, having been engaged to Ted for four years. Her desire for life and her strong sense of its worth endured till the end, and when she left, she was at peace.

"She was born into the other world the same day that my mother was born into this," Louisa wrote to Greville. "She died clinging to us, to her Ted, and to the beauty of the earth. Her dear sisters made her a covering from the silk of her wedding dress."

Louisa was shaken to the very foundations of her soul. She had spent so many years nursing, and now there was nothing more to do. Her arms were empty. Her daughter had been taken away. Life seemed intolerable, and it would take time to grow accustomed to the loss.

"Each Love of your brave mother's heart is a whole world placed in it," George told his children as they grieved. "And when these most urgent duties are torn from her, the loss is not less terrible that ten other darling worlds remain hungry for her care."

Marriage and childbearing, poverty and hardship, bitter losses and empty hands all culminated in Louisa's tears. She grieved for many months. Exhausted from caring for Mary and George, Louisa used a wheelchair when she needed to move about or leave the house. Greville, anxious for her, traveled to Italy for the summer. He was surprised to see his father in such good health and his mother frail and barely able to move about the house.

While he was there, Greville and his siblings, and sometimes their father, spent every day that summer in their little bay, where they would swim out to the peninsula. This gave Greville the chance to get to know his younger brother Maurice, and they had long talks about chemistry, physics, and evolution. Greville did not know then that this would be the last time he would ever see Maurice.

Louisa knew her family was concerned for her. "I must choose to join my husband in the rejoicing bondage of this world," she resolved, and slowly began the task.

During this period of sorrow, Octavia Hill came to visit. She was on the verge of a breakdown and traveled to Italy to recover from the strain of managing her housing plans for the poor. She didn't have a spouse in whom she could find support and solace, so she was beyond grateful that the MacDonalds welcomed her whenever she needed a respite.

George, seeing Octavia's strain, was grateful that Louisa had always been his support and comfort. Their marriage was strengthened by their spirits, which were awakened toward God and His grace. Through joy or sorrow, all true love is sacramental, they knew—each must abandon themselves to the other in order to participate in the reality that is God.

For Louisa's birthday, George wrote her a very personal poem to help with her grief.

Porto Fino, November 5, 1878.

To tell thee that our blessed child
Is watching thee from somewhere nigh,
Mourns with thee when thy agony grows wild,
Sits sometimes by thy bed while slow the hours go by,

Were but to mock thy weary pain
With pleasant fancies of a half-held creed,
To gather up and offer thee again
What thou hadst cast away as nothing to thy need.

But when the Shepherd great was dead
Death did but let the Shepherd's glory out:
She heard his voice and followed where he led—
He were no Shepherd now, not leading her about.

Take courage fresh, my Wife, this day
Step out with me to find her new abode;
We go together, cannot lose the way,
The wearier our feet, the shorter still the road.

Let us go on. We do not care
For aught but life that is all one with love:
We seek not death, but still we climb the stair
Where death is one wide landing to the rooms above.[7]

When their tenancy at the Palazzo Cattaneo ended, the MacDonalds moved to the Villa Barratta in Portofino. It was a romantic villa that overlooked the bay, which was filled with yachts and sailing vessels, and Rapallo on the other side. Miles of terraces, lush palms, and maritime pine filled the landscape.

Portofino rests on a little isthmus, and its quaint shops and outdoor restaurants add to its charm.

"We have such a domestic, secluded, wonderful life here," Lilia remarked, "and we see three times as much of Papa as we used to. But he's still hard at work writing all the time. And isn't it marvelous that even in the winter this country is lovely?"

While the climate had not cured Mary, Louisa saw that George was benefitting from the Italian sea and sun.

"I feel better than I have ever felt before," he said. "Today I climbed up the hill to breathe the clean air and it was an easy task. It seems as if both bronchitis and asthma have taken flight. It must be because this is the most beautiful area I have ever seen."

"Then I insist we stay," Louisa replied. "It's much cheaper than England, and the children have never had as much fun outdoors as they're having here. Also, I heard that there's a young lady from Florence, a Miss Verita, who cannot speak a word of English and is looking for a place to stay. I say we have her come and live with us and teach us Italian."

George spent a great deal of time in his study, examining Scripture and writing. He had become particularly interested in Greek and began comparing variations in the earliest Biblical texts. "Papa and Greville are Greek-Testamenting together," Louisa often announced to the others.

There in his study, George completed two more novels, *Paul Faber, Surgeon*, and *Sir Gibbie*. He knew he had to keep up a steady pace because he was being paid less and less for each novel. At the end of 1878, he found that he had only made approximately half of what he'd made the year before.

"Papa," Greville said after reading his father's newest works, "I think *Sir Gibbie* is the most picturesque of your Scottish stories. I enjoyed the deep truths you bring out from the commonest things, and through the dear, mute street creature—who would ever expect such a one to grow into a Christ figure?"

Readers also enjoyed *Sir Gibbie*, and it became one of George's most beloved novels.

It took about a year for the family to adjust to Mary's death. Then, in February 1879, fifteen-year-old Maurice was suddenly stricken by pneumonia. He battled it for eighteen days but died on March 5. Many believe that George based the character of Gibbie on Maurice's meek and gentle spirit.

George and Louisa had cherished Maurice and had often marveled at his blameless soul and great mind. Both had hoped he would become a Christian leader. Louisa sometimes referred to him as "angelic" because of his quiet, ready smile. But he also had a keen wit and a flair for the dramatic. He was adept at charades and drama, and his mother often chided him for being the "funny-man" of the family. His only fault, insisted Louisa, was that he overexerted himself. Thin and agile, he was never one to sit still, and he liked his reputation for being the best among his brothers at swimming and diving.

"My darling Maurice," she had often told him, "you do everything with such gusto! You walk too far, you swim too long, and you worry me so with the way you wander about in the wet and rain. This is why you are so often ill."

Throughout the eighteen days of Maurice's illness, Louisa nursed him tirelessly while Lily, Grace, Robert—by then called Bob—and Ronald helped as best they could. Ever by his side, Louisa never slept unless her children forced her to rest.

"I'm glad to say that your mother had an hour and a half of rest last night," George told the family. "She had begun talking nonsense—I'm hoping that bit of rest has restored her senses. We ask God for a little star of hope, but if not, may He give us strength to help our dear Maurice to die."

One morning, taking Maurice's hand, George quoted Scripture: "Let patience have her perfect work, that ye may be perfect and entire, wanting nothing."[8]

A minute later, Maurice looked up and asked, "Would you please repeat that verse, Papa?" George was deeply affected by this request.

Early in the morning on March 5, Maurice's screams startled the family awake. He was hemorrhaging from his lungs, and he died at two o'clock that afternoon.

The family used some silk that had been intended for Mary's wedding dress as a burial cloth. On the silk, Maurice's sisters stitched the emblem of a crimson cross, the same insignia they had stitched on Greatheart's costume for *The Pilgrim's Progress*, because Maurice had stepped into the role whenever George was unavailable.

They buried Maurice by moonlight on March 6. Ronald and Bob carried his coffin up the steep, stony path and placed it beneath a large boulder that would shield him from the sea spray. The rest of the family followed silently behind, and the Reverend Woodruff from Nervi presided over a simple graveside service while Robert held the lantern.

"I am enraged that the church will not allow us to bury him in their graveyard," George told Louisa. "And it is ridiculous that we cannot bury him with Mary."

"Dearest Bear, despite Rome's denial, Maurice will consecrate these Italian rocks for all time," Louisa said as she took his hand in hers. "And we will see him every day. The Castello Brown near the church is in sight of our home, and the maritime pine and cypress will keep solemn watch over him."

Reality is a harsh and stunning superintendent, which the MacDonalds realized after losing two children within a year. Day to night, birth to death—the magnificence of light can only be realized when darkness has overwhelmed one and is then overcome by the illumination of God's sovereignty.

> *Death, like high faith, levelling, lifteth all.*
> *When I awake, my daughter and my son,*
> *Grown sister and brother, in my arms shall fall,*
> *Tenfold my girl and boy.*
> George MacDonald, *Diary of an Old Soul,* January 4

CHAPTER 18

A SLOW AND CERTAIN LIGHT

But there is no veil like light—no adamantine armor against hurt like the truth.
George MacDonald, *The Marquis of Lossie*

After the loss of Mary and Maurice, Louisa did the one thing she knew to do: she knelt to pray and cried out to God.

"How shall I be patient? How shall I submit to this?" she asked her Savior.

She found some solace in the knowledge that Mary and Maurice were together. And despite everything, God had brought the family to Italy, where George found rest for his tired brain and health for his ailing body. Louisa now knew her primary duty was to keep him from returning to the harsh English winters.

"And what about my children?" she wondered. "How are they processing more loss? I must listen to their hearts and hurts."

Her hands gently smoothed the pages of her Bible as she sought solace in His word. "Have mercy on us, O God. Show us the way through this," she prayed.

The old, conventional forms of religion's comforting words were utterly useless—Louisa knew she must teach her children that it is fine to admit anger and doubt. They had to fight what George called "the Apollyon of unbelief" and wrestle through tragedy together. Years later, Greville wrote of his father and mother's tranquility during this time of grief. This characteristic, always present in George, also arose in Louisa whenever wisdom and courage were demanded of her.

But this time, George's grief was acute, overwhelming, and prolonged.

"I think if I am to come to terms with Maurice's death, I need to apply my grief to my writing," he decided. "I know of death and its trappings, but I believe in life and the resurrection."

Gradually, he found healing, mainly by writing a calendar poem with a new verse for each day of the year. In the verses—prayers to God—George addressed his doubts, anguish, and desire for insight and hope. He called the finished poem *A Book of Strife in the Form of the Diary of an Old Soul*, and it was published in 1880. When John Ruskin received a copy, he lauded it as "one of the three great sacred poems of the nineteenth century" during his Oxford Lectures.[1]

Seventy-two years later, on Christmas Day, 1952, C. S. Lewis gave his future wife, Joy Davidman, a copy of the book, by then known as *Diary of an Old Soul*. Lewis had somehow obtained a first-edition copy, with an inscription by George on the front page.

Not long after Maurice's death, the MacDonalds received word that Richard Gilder was ill and needed a change of climate. George and Louisa insisted that Richard, his wife Helena, and their son Rodman visit them at Villa Barratta. Louisa's deeply weary heart found respite in caring for Richard, and she even encouraged Richard and Helena to leave their little boy with her while they went to Pisa and Rome for a healing holiday.

Neither George nor Louisa ever hid their grief from their children—but they did not dwell upon it, either. They focused on their hope and on God's grace. George found a quiet joy in knowing that his books were increasingly influencing the spiritual lives of his readers, and Louisa kept her eyes on the horizon and continued on, doing the next thing. She knew that caring for Rodman was part of God's plan to heal her family.

"Isn't he bright and dear?" Louisa asked her family as she held the boy. "He's a darling of darlings, and we are all blessed to see his sweet face and be kissed by his little lips!"

Her family knew Louisa needed to stay busy, so they helped her with the plays while little Rodman watched and copied them. Acting in the two *Pilgrims Progress* dramas brought solace to the entire family—Bunyan's spiritual truths guided them through their grief. They also added *Macbeth* and Corneille's *Polyeuctus* to their repertoire.

During the summers between 1879 and 1887, the MacDonalds performed in Genoa and all over England and Scotland. With such a large company of performers, who often needed Mama's medical care, Louisa stayed busy, which was the best medicine for her sorrow. Everywhere they went, they were received with acclaim. Lilia was the most talented, and she sparkled in whatever role she played. When they performed *The Pilgrim's Progress*, she always played Christiana. The set was creatively crafted, worthy of high praise. Louisa and her daughters had sewn and embroidered the curtains that replaced the scenery backdrops, and for music there was a piano as well as the occasional violin to accompany the actors as they sang.

"I believe we have become a company of acting strollers— I mean strolling actors!" George said with a wink. "And while so many do not approve of our enterprise, I do believe, dear Louisa, that your interpretation of *Pilgrim's Progress* leaves a profound impression on those who see it."

Louisa chuckled at his play on words. She was glad to see her Greatheart happy again.

"It does touch my heart that our audiences always respond to Bunyan's message," she said. "And the words' beauty and joy are so very important for us to share. Besides, these plays have provided the funds to spend half of every year in Italy."

They were able to stay at Corage when they returned to England, and they even considered settling there again. They spent Christmas in Bournemouth, but George's ill health soon returned.

"We must return to Italy permanently," Louisa said one day as she wiped his brow. She needed to muster grit if she was going to accomplish this. She would have to pack and ship trunks full of personal belongings, travel across the English Channel with an invalid, find a new home in Italy, and learn Italian.

George agreed with her plan. "I'm not able to write here— my health prevents it."

Fortunately, they still had the large sum the Cowper-Temples had given them and specifically designated for a permanent home. Many prominent members of society had contributed to the gift: Princess Alice, the Earl and Countess of Ducie, Lord and Lady Darnley, Lord Lawrence, Baroness Paul Ralli, the Russell Gurneys, the Charringtons, the Mathesons, the Miss Hills, and Mr. and Mrs. C. Edmund Maurice. Relatives, friends, and even old servants contributed as well. With the funds, the MacDonalds were finally able to build a home in Bordighera, Italy, where they believed George's lungs would heal.

One can see the French coast from Bordighera, which is located on Cape Sant'Ampelio just twelve miles from France. The Maritime Alps meet the sea here and cause warm, dry winds that create a mild winter climate, so the town was the perfect place for George to live and work. An extensive beach separates the town from the sea, which is usually calm and serene. Twice as many English as Italians lived in Bordighera while the MacDonalds were there; the expats enjoyed the yellow stucco buildings and tiled streets of the picturesque town.

Because the temperature never falls below freezing, Bordighera is surrounded by fragrant, vibrant flowers, olive and citrus trees, and majestic palms whose fronds are used on Palm Sunday at the Vatican.

But Lily was not excited about returning to Italy. She'd have preferred to join Octavia Hill in her work with the poor. Nevertheless, she decided to remain with her family. Besides, she especially enjoyed portraying Christiana, a character whose personality was a mirror of her own.

"I shall never be able to work for Miss Octavia. How can I give up that hope?" she asked sadly.[2] But she did give up that hope, perhaps because she had a premonition of the future sorrows that would befall her family and require her healing touch of kindness.

The family stayed at Casa Patrick while George designed their new home, Casa Coraggio. They chose a lot directly across from a Scottish Presbyterian church, but not because they planned to attend services there—they chose to worship at All Saints Church instead.

Casa Coraggio was designed with the study George had always desired, more accommodations than the family required, and a giant living room that measured fifty-two feet by twenty-six feet by thirteen feet, with a third of it curtained off to hide a pipe organ. The space could also be used as a dining room.

A large, luminous kitchen was built so Louisa could cook for her sizeable family and numerous guests. The exterior of Casa Coraggio was lush with greenery; evergreen creepers and ivy hugged its walls.

Because their furniture would not arrive for many months, the family set to work making some. Following Louisa's can-do example, they each got busy using their gifts. While the boys assembled chairs and ottomans, Lilia learned to upholster. Louisa's sitting room was painted a soft red, and Grace added a eucalyptus-leaf motif to the walls. Everyone pitched in to paint rooms and stain woodwork.

Because they planned to use the great room for entertaining, the family took extra care in decorating it. The dark-blue velvet curtains complimented the olive-green walls, and colorful vases and carefully placed throws were spread about the room. The finishing touch was George's father's chair, judiciously placed at the center of the room for George to conduct his readings.

"Dante said the highest property increases to each by the sharing of it with others," George said as he looked about their finished home. "Louisa, we certainly have enlarged the place of our tent, as Scripture says!"

"This home will be perfect for gathering our family and anyone who wants to join us on Sundays," said Louisa. "Everyone loves to come and listen to you read and teach."

They had not been in Italy long before Louisa became acquainted with an Englishwoman, Mrs. Gertrude Desaint, who was destitute and quite ill. Her French husband had abandoned her and their two young daughters, Honey and Joan. Louisa insisted that Gertrude and her daughters come and live with the MacDonalds, and the MacDonald women immediately got to work loving and educating Honey and Joan.

When the MacDonalds returned to England in 1880 to earn enough money to ship the remainder of their possessions to Casa Coraggio, they brought the Desaints with them and placed Gertrude in a hospital so her consumption could be treated. After she had partially recovered, she lived with them for seven years, and Louisa cared for her until she passed away. The MacDonalds then adopted Honey and Joan—otherwise, the girls would certainly have been sent to a workhouse.

Another set of siblings, Percy Harrat and his little brother, also joined the MacDonald household. Percy and Irene could often be found wandering along the coast, painting and watching the sun as it danced on the water.

Although she knew the English colony at Bordighera gossiped about the orphans she took in, Louisa was duty bound to care for them. Her heart always had room for more. Throughout her life, she performed an almost uncountable number of kind and generous acts.

Once Casa Coraggio was complete, the family opened it to all who wanted to join them for Sunday gatherings and Wednesday afternoon "At-Homes," when George would read. During the winters, he taught courses on Dante and Shakespeare. Sometimes one hundred or more people would visit on Sundays, and all were deeply moved by the MacDonalds' personal, hospitable welcome.

To grow closer to the community and share her gifts, Louisa volunteered as the church organist and also trained the choir. On Sunday evenings, she would play the great-room organ and a few choir members would sing psalms and hymns. When the clock struck eight, George would sit in his chair by the open fire, beneath the carved mantle braced by wooden figures of St. Christopher and St. Elizabeth of Hungary, and read to the guests.

Because there were no evening services in Bordighera, men and women of various schools of thought came to Coraggio on Sunday evenings. Even the Duke of Argyll and the Archbishop of Canterbury visited. People flocked to hear George because he focused his Sunday evening teachings on love rather than on fear.[3]

Though the MacDonalds had very little to spare, they shared lavishly with the community. Bernard and George MacKay would greet visitors at the door, while Percy and his brother would usher them up the stunning staircase. Graceful, tactful Lily always had just the right greeting for her parents' many guests. Family and visitors alike would listen quietly as George taught; then he would kneel so all would join him in opening their hearts to God. Finally, he would speak a blessing that lingered in the visitors' hearts as they descended the stone stairs into the starry Italian night, accompanied by Louisa's rendition of Handel's "Largo."

"I was brought up on Handel," she would tell those who complimented her playing.

The MacDonald children would often gather around the piano and sing together. Irene, especially, had a beautiful, clear voice.

Years later, Prebendary Wilson Carlile[4] recalled spending a delightful evening at Casa Coraggio as a young man:

> *The picture of [MacDonald] sitting in his study is still fresh in my mind, though it is thirty years ago. His splendid hospitality with an almost empty pocket amazed me. His keen eye could see beauty and reveal it even when all around seemed ugly and repelling. He radiated Divine Love. . . . He often drew me to him and wanted to know the best I had recently seen in the worst criminals that were always passing through my hands and whose lives, so changed by God, shamed by their devotion the easy-going passivity of many religious people.*[5]

Christmas at Coraggio was always Louisa's favorite season, and it was especially wonderful when the children who were away at college were able to join the family. While preparing for the holiday, Louisa came up with a fantastic idea that would bless the entire community.

"My dear, Coraggio is the perfect place to present *tableaux vivants*," she told George.

"Tableaux vivants?" he asked.

"Yes." she replied. "You know, a 'living picture' put on by actors. They stay still and wear costumes and hold props—like living statues!"

She got to work, using her skills in stagecraft to create beautiful scenes, and at very little cost to the family. George played the aged Simeon who blessed the newborn King, and the other MacDonalds silently portrayed each person present at the Savior's birth.

The tableaux were a favorite of the Italian children of Bordighera, who joyfully came to see the silent scenes carefully positioned throughout the hall. Visitors were greeted by carols and a Christmas tree, and after the tableaux were done, the MacDonalds and their guests, young and old alike, would dance the Sir Roger de Coverley. Although Casa Coraggio was simply, even poorly, furnished, it did not lessen the beauty of the MacDonalds' hospitality. Lord Mount Temple even wrote of their generous hospitality in his *Memorial*s:

> ... *On Christmas Eve, we were dining in our little room looking on the olive wood, and we heard the sound of many voices, and looking out, lamps glimmered among the trees, and figures carrying lanterns and sheets of music. Who should they be but the dear MacDonald family visiting the houses of all the invalids in the place, to sing them carols and bring them the glad tidings of Christmas. The next day they had beautiful tableaux of the Annunciation, the Stable, the Angels, and the Shepherds, ending up with the San Sisto Madonna, in their wonderful room in the Coraggio, and they had invited the peasants to come and enjoy this, for them, novel representation of the event of the blessed Christmas-tide. That house, Coraggio, is the very heart of Bordighera, the rich core of it, always raying out to all around, and gathering them to itself.*[6]

These times of community were good for George. "Since I'm

so busy writing and have no time to call on others," George explained to Louisa, "I'm pleased that you don't mind opening our home one afternoon a week so I can see my friends."[7]

"Our friends enjoy it just as much," Louisa replied. "They wait in anticipation for you to ring the bell and seat yourself by the great fireplace."

Louisa was always there to receive the MacDonalds' evening guests. Once everyone had been welcomed, she and her children would flit about the room with trays of tea and cakes.

"This is wonderful!" Louisa told her family one night. "A local fisherman may find himself sitting next to an English aristocrat or even Lord Mount Temple himself!"

"And with the waltzes you play, Mama, our boys—in fact, all the young people in Bordighera—have gone mad over dancing!" Lilia remarked.

"We must never mind the trouble of hosting as long as we can bring others joy," Louisa often reminded her family. "And I think we should fly a flag from our rooftop when it's time for charades, just to make sure the town is prepared!"

The MacDonalds contributed greatly to the camaraderie of the little English colony; they always made sure no one was overlooked. As a result, the community adored Louisa and George. Some people even referred to George as "the blessed St. Mac" or "The Sage of Bordighera."

An example of the MacDonalds' outreach is the poem they distributed to their community. It was an invitation to a New Years' Eve bonfire:

Please come on Monday
The day after Sunday,
And mind that you start with
Something to part with;
A fire shall be ready
Glowing and steady
To receive it and burn it
And never return it.

We'll make it the tomb
For all sorts of gloom,
The out-of-door path
For every man's wrath.
All lying and hinting,
All jealous squinting,
All unkind talking
And each other balking,

Books that are silly,
Clothes outworn and chilly,
Hats, umbrellas or bonnets,
Dull letters, bad sonnets,
Whate'er to the furnace
By nature calls "Burn us!"
An ancient, bad temper
Will be noted no damper—
The fire will not scorn it
But glory to burn it!
Here every bad picture
Finds refuge from stricture;
Or any old grudge
That refuses to budge,

Let the fire's holy actions
Turn to ghostly abstractions.
All antimacassars,
All moth-egg amassers,
Old gloves and old feathers,
Old shoes and old leathers,
Greasy or tar-ry,
Bring all you can carry!
We would not deceive you:
The fire shall relieve you,
The world will feel better,
And so be your debtor.
Be welcome then—very—
And come and be merry!

Casa Coraggio,
Dec. 31st, 1885.

George and Louisa MacDonald
Bonfire at 7 p.m.
Dancing at 8.[8]

Creativity and intentionality were Louisa's gifts. She was able to pull things together in the most fun and unusual ways. Once, she invited everyone to Casa Coraggio for a night of dancing, but there was one requirement: all must arrive wearing white.[9]

"I don't care if they come wearing a sheet," she told her family. "Sheets, towels—they don't need anything expensive or elaborate, they just need to be covered in white! I'll make sure the supper table is covered with white, and all the food will be white too!"

"That was one of your finest, most amusing creations yet," George told her after the guests had gone home.

On another occasion, the family held a concert at Coraggio and used all the proceeds to help the local Catholic church pay its debts.

Eventually, the entire community wanted to see the plays they had heard so much about, so the MacDonalds erected a stage at the end of the great room.

"It's a good thing we designed this room to be so large,"

George mused one afternoon as he watched his favorite room shrink.

"Did you notice that when we were performing *Domestic Economy*, the audience laughed so hard we nearly broke down with them?" Lilia asked as they reviewed their latest production.

As their plays became popular in Italy, they rented the Theatre of Cannes on the French Riviera to perform Shakespeare's *Twelfth Night*. They charged thirty francs per seat.

"The manager said that when he has engaged the best of French artists, he can barely sell a seat, but with our troupe, the audience is beyond belief!" Louisa told George as she repaired costumes for their next production.

When one considers all that Louisa accomplished during those trying years, it's a remarkable testament to what God can do in and through people despite their circumstances.

Still, those years held some of the MacDonalds' happiest days. On the rare quiet ones, they would take walks to enjoy lazy afternoons, embrace the tranquility of the gardens, and explore the charming streets of Bordighera. Louisa's heart yearned for beauty and nature; they balanced all that she was creating and managing.

Meanwhile, George was writing—constantly writing. Between 1881 and 1883, he wrote seven books: *Mary Marston*, *Warlock O' Glenwarlock*, *Weighed and Wanting*, *A Dish of Orts*, *The Princess and Curdie*, *The Gifts of the Child Christ*, and *Donal Grant*. All were published during his time at Bordighera.

Now that the children were reaching adulthood, household changes were inevitable. Greville had finished medical school and decided to establish himself in London; Ronald enrolled as an undergraduate at Trinity College, Oxford to study history; and Robert, along with his cousin Frank Troup, joined the London office of J. J. Stevenson as architects.

Lilia, too, thought she would leave home; she had met Charlie Granet de la Rue, a handsome young man, when her family moved to the Italian coast. He was thin, with a distinguishable moustache, and he came from a prominent family who had made a fortune from cigarettes. He and Lilia were quite taken with each other, and the MacDonalds were fond of him too—Louisa especially, after Charlie agreed to appear in *Pilgrim's Progress*.

Charlie and Lilia's engagement was announced in August 1879, and Louisa was anxious to begin sewing clothes and decorations for the wedding. Unfortunately, the engagement did not last long. Although the couple was deeply in love, Charlie's family disapproved of Lilia's acting, and they threatened to cut off his inheritance. Most virulent was his aunt, who had charge of the family purse. She soon brought her nephew around to her view. He pleaded with Lilia to forsake the stage.

"I was taught that it is better to be poor and free than to be rich and in chains," Lilia told him. "You are choosing to be chained to your family's money and control."

Lilia was heartbroken, but she knew she had to say goodbye, and the engagement was called off in October 1880.

"Our poor Lily. I will never understand how that boy could turn around and side with his worldly old aunt who cares more for her money than anything or anyone. She never saw our Lily's golden heart," Louisa said to George.

"Well, he has his financial reward here on earth, and Lily has her suffering. But hers is a noble suffering, and she bears it as very few are able," George replied, his heart aching.

Although they were sad for Lilia, George and Louisa rejoiced when Grace met a young man named Kingsbury Jameson. He had just graduated from Cambridge, and he met Grace while she was on tour in England performing *Pilgrim's Progress*.

"Mama, what seemed like disaster struck when I was so suddenly taken ill—with the hall booked and the audience waiting. Wasn't it fortunate that Kingsbury agreed to help with the acting that evening? Otherwise our paths would never have crossed," Grace told her mother.

Kingsbury was about to be ordained as an Anglican priest and sent to the English community in Bordighera to act as assistant chaplain. It was a perfect match.

"Kingsbury is a good, true, earnest, and very loveable fellow," George said as he and Louisa watched the couple stroll hand in hand.

"His cousin Ellen tells me that he holds you in highest esteem and that your books greatly influenced his decision to become a minister," Louisa replied. "This is a true blessing."

That winter, Grace and Kingsbury became engaged. But it would be a long winter for Grace. Her lungs became diseased and her breathing was so severely affected that she was placed on a portable respirator. When she recovered, she and Kingsbury were married that April in Rome, which allowed the MacDonalds to finally see for themselves the sights of the Eternal City.

But there is a light that goes deeper than the will, a light that lights up the darkness behind it: that light can change your will, can make it truly yours and not another's—not the Shadow's. Into the created can pour itself the creating will, and so redeem it!
George MacDonald, *Lilith*

CHAPTER 19

A ROUGH SHAKING: SHIFTING GROUND AND GATHERED FRAGMENTS

... beauty is the only stuff in which Truth can be clothed; and you may, if you will, call Imagination the tailor that cuts her garments to fit her ...
George MacDonald, *A Dish of Orts*

Louisa woke to the moon shining on her face. Her anticipation made it hard to sleep. Quietly, she slid her legs over the edge of the bed and stood up. Putting on her shawl, she walked to the window and smiled at the light rising above the church steeple.

"Father, please be with our Grace tonight and with the precious baby she carries in her womb," she prayed.

The next day, March 17, 1882—St. Patrick's Day—Grace gave birth to Octavia Grace, George and Louisa's first grandchild, a little leprechaun. The new grandparents were delighted, especially because Kingsbury and Grace were living at Casa Coraggio, so Louisa could care for Grace and the baby. Grace was still not well, and her health was a constant source of concern for Louisa.

"Our granddaughter is a darling," Louisa told George as she held Octavia, gently caressing the curl peeking out from the wee girl's bonnet.

"But I am so worried about Grace," George replied.

Kingsbury decided to build a home just a few doors down from Casa Coraggio. It was his attempt to keep Grace's health from deteriorating further. They named it Casa Grazia, which means House of Grace. It was constructed of gray stones, with windows placed wherever possible to brighten the rooms, folding doors between rooms, and high ceilings to allow for airflow. They hung a hammock by the large bay window so Grace could spend time in the sun. But even with

all the accommodations, Grace died on May 5, 1884.
Little Octavia Grace was barely two years old.
Three days later, Louisa wrote to her sister Charlotte:

> *Her departure was far more terrible and difficult than Mary's. Oh—so terrible—but her cry of Father take me at the last was so fervent and strong. We knew it was a struggle after that. Surely sometimes Death comes to the saints in a Demon shape—especially those who have had no great knowledge of the struggles with him before."*[1]

The family buried Grace in the newly established Stranger's Cemetery in Bordighera. So many flowers were sent to Casa Coraggio that Louisa began to detest them, but when she saw how they flowed over Grace's grave, her heart found peace.

She and George would often visit their children's graves at Nervi and Portofino and remove the weeds so they could place fresh flowers on the headstones. Louisa found solace in planting lily roots on Grace's grave. They were Grace's favorite.

Although Grace was gone, Kingsbury and Octavia Grace remained in Bordighera, so Louisa took it upon herself to help her newly widowed son-in-law. She became a mother to Octavia, whom they called Little Grace, and this greatly helped Louisa as she grieved. Kingsbury remained close to his in-laws—he knew he desperately needed Louisa's help.

"Little Grace is a duck of ducks!" Louisa would often say. "She has the cutest pixieish laugh, and she coins the funniest words. She can be sweet and funny and naughty all in the span of four minutes!"

Every moment she spent with Little Grace shook Louisa further out of her grief. One morning, to wake Louisa, the girl announced, "Ou's are lazy 'ittle pigs, so get up!" Then she did her best imitation of the pigs she had recently seen. How could Louisa remain depressed when she had such a sweet child to love?

After the loss of their beloved Grace, the MacDonalds decided not to perform that summer. But as they did every year, they traveled to England, this time for George to give lectures and earn the money they always seemed to lack.

Greville moved to Italy to be closer to his family, but his hearing loss and inability to speak Italian meant he treated only three patients in the span of a year, so he returned to England. The following year, 1885, Bernard left for Christ's College, Cambridge, where he studied law, and George MacKay soon followed him to Cambridge to study natural science. He wanted to become a doctor like Greville. As for George, he published *The Tragedie of Hamlet*, *What's Mine's Mine*, and the second volume of *Unspoken Sermons*, which he lovingly dedicated to Louisa.

Throughout the late 1880s, the many rooms of Casa Coraggio were frequently filled with guests. Some were the children of wealthy parents, sent to Italy to be tutored and to study music with Louisa. Some were orphans or impoverished adults whom George and Louisa helped to become self-sufficient. Some were ill and needed nursing. Many friends and family members visited, too, which always made Louisa happy. As always, she enjoyed the busyness of caring for others.

The MacDonald home became known as the place where care was always available. Once, while walking down a street in Bordighera, Kingsbury and George MacKay were stopped by an elderly woman who asked, "Can you please direct me to the MacDonald Sanitorium? I hear that it is a very good one." Kingsbury and George assured her they had never heard of such a place and then scurried behind a wall to hide their amusement.

Casa Coraggio was a refuge when a great tragedy struck all of Italy. At five thirty in the morning on February 23, 1887, a terrible earthquake shook France and Italy and lasted almost four hours. The earth shook again the next morning, but less severely. The quake's epicenter was in Nice, its effects were felt from Milan to Marseille, and it triggered a tsunami that ran for two miles along the coast of Imperia, Italy. At least six hundred people were killed, mainly due to collapsing structures. Bordighera, only twenty miles from Nice, was hit with tremendous force.

The jolt was so violent that the MacDonalds had difficulty standing up as they clambered out of bed. Their hearts raced as the loud, rumbling earthquake rocked Coraggio, causing their furniture and other possessions to shift or fall.

"I remember some slight shakes we had at Algiers, but I never knew the real terror of one before this!" Louisa told her children.

"What a powerful shock!" George said. "It must be none other than God, for no lesser power could hold the earth like that, as if it were 'A very little thing,' and shake you as if your big house were a doll's fly!"[2]

Fortunately, they only had to deal with some broken jugs and vases, cracked plaster, and a defective tower as a result of the tremors.

"Well, I am glad that horrible tower has fallen," George said with a smile. "It must be because it wasn't built to my specifications!"

The following morning, as Louisa was sitting at the organ in the English church, a second fierce earthquake struck.

"The whole bulk of the building began to sway and shudder," she told the family, "just like the skin of a horse determined to get rid of a gadfly! And then the church began to shake so much that I felt sure it was going to collapse and bury me. So I pulled out all my stops and started playing the 'Hallelujah Chorus' as loud as I could!" She giggled as the family shook their heads in amazement.

"The earth shall quake 'neath them that trust the solid ground," George reminded them.

They busied themselves by bringing everything down to the ground floor, invited a family for meals, and did their best to avoid faints and hysterics. Each member of the family did all they could to calm the fears of Bordighera's visitors and native residents.

While most of the town's residents camped under Bordighera's olive trees, George remained in his study, writing, sound and firm—much like the figure of Christ that sat on top of one of his bookcases.

"Do you know, my Love," he asked Louisa, "that while all my books were flung to the floor during the quake, the Christ figure on the shelf was unaffected?"

The statue may have been spared, but devastation was everywhere.

"The English did not suffer any losses, unlike the Italians, and sadly, it is only the English who have behaved disgracefully," Louisa commented as she and the girls held a sewing party to help those who had lost clothing in the quake. "Such mystery shrouds suffering—we feel a holy awe when we are near those who are enduring so much. But like your Papa says, we shall trust in the Rock, our Savior, our solid ground."

George wrote through the upheaval and finished his next novel, *Home Again*. It was published soon after. As he worked in his study, he would often pause and listen to Louisa and the girls play their instruments and sing in harmony. He was quite proud of Louisa's musical abilities, especially because he could neither read music nor carry a tune. "All I understand about music," he often quipped, "is that some comes in and some stays out!"

Music had always been an important outlet for the MacDonald family. In addition to performing family concerts, Louisa and her daughters participated in musical events in the Bordighera community. Music provided Louisa with an important emotional channel and helped her cope as her children grew up and left home one by one.

Ronald had recently graduated from Trinity College and was now teaching at Clifton College, a boys' boarding school in Bristol. To his parents' joy, he announced his engagement to Louise Vivenda Blandy, a former student of John Ruskin. She was the daughter of Dr. Alfred and Ozillah Blandy and had been born in Baltimore, Maryland.

Dr. Blandy, originally from Bristol, was a professor of dental practice at the Baltimore College of Dental Surgery. When the Civil War broke out, Blandy, a secessionist,[3] brought his family back to England and set up a practice in London. The Blandys became part of the Victorian art world, and Louise exhibited promising artistic talent herself. In 1874, she began taking lessons from Ruskin and was soon invited to exhibit her paintings, which is probably how she met Ronald. They began dating during the fall of 1886. Because Ronald had been exposed to the arts while growing up, it was a perfect match. Louise remained an artist, and Ronald became a novelist and playwright.

After becoming engaged to Louise, Ronald was invited to teach at the Hill School in Pottstown, Pennsylvania. Before leaving for the United States, he brought Louise to Italy to stay at Coraggio for the winter. Although Louise was vivacious, she was also frail, and Ronald knew that she would benefit from Bordighera's climate and the tender care of his mother and sisters.

Everyone at Casa Coraggio adored Louise. After Ronald returned from his teaching post, he and Louise were married on July 7, 1888, in Hendon, London. In 1889, the newlyweds emigrated to America, where Ronald became the headmaster of Ravenscroft School in Asheville, North Carolina.[4]

The next MacDonald child to announce an engagement was Greville. In March of 1888, Greville, now practicing medicine in London, informed the family that he was about to marry Phoebe Winn, a nurse who was the matron of the hospital where he worked as an ear, nose, and throat surgeon.

Greville had always been the one about whom the family was most concerned, particularly because he struggled to prudently manage his affairs and projects. "He sorely needs an efficient, well-organized wife who will keep him in line," Irene often said.

But Greville's engagement didn't receive the same approval that Ronald's had.

"Phoebe is powerfully built, gentle as any woman need be in spite of a rather defiant mouth, sensible on every practical subject, and devoid of sentimentality," he wrote to his family.

Louisa was horrified by his description. "What a woman for a gentleman to marry! Come, Lily, we're going to London to put a stop to this!" She was much less willing to accept Greville's union than George was.

When they arrived in London, Greville was already married. To her credit, Louisa found Phoebe to be the perfect partner for her son. Phoebe was devoted to her new husband and proved herself again and again. She nursed Greville through his many ear problems and the serious blood poisoning he battled in 1891. Most importantly, she was practical and organized, so she complemented Greville's personality well.

Amid these additions to his family, George continued to write. He published *The Elect Lady* and the third volume of *Unspoken Sermons* and completed the first draft of *Lilith*.

But for the first time, Louisa disliked one of his books. She and George were at odds over *Lilith*. She found the narrative distressing and its hidden meanings too obscure. "I know you must walk where angels fear to tread, but this is a terrible book, though parts are beautiful," she told him.

George was not pleased.

"I think we should have Greville adjudicate," he told Louisa. "I am so tired of everything, yet I have so much more to learn. I wanted to show how sadness can harmonize with the far-calling chimes of our unfathomable faith, and to represent the return of mankind to our ultimate source in the Creator."[5]

George and Louisa always sought to agree, and if they could not, they would defer an issue and trust each other. Their marriage was a rare and remarkable example of the Biblical command to become one.

Honored that he should be trusted with such an important assignment, Greville read *Lilith* with gusto. After his parents' concern about his marriage, their trust in his judgement gave him the assurance he needed of his place in their hearts.

"Papa, Mama," Greville said when he had finished the book, "I was gripped by the story's uplifting mysticism and the way it fearlessly faces the questions that, for many, are obstacles to faith. So far from its being Papa's last book, as he keeps opining, I believe it is his finest, the Revelation of St. George the Divine."

Evidence of the book's brilliance also came in the form of a letter from H. G. Wells:

> From H. G. Wells to George MacDonald
> Working,
> Sept. 24/95.
>
> Dear Sir,
>
> I have been reading your Lilith *with exceptional interest. Curiously enough I have been at work on a book based on essentially the same idea, namely that, assuming more than three dimensions, it follows that there must be wonderful worlds nearer to us than breathing and closer than hands and feet. I have wanted to get into such kindred worlds for the purposes of romance for several years, but I've been bothered by the way. Our polarization and mirror business struck me as neat in the extreme. For my own part I've never quite got out of this world. In my own book* The Wonderful Visit *(of which I will send you a copy in the course of a week or so—so soon as it is published, that is) I have done the complement of* Lilith. *You make a man go out of this world of three-dimensions and I make a visitor from outside come into it. But different as the books are, the mother idea is the same beyond question. It's curious, is it not, that after this new idea has been lying neglected for years, it should be worked at simultaneously in this way?*
>
> *Yours very truly,*
> H. G. Wells.

Years later, Wells confided to Greville that he was always pleased to be associated with the memory of George MacDonald.[6]

Every year brought new challenges. The struggle to provide for the family's needs never seemed to end, and now the MacDonalds had their sons' college expenses to deal with as well. To avoid debt, George faithfully kept up his arduous writing schedule and his numerous speaking engagements. Louisa managed their drama performances and continued the family's outreach to the community.

"So many changes," Louisa sighed as she tried to sleep.

Even with all these transitions, the comings and goings, the sorrows and joys, the family's happiest years had been spent at Casa Coraggio. Louisa lay in bed one warm Italian night, thinking about it all. Her heart was full. She prayed for each child, then for her granddaughter Grace, and of course for her snoring husband who was sleeping beside her. She also thanked God for her new son-in-law and daughters-in-law. Her heart readily expanded to embrace these new additions.

How little are we our own! Existence is decreed us; love and suffering are appointed us. We may resist, we may modify; but we cannot help loving, and we cannot help dying. . . . Great in goodness, yea absolutely good, God must be, to have a right to make us—to compel our existence, and decree its laws!
George MacDonald, *What's Mine's Mine*

CHAPTER 20

THE PERFECTION OF SELFLESS LOVE

The good Father made his children to be joyful; only, ere they can enter into his joy, they must be like himself, ready to sacrifice joy to truth.
George MacDonald, "Self Denial" from *Unspoken Sermons*

Louisa shed silent tears as she read Ronald's letter by the light of a candle. Her elegant hands tried to smooth the pages, but she only smeared the heartbreaking words.

> *Dear Mammy, pray for me. It is curious that in this my greatest trouble I feel God's goodness & presence more sweetly & closely than ever before—thanks be to him. And yet I suffer awfully. . . . I would I had Greville to doctor & Lily to nurse.*[1]

Ronald was beside himself. His wife was severely ill. After giving birth to a daughter, Ozella, once-lively Louise was now just a broken shell. While trying to manage Ravenscroft, Ronald also had to care for baby Ozella and could only prepare for lessons when Louise was sleeping because she was hysterical and delirious and would not let him leave her side.

"We must see if Lily would want to go to America," Louisa told George.

Lilia agreed to the plan. "I'll be glad to go to them—I can't imagine that Ronald would want anyone there to help him besides me, though of course he would prefer you and Father."

Louisa wanted Lilia to wait until George MacKay and Irene returned to England, but Lilia preferred to leave immediately. On September 3, 1890, she boarded the SS *City of New York*. In her pocket she carried a note from her father:

> *I have thought of something to send you out of my waist-coat pocket—a valuable coin of the year you were born. I hope the post office will let it pass. My love to you all the voyage and to all eternity, forever and always. When you feel ill think how*

> *happy Ronald will be to see you. One of the handkerchiefs in the box your mother sends him is one of those Mr. Wylde gave me with my initials. Give my dear love. Nothing else is any good. Your loving father.*[2]

In Lilia's trunks were all sorts of handmade goodies Louisa had lovingly made for Ronald, Louise, and Ozella. But Lilia arrived too late. Louise had died on August 27.

Ronald greeted Lilia at the train in Asheville looking worn and thin.

Lilia wrote to her mother upon arriving.

> *The baby is indeed a little gem. The gentlest & most gracious little child I ever saw—every movement is full of sedate simplicity & she can hardly move her hands & arms without giving one a sense of benediction. . . . She is very pleased with the woolen ball you sent her . . .*[3]

"Oh!" Louisa said to George as she read the letter. "What lovely children we have. Ronald is wonderful. God must have something grand planned for him in his sufferings."

Indeed, the perfection of selfless love, the only eternal thing, was evident to Ronald in the life of his sister Lilia. In his grief, he learned that selfless love ignites the heart of every living thing in times of beauty, joy, wisdom, pain, and death.

Lilia stayed in America for eight months, until the school term had ended and Ronald had found a suitable helper. She returned to Bordighera in April 1891 to care for a dear friend, Eva Pym, who was suffering from advanced lung disease. Lilia was also concerned about her niece, Octavia Grace, who also suffered from lung disease. Sadly, Little Octavia died before Lilia arrived in Italy.

Little Octavia "was the young light of her Grannie's eyes," George wrote in a letter to C. E. Maurice. "She had had a sort of intermittent fever, for several weeks, but there seemed no immediate danger when she was seized with convulsions and died in half an hour. . . ."[4]

"I fear that Mother will never care for anything again,"

Lilia remarked to Winifred. "She virtually raised Little Octavia, and they were quite close."

By and by, Louisa's heart did heal, and she came to accept the tragic loss of her granddaughter.

George, reflecting on the loss of so many in his family, told Louisa, "Sometimes I want to ask, like Tolstoi, 'What is it all for?' but for the hope of the glory of God."[5]

Another tragedy occurred when the English Bank of the River Plate failed and Louisa's inheritance was lost—all two thousand pounds.

"There's a nut for us to crack without any kernel," said Louisa, trying to lighten the blow. "It doesn't seem very hard except for the children."[6]

But much happier events also occurred that year. Bernard, now practicing law, married Belinda Bird, and George wrote three books: *A Rough Shaking*, *The Flight of the Shadow*, and *There and Back*.

After Lilia returned from America, she immediately got to work caring for Eva. Louisa had also tried to help Eva, but Eva would only allow Lilia at her bedside. The tuberculosis spread rapidly through Eva's body, but Lilia never left her friend. Despite Lilia's valiant efforts, Eva died an agonizing death that summer.

Not surprisingly, Lilia had been exposed to the deadly disease, and soon afterward, she began to cough up blood.

"We must send for Greville," Louisa told George.

It seemed to everyone that all her life, Lilia had given, served, and sought to honor her parents and God. She never wavered in her faith, even when her engagement ended. Whenever she was asked about it, she always responded, "Things must have been for the best with me—and not me only—that is my comfort. And God gives me a light heart. I thank Him."[7]

Greville cared for Lily through the fear, anguish, hope, and courage she experienced during the course of her illness. He diagnosed her with tuberculosis, which had come on quickly and severely. Deeply distressed, her family prayed and hoped that she would recover. "Lilia has always been the most perfect woman we have ever known," said Greville with sorrow.

Throughout Lilia's illness, because of the family's financial needs, George was lecturing in Scotland. It was to be his final lecture series.

Brave Louisa kept him updated through detailed letters. Her children always marveled that she could muster new vigor from some fountain of youth whenever seemingly impossible demands were placed on her.

> *Mrs. G.M.D. to her Husband.*
> *Stock Rectory,*
> *July 15. Bob's birthday. [1891.]*
>
> *So very many thanks to you, my dearest, for your lovely letter this morning with bits in it about your country and the white clover (we have a good deal of it here—Irene put out a little vase full of it yesterday) and the words and thoughts about the Glory of the Lord—being the end of all—made Handel's "And the Glory of the Lord" go in my head right gloriously and preach lovely to me with your having shot it to me from your bow. Lily advances, though slowly.*
>
> *. . . Indeed it must come all right some day. . . . MacKay [now a medical student at Christ's College, Cambridge] is very sweet and helpful and combs Lily's hair or plays picquet with her and helps me with Orange Jelly and reads in your study and is generally good and slow and dull and funny and kind as his head allows him. . . . I think it is quite delightful your having this quiet bit of old world time, Dearest and Beautifullest. Yes I feel too very strongly what you say about its all being so futile . . .*[8]

Whenever Lilia felt up to it, Irene and Winifred would help Louisa carry her in her wheelchair to a nearby hillside to see the pines and breathe in the clear air. But as autumn progressed, a convulsive cough, lack of appetite, and high fever took over her frail body. Their "White Lily" revived long enough to welcome her father home from Scotland, and she died in his arms on Sunday, November 22, 1891, at the age of thirty-nine. Their very own Christiana was called to the riverside.

> ....*a post come from the Celestial City, with matter of great importance to one Christiana, the wife of Christian the pilgrim....The contents were, Hail,good woman; I bring thee tidings that the Master calleth for thee, and expecteth that thou shouldst stand in his presence in clothes of immortality within these ten days. presented her with a letter. When he had read this letter to her, he gave her therewith a sure token that he was a true messenger, and was come to bid her make haste to be gone. The token was, an arrow with a point sharpened with love, let easily into her heart, which by degrees wrought so effectually with her, that at the time appointed she must be gone.... she called for Mr. Great-heart, her guide, and told him how matters were. So he told her he was heartily glad of the news, and could have been glad had the post come for him, saying, Thus and thus it must be; and we that survive will accompany you to the river side.*[9]

Louisa wrote to Greville, who had returned to England at the end of the summer:

> *... Her beautiful body looked oh! so lovely—grand, gentle radiant almost though, more than all, peaceful.... Strange that W. J. Matheson should have been buried at the same hour! ... We have been terribly dazed, dear; it was so sudden, awful for us, but for her, how blessed!—scarcely any distress, and just quietly saying, 'I think I'm going, Mammy—to the others, you know, to join them.' After one dead faint, she spoke as if she had seen Maimy; and then the quiet clasp of the hands saying, 'If God wills'. But oh! my Greville, it's dreadfully hard to bear.*[10]

George and Robert lifted Lilia's body into a plain wooden coffin adorned with one long red cross. Singing "My God, My

Father, While I Stray," the congregation watched as Lilia's coffin was carried into the church. In packed pews, reverently silent, they mourned their cherished friend, the woman who had been a mother to everyone. She was buried beside Grace, and the sisters rest at the top of the cemetery under a few shady trees, watched over by delicate gravestones designed by Edward Hughes. George and Louisa's firstborn child, the center of family life, beloved by everyone, was no longer with them.

"Come, my Dear," Louisa said, taking George's arm as she gently led him away from the grave. He could not seem to leave Lily. "It's beginning to rain, my dear Greatheart. It reminds me of *Pilgrim's Progress* and Christiana saying, 'Come wet, come dry, I long to be gone; for however the weather is in my journey, I shall have time enough when I come there to sit down and rest me and dry me. I come, Lord, to be with Thee, and bless Thee.' Our very own Christiana has departed to the Celestial City."

"An arrow with a point sharpened with love," he replied.

Thy great deliverance is a greater thing
Than purest imagination can foregrasp;
A thing beyond all conscious hungering,
Beyond all hoe that makes the poet sing.
It takes the clinging world, undoes its clasp,
Floats it afar upon a mighty sea,
And leaves us quiet with love and liberty and thee.
George MacDonald, *Diary of an Old Soul*, May 5

CHAPTER 21

THE ONE WHO IS THE LIFE AND LIGHT

A star shining in one man's soul may, like a lantern, shed light for many a wayfarer.
Greville MacDonald, *George MacDonald and His Wife*

It was a quiet afternoon. By the hearth, the copper kettle was filled with tea, and Coraggio's warm, inviting kitchen shone like a pearl. Outside, the leaves of the olive trees looked like clusters of gold dust as the sun shone on them. Louisa sat at the table and read through fifty years of letters from her George—the most beautiful letters, full of divine love.

Looking back at distant years, Louisa pulled her memories together like patches pieced in a quilt. "His letters to me ring with the eternities of truth—that the dying of this outer garment must take place before we can rise again, as full of life as ever," she thought. "He always pointed me to the One who is the Life and Light."[1]

After Lilia's death, Louisa, severely shaken, kept to her wheelchair for a long time. To get away and help Louisa regain her strength, the family went to Arth, Switzerland, during the summer of 1892. The clean, clear air slowly revived her.

Greville later diagnosed his mother with an enlarged thyroid, which he thought was delaying her recovery, but he was reluctant to let her know for fear it would upset her. Louisa found respite in devotedly caring for George; she always hoped he would get back to his old self if she nursed him well and faithfully. But she did admit to Greville that she wondered "whether I shall live long enough to go on tending him till he gets better...."[2]

George continued to write, and he published both *A Cabinet of Gems* and *The Hope of the Gospel* in 1892. In 1893, he published *Scotch Songs and Ballads*, *The Poetical Works of George*

MacDonald in Two Volumes, and *Heather and Snow*. These were followed by *Rampolli* and *Salted with Fire* in 1897. His very last book, *Far Above Rubies*, appeared in the Christmas issue of *The Sketch* in 1898.

Although *Far Above Rubies* has never been considered one of George's better books, it is a sweet reflection of the relationship that blossoms between husband and wife as they navigate life's difficulties and are strengthened through faith in their Creator. It is, perhaps, a reflection of George's life with Louisa, and no accident that it was his last work.

Determined to keep his mind and memory from waning, George even began studying Dutch and Spanish. But Lily's death left a vacuum that could never be filled. Four of their children and one grandchild were gone. George and Louisa's arms felt terribly empty.

"No story, however, ends in this world," George often said.

With George's popularity waning and his income diminishing, Greville, now financially secure, decided to match his father's annual income. Although they knew Greville did this out of love and were extremely grateful, both George and Louisa, always wanting their children to seek godliness before all else, worried that their son was pursuing wealth rather than the Kingdom.

"The world is very different since Lily left," George told Louisa one afternoon. "It's a twilight world now. I think we both shall be glad when our time comes to join her."

But despite their sorrow and the approaching sunset of life, Louisa kept herself busy. She continued putting on plays in the great room at Casa Coraggio throughout the 1890s, even as late as 1898, when she was almost eighty years old. The MacDonalds also continued their Sunday evening gatherings and Wednesday afternoon readings, and Christmas remained a special time for them all. And as she had done during all their years at Bordighera, Louisa found joy in leading the choir and playing the organ at All Saints' Church.

She remained sharp and alert, and was often seen flitting about like a bird, her silver hair peeking out from beneath her cheerful bonnet. The family continued to host boarders, which helped with their finances and kept Louisa busy. She even threw a grand birthday party for her sister Charlotte. It was such a great event that it was covered in the local paper.

> On Friday afternoon Mrs. MacDonald gave an afternoon party in honour of the 84th birthday of her sister Mrs. Godwin. The guests were asked to come in "Whitechapel Costume. . . . [One] excellent get-up was that of a sandwich man bearing a highly adorned but very clever likeness of Mrs. Godwin, and one of our most popular residents not only dressed herself up as a "dirty old woman" but also mimicked the speech and action of a Whitechapel "lidy."[3]

Of course, the MacDonald children continually popped in and out of Coraggio, bringing their growing families with them.

"Just wait till you taste your Granny's cooking," they'd tell their little ones. "She'll be so happy to see her wee bairns again!"

For all the MacDonald children, hearing the words "mother" and "home" was akin to eating a golden treacle tart or treacle sponge pudding. And no matter where they were, they knew they were always within reach of their mother's compassionate fortification.

Their family steadily grew. Robert Falconer married Mary St. Johnstone in 1894, and George MacKay married Blanche Bird, the sister of Bernard's wife Belinda. On January 2, 1897, Winifred married Edward Troup, the son of the family's old friend Robert Troup and George's cousin Margaret MacDonald. Soon after their wedding, Winifred and Edward moved to Earls Terrace, the home in which she had lived as a child.

The only children who remained with George and Louisa at Coraggio were Irene, Honey, and Joan. It was not until May 1904 that Irene married Cecil Brewer, a celebrated architect. The last to marry was the MacDonalds' adopted daughter Honey. She was wed to Justin Herring. Her sister Joan never married.

In all, the MacDonalds were blessed with nine grandchildren. Octavia Grace was their first. Then came Robert's Ozella, the only one able to coax Grandpa George out of his moodiness. When Ronald remarried in 1897, taking Constance Robertson as his wife, they added Philip and Mary. George MacKay and Blanche had a daughter named Iris, while Greville and Phoebe adopted their daughter Mary, affectionately called Molly. Bernard's son, named after his beloved brother Maurice, was born on St. George's Day, 1892, the day also known for being Shakespeare's birthday. The significance of this date pleased George immensely. Later, Bernard had two more children, Lilia Mary and Richard.

"Why is it that grandparents always spoil their grandchildren?" George asked Louisa, smiling.

"Perhaps it is because as we grow older we have more faith," she answered. "When we were young, we thought everything depended on ourselves—and on our training. Now we see that God has a hand in the education, and we leave matters more to Him."[4]

As time went on, George began to lose his mental faculties—something he'd always feared. He found it increasingly difficult to remember things, and this was becoming more and more evident to those closest to him. In addition, his eczema caused unbearable suffering and hindered his ability to sleep and concentrate.

"Oh, I don't understand these interfering tricks of age. I'm becoming an old fool," he often lamented. Old age seemed to be his greatest trial.

"Louisa, I want to finish well. And what will be well is even now well. But my moods go from the very low of a mere man to the grand emotions that come from God. It is so difficult to manage," he confessed one morning as she brought him his tray. "This world seems full of dark and strange things, which drive me more and more to believe that He orders all things in a way that we can but partially understand because of its goodness." He signed and sipped his tea.[5]

"And I sense that visitors are coming great distances for

our Wednesday and Sunday evenings merely out of curiosity now. I feel as though they just want to see the aging prophet perform. I don't in the least care to amuse people; I truly desire to help them. My only hope is that I can show them that all they need to do is follow the advice of Jesus—to 'Enter into thy closet, and shut thy door, and pray to thy Father in secret' and pour out their hearts to God—to actually get down on their knees and let Him help them as no one else can."[6]

"I think we shall have to open our doors only halfway from now on," Louisa said. "You need your rest and time to write. But my hope is that we have lived graciously and loved each who entered here."

Everyone sensed that something seemed to have broken within George.

"Louisa, am I losing my wits?" he asked frequently.

"No, my dear. Your wits are only 'ben the hoose'—within the house!" she would tease.

Finding his care increasingly difficult was a bitter pill for Louisa to swallow. Her indomitable love and hope for his recovery drove her to continue, but eventually she knew he needed more care than she was able to give.

Fortunately, a kind couple came to help. They were well trained and devoted to George. Both Louisa and George greatly appreciated their care, and George always voiced his thanks for even their simplest services.

"They are saying that my wits are all gone again," George lamented one evening.

"No, dearest Bear," Louisa replied, "your wits are out in the backyard at present. We all know that."

A look of despair came over his face. "I know you are all going to leave me, and I am going to be left in a strange home."

Louisa put her arms around him. "I shall never leave you. I love nothing in the world than to be with you. All will be well. Now, would you like Irene to sing?"

George nodded. His face transformed as he listened to the sound of Irene's voice. She sang "O Salutaris Hostia," and

George changed from an unhappy creature to a wondering, loving soul. "Beautiful, beautiful!" he exclaimed as he folded his hands in prayer.

Music often calmed his emotions and brought the old George back to his family.

One morning, he woke to find that his skin had cleared. No longer afflicted with eczema, he was able to sleep again. But for the next five years, he barely spoke at all. He had most likely suffered a stroke. The final shadow had come. But his wide blue eyes, "those blue eyes that seemed rather made for other people to look into them than for himself to look out of,"[7] still watched, still waited, always aware of when Louisa left the room and always watching the door for her return.

Finally the time came when the MacDonald children decided that their parents needed to move back to England and, in 1899, took charge. Robert, the architect, drew up the plans, and Greville built their home. He named it St. George's Wood. It was a lovely place, but George and Louisa always returned to Casa Coraggio and the warmer climate of Italy in the winter.

Lovely gardens and three acres of magnificent beech trees, their branches arching over the road to the house, greeted George and Louisa as they arrived at their new home. Louisa hoped the change of scenery would bring George back to her and that she would hear his voice once again.

But he remained silent.

"To have one we love with us, and not with us consciously, not to be able to reach them, and yet to see them here is a terrible feeling. One has to cling on to the knowledge of how the soul lives independent of the body, and how sure the future is for us all," Octavia Hill wrote, trying to encourage and console the MacDonalds.[8]

George slowly adjusted to their new home. In the summertime, he was often wheeled about the grounds, always wearing his red cloak, white serge suit, and grey felt hat.

"Doesn't he look like a regal old saint?" the neighbors would remark.

All the MacDonalds found delight in the boy who rode

back and forth in front of St. George's Wood on his bicycle every day.

"Here he comes again," Louisa would say with a wink. Then the boy would wave and ride away.[9]

Although Louisa no longer heard the voice of her beloved, she still heard his heart. Faith, hope, and charity had always been the substance of his words, and now they were the substance of his silence. But he and Louisa both keenly felt the long vigil, for "All the night long the morning is at hand."[10]

When George and Louisa's golden anniversary arrived in March 1901, they were at Bordighera, but they officially celebrated on June 8 at their new residence.

Fifty years together.

Fifty years shouldering the plow and serving their Savior together.

Louisa was radiant, bright-eyed, and surrounded by her children, grandchildren, nieces, nephews, and dear friends. Octavia Hill and Mr. and Mrs. C. E. Maurice were among the celebrants. It was truly a momentous occasion.

George did not speak a word. He sat in his father's chair and watched as Louisa joyfully embraced their dear loved ones who had come to celebrate. Whenever she left the room, his gaze would follow her. He wouldn't look away until she returned, and then he would smile and sigh contentedly.

Greville, having taken lessons from a goldsmith, made a fifty-link gold chain for Louisa to celebrate the anniversary, and she was enthralled. In its clasp, he placed a star sapphire. This had always been George's favorite stone and symbolized his and Louisa's fifty years together. At various intervals in the links, Greville placed eleven stones that represented his parents' eleven children, each one unrepeatable. For the four children who had already gone ahead, he used four flawless pearls.

"It's rough, and not the quality I wished, but it's made with love," Greville said as he carefully closed the clasp around his mother's neck.

"Stop saying your craftsmanship is poor," insisted Louisa

as she held the chain and admired each inch. "It's perfect."

"Fifty long, laboring, striving, rejoicing, weeping years! Fifty links in your chain of life!" Greville beamed as he raised his glass for a toast. "And though you have grown old together in sorrow, you will ever be growing young in the living Joy. We need both of you more than ever—and all the more because you now need our upholding. And to you, our utterly beloved Mother, we can never give what you have given us. All we are, I do believe, is of your substance—soul and body, mind and character. To you and to God we are responsible for our gifts and talents. May God help us to live by the Light as you have done!"[11]

"I don't believe in all these fifty years since your father and I were made one, that my heart has ever been quieter, more grateful for all the lovely loves heaven has given us, than it is now," Louisa said as she raised her glass in return.[12]

Just after her and George's golden anniversary, Louisa's health began to fail. She lost her appetite and was gripped by frequent bouts of sciatic pain, but she never let George know. Every night, she read or sang to him.

"And in this love, more than in bed, I rest," she would say to herself, quoting George Herbert's "Even-song" as she fell asleep.

In the summer, George and Louisa would often be taken outside to sit under the magnificent beeches—he in his green armchair and Louisa beside him—while the canopy of leaves above them sang their psithurism.

"Oh! The joy of fifty years of interminable love," Louisa would say with a sigh and a smile.

Louisa felt useless while George was being cared for by others. Yet even as her health rapidly deteriorated, her children agreed that, even in her old age, her wrinkles were actually furrows of grace, etched by the Master Himself. Radiant in old age, unlike anyone else they knew, their mother was now putting on the beauty of immortality. And even though her strength was waning, she continued to faithfully write to her loved ones.

As her sun began to descend, like it had in the story of

Hezekiah, Louisa "turned [her] face to the wall and prayed to the Lord."[13]

On January 13, 1902, Louisa Powell MacDonald went home to be with her Savior and the children who had gone before her. Sunrise had finally swept away the shadows. She was laid to rest under a rough white stone cross in the quiet cemetery in Bordighera, beside Lilia and Grace. Their three stones rest against an old rock wall, shaded and protected by dark green cypress trees. This is the perfect place for Louisa to lie, surrounded by nature and her children. In ancient Israel, the cypress represented healing, uprightness, and eternal life. Cypress trees are resilient, known for their ability to withstand harsh climates and poor soil. They endure and bring comfort wherever they are planted—so very much like Louisa MacDonald.

For several days, Winifred and Irene kept the news of their mother's death from their father. When they finally found the courage to tell him, he broke down and wept.

Irene cared for her father at Bordighera until her marriage to Cecil Brewer in 1904, after which George went to be with Winifred and her husband, who lived at Ashtead in Surrey. Then, on September 18, 1905, after a short bout of pneumonia, George MacDonald followed his beloved Louisa in death. He slipped away quietly, serenely, leaving behind only an aura of peace.

Mary's silk cloth and George's tartan shrouded his flower-covered coffin. Ronald, Robert, Bernard, and George MacKay carried the coffin into the chapel while choirboys sang "Thou Art the Way." George's son-in-law Kingsbury Jameson presided. It was a small, simple, quiet service. The following January, George's ashes were placed in Louisa's grave, unifying them in death as they had been in life.

This is my wife. You cannot see her very well, for, like Hamlet, I wear her "in my heart's core, aye, in my heart of hearts!"
George MacDonald, *Far Above Rubies*

ACKNOWLEDGEMENTS

I wish to acknowledge my indebtedness and grateful thanks to the following individuals for their support during the writing of this book. Jess Lederman, I am deeply grateful to you for believing in me and in this project, and for supporting and expertly guiding this endeavor. To Dr. Rolland Hein, my friend and mentor, thank you for wisely advising me about the life and legacy of George MacDonald. To Christopher MacDonald, I am grateful for your encouragement, your kindness, and for sharing letters and photos of your great-great granny.

Finally, I am most grateful for the faithful love and encouragement of my husband, Earle and for the prayers of our children, Desiree, Samuel, Hannah, Ethan, Colin, and Timothy. I have been upheld. May your lives forever be songs and lights that glorify our Savior.

NOTES

The majority of the papers and letters relating to George MacDonald and his family are kept at Yale, in the Beinecke Library. It is these letters, and the biographies written by their sons, Greville and Ronald, that I have used for conversations in this book. I have, to the best of my ability, tried not to add anything that cannot be found in the letters or works of MacDonald.

CHAPTER ONE
The Near Loss of Everything
1. *George MacDonald and His Wife* by Greville MacDonald, M.D., London, 1924 pg. 155.

CHAPTER TWO
The Becoming of Louisa
1. *George MacDonald and His Wife by Greville MacDonald, M.D., London, 1924 pg. 102.*
2. George MacDonald and His Wife *by Greville MacDonald, M.D., London, 1924 pg. 102.*
3. *George MacDonald, as quoted in John Thomas Dale:* The Way to Win Showing How to Succeed in Life *(1887)*, pg. 89.

CHAPTER THREE
Struck from The Eternal Light
1. *George MacDonald and His Wife* by Greville MacDonald, M.D., London, 1924 pg. 106.
2. *George MacDonald and His Wife* by Greville MacDonald, M.D., London, 1924 pg. 98.
3. *George MacDonald and His Wife* by Greville MacDonald, M.D., London, 1924 pg. 99.
4. *George MacDonald* by William Raeper, Batavia, IL: Lion Publishing, 1987 pg. 21.
5. 15 May 1949, Beinecke Rare Book and Manuscript Library, Yale University.
6. *George MacDonald: Victorian Mythmaker* by Rolland Hein, Nashville, TN: Star Song Publishing Group, 1993, pg. 37.

Notes

7. *George MacDonald and His Wife* by Greville MacDonald, London, 1924 pg. 27.
8. 5 October 1849, Beinecke Rare Book and Manuscript Library, Yale University.
9. GMD to Louisa, 27 December 1850 (ALS Yale).
10. 31 May 1849, Beinecke Rare Book and Manuscript Library, Yale University.
11. *George MacDonald: Victorian Mythmaker* by Rolland Hein, Nashville, TN: Star Song Publishing Group, 1993, pg. 39.
12. *George MacDonald and His Wife* by Greville MacDonald, M.D., London, 1924 pg. 117.

CHAPTER FOUR
The Whole Universe Is Tented with Love

1. Chartism was a United Kingdom parliamentary reform movement that occurred between 1837-1848. Its aim was to gain political rights and influence for the working classes.
2. *George MacDonald and His Wife* by Greville MacDonald, M.D., London, 1924 pg. 53.
3. N.d. Beinecke Rare Book and Manuscript Library, Yale University.
4. *George MacDonald and His Wife* by Greville MacDonald, M.D., London, 1924 pg. 116.
5. *George MacDonald and His Wife* by Greville MacDonald, M.D., London, 1924 pg. 121.
6. *George MacDonald and His Wife* by Greville MacDonald, M.D., London, 1924 pg. 122.
7. *George MacDonald: Victorian Mythmaker* by Rolland Hein, Nashville, TN: Star Song Publishing Group, 1993, pg. 47.
8. *George MacDonald and His Wife* by Greville MacDonald, M.D., London, 1924 pg. 120.
9. *George MacDonald: Victorian Mythmaker* by Rolland Hein, Nashville, TN: Star Song Publishing Group, 1993, pg. 60.
10. GMD to Louisa, 5 February 1855 (ALS Yale).
11. *George MacDonald and His Wife* by Greville MacDonald, M.D., London, 1924, pg. 140-141.
12. *George MacDonald: Victorian Mythmaker* by Rolland Hein, Nashville, TN: Star Song Publishing Group, 1993, pg. 56.

13. GMD to Caroline Chase Powell, 10 December 1850 (ALS Yale).
14. Louisa to GMD n.d. 1850 ALS Yale.

CHAPTER FIVE
Called to Preach: Te Deum
1. *George MacDonald and His Wife* by Greville MacDonald, M.D., London, 1924 pg. 137.
2. Coleridge died in 1832, and he had been professionally close with James Powell's oldest son, also named James, from his first wife. James was a practicing surgeon in Hackney, who, Louisa later told her son Greville, often incurred Coleridge's displeasure, and sometimes anger, by effusing to supply him with laudanum or crude opium. Coleridge was living in Highgate at the time.
3. *George MacDonald and His Wife* by Greville MacDonald, M.D., London, 1924 pg. 137.
4. Stock-cravats were scarf-like articles which were wrapped around the neck with high collars and pointed edges around the chin and cheeks, ending in bows or various types of knots.
5. *George MacDonald and His Wife* by Greville MacDonald, M.D., London, 1924 pg. 138.
6. *George MacDonald and His Wife* by Greville MacDonald, M.D., London, 1924 pg. 139.
7. *George MacDonald and His Wife* by Greville MacDonald, M.D., London, 1924 pg. 142.
8. *George MacDonald and His Wife* by Greville MacDonald, M.D., London, 1924 pg. 142.
9. *England's Antiphon* by George MacDonald, Good Press, London, 1868 p. 329.
10. Leeches are hermaphroditic parasites which live on blood. They were used for medical purposes for centuries to drain blood and relieve swelling.
11. Mrs. New was George MacDonald's landlady in Arundel, who became a true friend in the sufferings that fell so soon on the new minister.
12. *George MacDonald and His Wife* by Greville MacDonald, M.D., London, 1924, pg. 145.

13. *Castle Warlock* by George MacDonald, London, 1883, vol. 2 pg. 127.
14. *Castle Warlock* by George MacDonald, London, 1883, vol. 1, pg. 124.
15. *George MacDonald and His Wife* by Greville MacDonald, M.D., London, 1924, pg. 148.

CHAPTER SIX
By and By Becoming Thoroughly One
1. GMD to Louisa, 23 May 1849 (ALS Yale).
2. *George MacDonald and His Wife* by Greville MacDonald, M.D., London, 1924 pg. 125.
3. *Poetical Works* by George MacDonald, Chatto & Windus, 1893, vol. 1, pg. 79.
4. *What's Mine's Mine* by George MacDonald, D. Lothrop, 1886.

CHAPTER SEVEN
For Richer, for Poorer, in Sickness and In Health
1. *George MacDonald and His Wife* by Greville MacDonald, M.D., London, 1924, pg.199.
2. *George MacDonald and His Wife* by Greville MacDonald, M.D., London, 1924, pg. 171.
3. *George MacDonald and His Wife* by Greville MacDonald, M.D., London, 1924, pg. 173.
4. *George MacDonald and His Wife* by Greville MacDonald, M.D., London, 1924 pg. 181.

CHAPTER EIGHT
Salted with Fire
1. 21 Dec.1853, Beinecke Rare Book and Manuscript Library, Yale University.
2. *George MacDonald and His Wife* by Greville MacDonald, M.D., London, 1924 pg. 202.
3. N.d. Beinecke Rare Book and Manuscript Library, Yale University.
4. May 30th, 1854, Beinecke Rare Book and Manuscript Library, Yale University.
5. *George MacDonald and His Wife* by Greville MacDonald,

M.D., London, 1924, pg. 226.
6. *George MacDonald and His Wife* by Greville MacDonald, M.D., London, 1924, pg. 226.
7. *George MacDonald and His Wife* by Greville MacDonald, M.D., London, 1924, pg. 230.
8. *George MacDonald and His Wife* by Greville MacDonald, M.D., London, 1924, pg. 232.
9. *George MacDonald and His Wife* by Greville MacDonald, M.D., London, 1924, pg. 251.

CHAPTER NINE
The Chalice and The Paten: Parenting, Poverty, and Pilgrimage
1. *George MacDonald, An Anthology* by C.S. Lewis, MacMillan, 1947, #296.
2. *George MacDonald, An Anthology* by C.S. Lewis, MacMillan, 1947, #296.
3. *The Vicar's Daughter* by George MacDonald, Tinsley Brothers, 1872, ch.40.
4. Is. 58:6-9, English Standard Version.
5. *Reminiscences of a Specialist* by Greville MacDonald, M.D., London, 1932, pg. 13.
6. *Reminiscences of a Specialist* by Greville MacDonald, M.D., London, 1932, pg.41.
7. *Reminiscences of a Specialist* by Greville MacDonald, M.D., London, 1932, pg. 304.
8. *A Player Under Three Reigns* by Johnston Forbes-Robertson, Boston, Little, Brown, and Company, 1925, pg. 10.
9. *Reminiscences of a Specialist* by Greville MacDonald, M.D., London, 1932, pg. 27.
10. *Reminiscences of a Specialist* by Greville MacDonald, M.D., London, 1932, pg. 303.

CHAPTER TEN
Limping Toward Jerusalem
1. *George MacDonald and His Wife* by Greville MacDonald, M.D., London, 1924, pg. 259.
2. *Adela Cathcart* by George MacDonald, London, 1864, pg.

73.
3. *George MacDonald and His Wife* by Greville MacDonald, M.D., London, 1924, pg. 261.
4. *George MacDonald and His Wife* by Greville MacDonald, M.D., London, 1924, pg. 261-262, reformatted as dialogue.
5. *George MacDonald and His Wife* by Greville MacDonald, M.D., London, 1924, pg. 263.
6. *George MacDonald and His Wife* by Greville MacDonald, M.D., London, 1924, pg. 264.
7. *George MacDonald and His Wife* by Greville MacDonald, M.D., London, 1924, pg. 268.
8. *George MacDonald and His Wife* by Greville MacDonald, M.D., London, 1924 pg. 271.
9. *George MacDonald and His Wife* by Greville MacDonald, M.D., London, 1924, pg. 272.

CHAPTER ELEVEN
Adeste Fideles
1. *George MacDonald and His Wife* by Greville MacDonald, M.D., London, 1924, pg. 281.
2. *George MacDonald and His Wife* by Greville MacDonald, M.D., London, 1924, pg. 286-287.
3. *George MacDonald and His Wife* by Greville MacDonald, M.D., London, 1924, pg. 288.
4. *George MacDonald and His Wife* by Greville MacDonald, M.D., London, 1924, pg. 289.
5. *George MacDonald and His Wife* by Greville MacDonald, M.D., London, 1924, pg. 295.
6. *George MacDonald and His Wife* by Greville MacDonald, M.D., London, 1924, pg. 299.
7. *Surprised by Joy* by C.S. Lewis, Geoffrey Bles, 1955, pg. 172.

CHAPTER TWELVE
Faithful, Forever Friends
1. *Reminiscences of a Specialist* by Greville MacDonald, M.D., London, 1932, pg. 19,20.
2. *Reminiscences of a Specialist* by Greville MacDonald, M.D.,

London, 1932, pg. 20.
3. *George MacDonald and His Wife* by Greville MacDonald, M.D., London, 1924, pg. 318.
4. *George MacDonald and His Wife* by Greville MacDonald, M.D., London, 1924, pg. 313.
5. *George MacDonald and His Wife* by Greville MacDonald, M.D., London, 1924, pg. 321.
6. Edith Lazaro Honig, *Breaking the Angelic Image: Woman Power in Victorian Children's Fantasy*, pg. 92.
7. *Aberdeen Free Press and Buchan News,* February 2, 1869.
8. *Adela Cathcart* by George MacDonald, London, 1864.
9. The Royal Polytechnic Tales are a collection of giant magic lantern slides painted by H.G. Hine, and now reside in the museum of the History of Science, Oxford, England.
10. *David Elginbrod,* by George MacDonald, Hurst and Blackett, 1863, Book 3, Ch. 12.

CHAPTER THIRTEEN
Do the Next Thing
1. N.d. . Beinecke Rare Book and Manuscript Library, Yale University.
2. *George MacDonald and His Wife* by Greville MacDonald, M.D., London, 1924, pg. 347-348.
3. *George MacDonald and His Wife* by Greville MacDonald, M.D., London, 1924, pg. 350.
4. *Wilfrid Cumbermede* by George MacDonald, Hurst & Blackett/Scribner, 1872, pg. 244.
5. *George MacDonald and His Wife* by Greville MacDonald, M.D., London, 1924, pg. 358.
6. *George MacDonald and His Wife* by Greville MacDonald, M.D., London, 1924, pg. 226.

CHAPTER FOURTEEN
The Sound of a Far-Off Song
1. *George MacDonald and His Wife* by Greville MacDonald, M.D., London, 1924, pg. 363.
2. *George MacDonald and His Wife* by Greville MacDonald, M.D., London, 1924, pg. 370.

Notes

3. *George MacDonald: Victorian Mythmaker* by Rolland Hein, Nashville, TN: Star Song Publishing Group, 1993, pg. 205.
4. McComb, Samuel, 1864-1938: *Preaching in Theory and Practice* (New York, London Oxford University Press, 1926.
5. *George MacDonald: Victorian Mythmaker* by Rolland Hein, Nashville, TN: Star Song Publishing Group, 1993, ch. 19.
6. N.d. . Beinecke Rare Book and Manuscript Library, Yale University.
7. N.d. . Beinecke Rare Book and Manuscript Library, Yale University.
8. *George MacDonald and His Wife* by Greville MacDonald, M.D., London, 1924, pg. 395.
9. *George MacDonald and His Wife* by Greville MacDonald, M.D., London, 1924, pg. 395.
10. *Castle Warlock* by George MacDonald, London, 1883, ch. 23, pg. 115.
11. George MacDonald, as quoted in Greville McDonald, *George MacDonald and His Wife* (1924), pg. 375.

CHAPTER FIFTEEN
America

1. *George MacDonald and His Wife* by Greville MacDonald, M.D., London, 1924, pg. 421.
2. *George MacDonald and His Wife* by Greville MacDonald, M.D., London, 1924, pg. 422.
3. *Reminiscences of a Specialist* by Greville MacDonald, M.D., London, 1932, pg. 50.
4. *Reminiscences of a Specialist* by Greville MacDonald, M.D., London, 1932, pg. 51.
5. *Reminiscences of a Specialist* by Greville MacDonald, M.D., London, 1932, pg. 51.
6. *George MacDonald and His Wife* by Greville MacDonald, M.D., London, 1924, pg. 426.
7. *Reminiscences of a Specialist* by Greville MacDonald, M.D., London, 1932, pg. 47.
8. *George MacDonald and His Wife* by Greville MacDonald, M.D., London, 1924, pg. 430.

9. *George MacDonald and His Wife* by Greville MacDonald, M.D., London, 1924, pg. 435-436.
10. *George MacDonald and His Wife* by Greville MacDonald, M.D., London, 1924, pg. 454.
11. *George MacDonald and His Wife* by Greville MacDonald, M.D., London, 1924, pg. 449.
12. *Unspoken Sermons,* The Hardness of The Many, Series Two, by George MacDonald, Longmans Green, 1867.
13. *George MacDonald and His Wife* by Greville MacDonald, M.D., London, 1924, pg. 459-460.
14. Newspaper clipping, Beinecke Rare Book and Manuscript Library, Yale University.

CHAPTER SIXTEEN
Tethered to The Cross
1. *George MacDonald and His Wife* by Greville MacDonald, M.D., London, 1924, pg. 465.
2. *George MacDonald and His Wife* by Greville MacDonald, M.D., London, 1924, pg. 468.
3. *George MacDonald: Victorian Mythmaker* by Rolland Hein, Nashville, TN: Star Song Publishing Group, 1993, pg. 273.
4. *At the Back of the North Wind* by George MacDonald, Strahan & Co., 1871, pg. 280.
5. July 24, 1875, Beinecke Rare Book and Manuscript Library, Yale University.
6. 27 October 1875, Beinecke Rare Book and Manuscript Library, Yale University.
7. *George MacDonald: Victorian Mythmaker* by Rolland Hein, Nashville, TN: Star Song Publishing Group, 1993, pg. 472. MacDonald's robe and the Beulah curtains were previously in the possession of Freda Levson of London. Freda Levson donated them to the William Morris Society in April, 1986.
8. "Notes Referring to Family Letters," Beinecke Rare Book and Manuscript Library, Yale University.
9. *George MacDonald and His Wife* by Greville MacDonald, M.D., London, 1924, pg. 473.
10. 6 January 1878, The Trustees of the National Library of

Scotland.
11. 2 Aug. 1877, Beinecke Rare Book and Manuscript Library, Yale University.

CHAPTER SEVENTEEN
Through the Valley of the Shadows
1. *George MacDonald and His Wife* by Greville MacDonald, M.D., London, 1924, pg. 475.
2. George MacDonald, *Diary of an Old Soul,* Nov. 3.
3. George MacDonald, *Diary of an Old Soul,* May 6.
4. *George MacDonald and His Wife* by Greville MacDonald, M.D., London, 1924, pg. 479.
5. *George MacDonald and His Wife* by Greville MacDonald, M.D., London, 1924, pg. 480.
6. *George MacDonald and His Wife* by Greville MacDonald, M.D., London, 1924, pg. 481.
7. *George MacDonald and His Wife* by Greville MacDonald, M.D., London, 1924, pg. 485.
8. *James 1:4, The Bible*, King James Version, 1900.

CHAPTER EIGHTEEN
A Slow and Certain Light
1. George MacDonald: Victorian Mythmaker by Rolland Hein, Nashville, TN: Star Song Publishing Group, 1993, pg. 318.
2. 6 May 1898, Beinecke Rare Book and Manuscript Library, Yale University.
3. *The Beautiful Arabella Phipps and Others* by Gina Rose, London, 1914, pg. 171.
4. A Prebendary is a canon of a cathedral or collegiate church whose income originally came from a prebend, or stipend furnished by a cathedral or collegiate church.
5. *George MacDonald and His Wife* by Greville MacDonald, M.D., London, 1924, pg. 506.
6. *George MacDonald and His Wife* by Greville MacDonald, M.D., London, 1924, pg. 510.
7. *The Beautiful Arabella Phipps and Others* by Gina Rose, London, 1914, pg. 172.
8. *George MacDonald and His Wife* by Greville MacDonald,

M.D., London, 1924, pg. 512.
9. *The Beautiful Arabella Phipps and Others* by Gina Rose, London, 1914, pg. 174.

CHAPTER NINETEEN
A Rough Shaking
Shifting Ground and Gathered Fragments
1. 8 May 1884, Beinecke Rare Book and Manuscript Library, Yale University.
2. *George MacDonald and His Wife* by Greville MacDonald, M.D., London, 1924, pg. 514.
3. A secessionist was a person who favored formal withdrawal from membership of a federation or body, especially a political state. In this case, Blandy favored the withdrawal of 11 slave states from the Union during 1860-1861 following the election of Abraham Lincoln as president.
4. *In the Near Loss of Everything* by Dale Wayne Slusser, Zossima Press, 2009, pg. 9-21.
5. *Reminiscences of a Specialist* by Greville MacDonald, M.D., London, 1932, pg. 320.
6. *Reminiscences of a Specialist* by Greville MacDonald, M.D., London, 1932, pg. 320-324.

CHAPTER TWENTY
Perfection of Selfless Love
1. Letter from Ronald MacDonald to Louisa MacDonald, July 15, 1890, George MacDonald Collection, General Collection, Beinecke Rare Book and Manuscript Library, Yale University.
2. *In the Near Loss of Everything* by Dale Wayne Slusser, Zossima Press, 2009, pg. 41.
3. *In the Near Loss of Everything* by Dale Wayne Slusser, Zossima Press, 2009, pg. 46.
4. *George MacDonald and His Wife* by Greville MacDonald, M.D., London, 1924, pg. 519.
5. *George MacDonald and His Wife* by Greville MacDonald, M.D., London, 1924, pg. 520.
6. *George MacDonald and His Wife* by Greville MacDonald,

Notes

    M.D., London, 1924, pg. 524.
7. *George MacDonald and His Wife* by Greville MacDonald, M.D., London, 1924, pg. 517.
8. *George MacDonald and His Wife* by Greville MacDonald, M.D., London, 1924, pg. 520.
9. *The Pilgrim's Progress* by John Bunyan, London, 1678, Part II, Section 4, Step 8.
10. *Reminiscences of a Specialist* by Greville MacDonald, M.D., London, 1932, pg. 309.

CHAPTER TWENTY-ONE
The One Who Is the Life and Light
1. *Reminiscences of a Specialist* by Greville MacDonald, M.D., London, 1932, pg. 335.
2. *Reminiscences of a Specialist* by Greville MacDonald, M.D., London, 1932, pg. 336.
3. *Journal de Bordighera,* Jeudi 19 Janvier 1899.
4. *George MacDonald and His Wife* by Greville MacDonald, M.D., London, 1924, pg. 539.
5. GMD to Susan Scott, June 1, 1894, *An Expression of Character, The Letters of George MacDonald* by Glenn Edward Sadler, Editor, Eerdmans, 1994, pg. 360, Autograph Letter Signed, Huntington Library.
6. *George MacDonald and His Wife* by Greville MacDonald, M.D., London, 1924, pg. 538.
7. *At the Back of the North Wind* by George MacDonald, Strahan & Co., 1871, pg. 345.
8. Octavia Hill to Winifred L. Troup (MacDonald), 4 July 1904, (ALS Yale).
9. *George MacDonald and His Wife* by Greville MacDonald, M.D., London, 1924, pg. 561.
10. *Lilith* by George MacDonald, Chatto & Windus/Harper, 1895, pg. 332.
11. *Reminiscences of a Specialist* by Greville MacDonald, M.D., London, 1932, pg. 350.
12. *Reminiscences of a Specialist* by Greville MacDonald, M.D., London, 1932, pg. 350.
13. Isaiah 38:2, English Standard Version

Made in the USA
Middletown, DE
28 June 2021